LONDON AND THE (
HOMOSEXUALIT

London and the Culture of Homosexuality explores the relationship
between London and male homosexuality from the criminalisation
of all 'acts of gross indecency' between men in 1885 to the outbreak
of the First World War in 1914 – years marked by an intensification
in concern about male–male relationships and also by the emergence
of an embryonic homosexual rights movement. Taking his cue from
literary and lesbian and gay scholars, urban historians and cultural
geographers, Matt Cook combines discussion of London's homosexual
subculture with a detailed examination of its representation in the
press, in science and in literature. The conjunction of approaches
used in this study provides fresh insights into the development of ideas
about the modern homosexual and into the many different ways of
comprehending and taking part in London's culture of homosexuality.

MATT COOK is Lecturer in Modern British History at Keele University.

CAMBRIDGE STUDIES IN NINETEENTH-CENTURY
LITERATURE AND CULTURE

General editor
Gillian Beer, *University of Cambridge*

Editorial board
Isobel Armstrong, *Birkbeck College, London*
Leonore Davidoff, *University of Essex*
Terry Eagleton, *University of Manchester*
Catherine Gallagher, *University of California, Berkeley*
D. A. Miller, *Columbia University*
J. Hillis Miller, *University of California, Irvine*
Mary Poovey, *New York University*
Elaine Showalter, *Princeton University*

Nineteenth-century British literature and culture have been rich fields for interdisciplinary studies. Since the turn of the twentieth century, scholars and critics have tracked the intersections and tensions between Victorian literature and the visual arts, politics, social organisation, economic life, technical innovations, scientific thought – in short, culture in its broadest sense. In recent years, theoretical challenges and historiographical shifts have unsettled the assumptions of previous scholarly synthesis and called into question the terms of older debates. Whereas the tendency in much past literary critical interpretation was to use the metaphor of culture as 'background', feminist, Foucauldian, and other analyses have employed more dynamic models that raise questions of power and of circulation. Such developments have reanimated the field.

This series aims to accommodate and promote the most interesting work being undertaken on the frontiers of the field of nineteenth-century literary studies: work which intersects fruitfully with other fields of study such as history, or literary theory, or the history of science. Comparative as well as interdisciplinary approaches are welcomed.

A complete list of titles published will be found at the end of the book.

LONDON AND THE CULTURE OF HOMOSEXUALITY, 1885–1914

MATT COOK

CAMBRIDGE
UNIVERSITY PRESS

CAMBRIDGE UNIVERSITY PRESS
Cambridge, New York, Melbourne, Madrid, Cape Town, Singapore, São Paulo, Delhi

Cambridge University Press
The Edinburgh Building, Cambridge CB2 8RU, UK

Published in the United States of America by Cambridge University Press, New York

www.cambridge.org
Information on this title: www.cambridge.org/9780521822077

First published 2003
This digitally printed version 2008

A catalogue record for this publication is available from the British Library

Library of Congress Cataloguing in Publication data
Cook, Matt.
London and the culture of homosexuality, 1885–1914 / Matt Cook.
p.   cm. – (Cambridge studies in nineteenth-century literature and culture; 39)
Includes bibliographical references and index.
ISBN 0 521 82207 6
1. Homosexuality, Male – England – London – History – 19th century.   2. Homosexuality,
Male – England – London – History – 20th century.   3. London (England) – Social
conditions – 19th century.   4. London (England) – Social conditions – 20th century.
5. London (England) – Moral conditions.   I. Title.   II. Series.
HQ76.3.G72L653   2003
306.76´62´0942109034 – dc21   2003046120

ISBN 978-0-521-82207-7 hardback
ISBN 978-0-521-08980-7 paperback

For Nick
And in memory of Dad

Contents

Illustrations

Tables

Acknowledgements

I began work on the PhD thesis that forms the basis of this book in 1995 at Queen Mary College, University of London, and since then many people have offered help, advice and support. I was fortunate to have three supervisors during my time at QMUL: Cornelia Cook and Daniel Pick supervised the whole project; Sarah Waters helped to oversee the first year. I owe them special thanks for their encouragement, intellectual rigour and enduring support and interest. Allegra Madgwick inspired me to set out on doctoral study in the first place, and she and other members of the postgraduate reading group helped me to hone and think critically about my ideas. Discussions with Christopher Breward, Amber Jacobs, Catherine Maxwell, Lynda Nead, Miles Ogborn, Suzanne Raitt, Matthew Weait and Chris Waters were extremely helpful, and the insights of my examiners Gillian Beer and the late Roy Porter set me on the road to reworking the thesis.

Ivan Crozier, Anna Davin, Lesley Hall, Marybeth Hamilton, Morris Kaplan, Lisa O'Sullivan, Katharina Rowold, Gareth Stedman Jones, Peter Swaab, Rebecca Spang, Sadie Wearing and Judith Walkowitz read my work in various forms and at various stages; their comments and advice helped me to think and rethink the project's scope and direction. Students at Keele University over the past two years have helped me to reconsider certain issues and arguments. Colleagues there have also been very supportive. Nick Brigmont, Sally Cook and Matt Houlbrook read the book typescript (and parts of it several times!) in the fraught final stages; their help and suggestions were invaluable. I am grateful to Linda Bree, Rachel De Wachter, Audrey Cotterell and Jackie Warren at Cambridge University Press, and to the readers for their guidance.

The librarians and staff at the Bodleian Library, British Library, Colindale Newspaper Library, Harry Ransom Humanities Research Center, the London Library, London Metropolitan Archive and Wellcome Institute all smoothed the research process. Maggs & Co. Booksellers gave me access to George Ives' scrapbooks before they were sold to the Rare Book and Manuscript Library, Yale University. H. G. Cocks kindly allowed me to read the typescript of his forthcoming book. I am grateful to the Harry Ransom Humanities Research Center at the University of Texas at Austin for allowing me to quote from George Ives' papers and diary. All reasonable attempts were made to contact the copyright holders, but it has not been possible to trace them. The British Academy funded my doctoral work and my trip to Texas, and Gwladys Cook and Dorothy Cook provided additional financial help.

Sections of chapters four and five and the Epilogue appear in a piece in *History Workshop Journal* (Autumn 2003). I am grateful to the *HWJ* collective for allowing me to reprint here.

Friends and family have been hugely supportive throughout – and I especially want to thank Gwladys, Allegra, Pam, John and Madeline. As I was finalising the doctoral thesis Jaya was born; Chetan came along just before I submitted the typescript for the book. They brought new joy into my life – and unwittingly helped me finish up.

Above all, thanks to Nick, who has seen me through the whole process with his friendship and care. This book is dedicated to him and to my Dad, Humphrey Cook, who died as I was starting out on postgraduate work but continues to inspire me in so many ways.

Note on terminology

Whilst 'homosexual' and 'homosexuality' are familiar terms now, they were only coined in the late 1860s and were little used until well into the twentieth century. The medicalised conception of sexuality they represent was also slow to take hold: the heterosexual/homosexual or gay/straight binary that structures our understandings of sexuality now was not so familiar in the late nineteenth century and cannot simply be imposed retrospectively. A number of terms were in use during the period and they were not necessarily premised on this dialectical understanding. 'Homosexual' identities were outlined, but there was no clear overarching term which encompassed them all. For the purposes of this book I have used different labels as they are appropriate to the material, but for pragmatic reasons use 'homosexuality' and 'homosexual' (as an adjective) in more general discussion. They are used in the widest sense: denoting, to use historian John Boswell, 'sexual phenomena between persons of the same gender, whether the result of conscious preference, subliminal desire, or circumstantial exigency' (*Christianity and Social Tolerance*, p. 44). There is not the presumption of a self-consciously assumed or applied identity. It is important to note finally that in general neither 'homosexual' nor 'homosexuality' should be seen automatically to refer to men. However, this book centres exclusively on male homosexuality in order to avoid collapsing two distinctive sexual subjectivities and relationships to the city. Consequently, I have tended to omit the additional adjective 'male' as long as the discussion obviously refers to sexual and emotional relations between men.

Introduction

In 1886 *Reynolds Weekly News* reported that Arthur Brown, 'a gentleman of means', had been sentenced to two years with hard labour for 'disgusting and filthy acts of indecency' with a guardsman in Victoria Station toilets.[1] Twenty-five years later the Irish nationalist Roger Casement recorded his longings for a 'nice, respectable' twenty-year-old 'who looked often and often' from across the platform at Gloucester Road Station.[2] Charles Ashbee, the architect and romantic socialist, met his lover, a guardsman called George Robson, at Charing Cross,[3] and in the boat train from the same station George Ives, founder of the first support and pressure group for 'homosexual' men, reported being courted by a Frenchman, who kissed his hand in the darkness when the lights of the sleeping cabin were put out. He was, Ives felt sure, 'sympathetic to our movement'.[4]

The stations and trains where these meetings and flirtations took place were relatively new urban spaces. The construction of the railways, chiefly in the years between 1837 and 1876, caused massive disruption in London and set in chain wide-ranging social and cultural change.[5] Communities were destroyed or split apart by the building works, while new suburban developments were facilitated and sustained by the railways.[6] Commuting became a common and characteristic urban experience, separating work and home life, and bringing strangers into close proximity as they travelled in and out of the city. The West End became more accessible, and new shops, theatres and restaurants were built, catering for an increasingly diverse clientele. The new transport infrastructure, which from 1863 incorporated the developing Underground,[7] altered the way time, space and the city were experienced. It was central to ideas about London's modernity and intrinsic to notions of a new pace and complexity to urban life.[8] The vast new termini which circled the central area, for example, combined monumental architectural rhetoric with chaotic scenes. They defiantly proclaimed London and Britain's technical, economic and cultural prowess. Yet with their cosmopolitan crowds, 'shifting scenes' and 'low life' they also threatened impropriety and a breakdown in social order.[9] As Henning Bech observes, they 'compacted and condensed' the experience of the modern city.[10] For men on the lookout for sex and relationships with other men, the mass of diverse strangers – hurrying or waiting – and the sense of transition and flux promised new erotic experiences.[11] They seemed to prompt the kind of longings and invite the intense fleeting encounters described by Casement in his diary. Empty railway carriages or the station toilets offered relative privacy for a while, albeit tinged with a danger that was itself titillating for some. For others – like the subject of one of Charles Féré's sexological case studies who reached 'the apogee of genital excitation and emission' on a crowded train – it was the lack of privacy and the forced proximity to unknown men which was exciting.[12]

The various homoerotic possibilities associated with London's stations and trains intersected with competing ideas about homosexuality. Whitmanesque and romantic socialist notions of cross-class comradeship shaped Ashbee's understanding of his relations with other men, and the fraternity of the ancient Theban bands structured Ives' concept of homosexual love and his fight for the 'cause' of decriminalisation and social acceptance. Ives also linked his desires to the distinctive urban identities outlined by the sexologists. Casement finally seems to have been enticed by the perceived scope for casual sex in the city. The French traveller, the guardsman and the 'respectable' young man at Gloucester Road may have brought other ideas to these encounters – about the possibilities and romance associated with travel and tourism, about sexually dissolute 'gents' or older men, about ploys for extra earnings, or about the desire for masculine intimacy, whether or not a distinctive sexual identity was owned or acknowledged. What is certain is that the encounters meant somewhat different things for each of the men involved.[13] The brief details of Brown's case in *Reynolds*, meanwhile, potentially reinforced notions about the type of man liable to commit 'acts of gross indecency' with other men, about the activities of soldiers and sailors stationed or on leave in the city – the latter famously disembarking at Victoria from Portsmouth[14] – or about the dangers and possibilities associated with London's stations.

The interplay of ideas and practices associated with the quintessentially modern sites of the railway station and train carriage underscore the axiomatic connection between urban material and cultural change and the proliferating discourses of homosexuality. The link would seem to be self-evident: think of 'gay' men and 'gay' culture and we think of cities, from ancient Athens through biblical Sodom and Renaissance Florence to Armistead Maupin's San Francisco or Pedro Almodovar's Madrid. Yet as the analysis above suggests, the apparent ubiquity of the connection is deceptive and diverse stories have been told about the place and experience of homosexuality in the metropolis. This book explores the contours of the relationship for one city and one short period – London from the criminalisation of all 'acts of gross indecency' between men in 1885 to the outbreak of the First World War in 1914. These years were marked by burgeoning debate and concern about homosexuality and came towards the end of half a century of massive upheaval in the rapidly expanding British capital.[15] Following Michel Foucault and Jeffrey Week's pioneering work in the 1970s, literary and lesbian and gay scholars have variously examined the significance of the law, the newspapers, sexology, aestheticism and decadence, and Hellenism to shifting ideas of homosexuality during the period under discussion here.[16] These fields of debate and writing provided distinctive frames of reference through which homosexual relations were experienced, condemned and celebrated. A similar complexity attended the representation of London, which was figured as a modern, imperial capital, a cosmopolitan and frivolous metropolis and a degraded and degenerate city, blighted by poverty and immorality. These and other conceptions of London, and the complex dynamics which existed between them, were repeatedly caught up in accounts of homosexual activity. Stations, theatres, public toilets, particular streets and parks, restaurants, pubs and hotels, university settlements, sports clubs, swimming pools and even the British Museum were loaded with expectations and associations which intersected with the different ways of thinking about homosexual encounter. These places were each implicated in the social, sexual and political aspects of emerging homosexual identities.

The book is informed by work in a number of disciplines. Cultural geographers and architectural theorists have demonstrated the constitutive power of the built environment and its importance to cultural and individual conceptions of self and sexuality. In consequence they have argued for the reintegration of space into social and cultural analysis.[17] Scholars working on specific cities – Tony Tanner on Venice, Christopher Prendergast on Paris, Catherine Edwards on Rome, and Elizabeth Wilson, Erica Rappaport, Judith Walkowitz and Lynda Nead on London – have taken up this challenge and shown how space and time might intersect in historical analysis.[18] Their interdisciplinarity has moreover allowed for complex understandings of the interaction of material change, representation and subjectivity. Such an approach acknowledges that we live, as Gillian Beer observes, 'in a variety of conflicted epistemologies' which intersect in different forms of writing and in our everyday lives.[19] This book follows a similar path. It attends carefully to the post-structuralist invocation to look closely at discourse and representation in a consideration of culture, society and identity, yet also seeks to resist the impulse to apply these ideas formulaically. What the encounters in the stations show is that understandings and behaviours were various and unpredictable. Circulating ideas about homosexuality were often contradictory and did not map straightforwardly on to an individual's self-perception and choices. Moreover, shifts over time in understandings of homosexual behaviour were neither universal nor even.[20] The criminalisation of acts of gross indecency between men in 1885 did not mark the initiation of a homosexual subculture or of a distinctive homosexual 'type', as the first chapter will show. There was not a wholesale revolution in attitudes or a sudden coherence in perspective in this year, and different views and experiences necessarily co-existed in domestic, work and recreational spaces across the capital.

People reacted to prevailing ideas and representations in many different ways. Newspaper coverage of the Wilde case, to take an obvious example, noisily rearticulated what should not happen between two men, but just as noisily proclaimed that it did and outlined where it took place and who was involved. The coverage may have induced self-doubt, fear, disgust or anger, but also provided solace and reassurance, and perhaps a role model and map for those who related to Wilde's desires. Such writing had numerous and conflicting meanings and effects, which existed beyond the control or intent of the writer and publisher, and exposed contradictions and inconsistencies in prevailing norms and values.[21] Its impact was modulated by an array of complex variables, which might themselves be in flux, among them the reader's social and economic status, profession, literacy, education, faith, their family's expectations and dynamic, and prevailing concepts of class, gender and nationality. These ideologies, values and pressures shaped the individual's sense of themselves and their relations with others, even if at a conscious level they were – to use Kaja Silverman – 'morally and ironically detached' from them.[22] They set up competing claims on the individual, so that his or her feelings, opinions and behaviour might change between places and between what Barbara H. Rosenwein calls 'emotional communities'.[23] Ives, for example, acted differently with his family, his friends and his associates in the Order of the Chaerona.

The men discussed in this book necessarily existed within complex and interlocking discursive frameworks, the precise impact of which is impossible to track. Even if we could, however, it is important to remember that the writing, speech and behaviour of an individual will always have elements which are beyond his or her conscious grasp, let alone the analytical powers of the biographer, historian or critic. Their, our, sexual identities, Lyndal Roper notes, 'nearly always lack the coherence – or the comforting contradictions – of discourse'.[24]

The chapters that follow describe and refer to a heady brew of ideas, ideologies, writings and debates which preclude any simplistic account of behaviour and choice. This is not to discount the power of language and representation in shaping subjectivity and marking limits to the conceptualisation of sexuality, identity and the city. Instead, it is to suggest that their effect was not uniform and that individuals responded in many different ways because of a complex nexus of variables. The book demonstrates the impossibility of conjuring a unitary 'gay' metropolis or a singular 'gay' urban type, and indicates instead the controlled plurality which characterised the relationship between London and homosexuality.

There have of course been other explorations of homosexuality and London. The important work of H. Montgomery Hyde and Rupert Croft-Cooke in the 1960s and 1970s suggested a pragmatic relationship between homosexuality and the city; it was a context for, rather than a component of, their analyses.[25] Neil Bartlett's *Who Was that Man? A Present for Mr Oscar Wilde* (1988) came as an inspiring and deeply personal corrective, exploring the 'signs' of homosexuality in London in the 1880s and 1890s as part of a meditation on the place of history and the history of places in the formation of ideas about the self and identity.[26] Further work on urban homosexuality in general and on other cities and other periods in London's homosexual history followed, notably George Chauncey's *Gay New York* (1995), Garry Wotherspoon's *City of the Plain* (1991) (on Sydney), and Alan Bray, Randolph Trumbach and Rictor Norton's studies of London in the Renaissance and early modern periods.[27] More recent scholarship has refocussed on the configuration of London and homosexuality during the nineteenth century. Morris B. Kaplan explores the relationship between homosexual subjectivity, the city and concepts of class and gender in a series of case studies from the 1870s and 1880s.[28] H. G. Cocks has combined an attentiveness to the representation of homosexuality – especially in the newspapers – with a rigorous analysis of arrest and prosecution patterns across the nineteenth century.[29] Both scholars suggest the complexity of forms of homosexual identity and self-making, something which has tended to be obscured by the attention devoted to Oscar Wilde.

This book complements and supplements these other studies. It moves the discussion beyond the Wilde trials to 1914 to counter the largely unchallenged orthodoxy that in their wake there was renewed repression and a recession in the urban homosexual subculture.[30] It also focusses specifically on the relationship between shifting conceptions of the metropolis and the intensifying debate on homosexuality from the 1880s onwards, moving between a range of writings and representations, from the scientific to the literary, to show how dissonant and overlapping images of urban homosexuality were propagated and circulated.

The first chapter looks at London's homoerotic geography from *c.*1700 through to 1914. Those that follow draw on this mapping and history, and discuss the law and the newspaper press, sexology, aestheticism and decadence, and Hellenism and pastoralism in turn. In some ways this structure is problematic, suggesting an inappropriate cultural compartmentalisation. It is nonetheless useful, because although the bodies of writing and debate were interrelated, they were not equivalent. They had different purposes, different power to influence ideas and behaviour, and different audiences. The separate treatment also allows internal dissonances to emerge; newspapers took up different ideological positions and sexologists disagreed about the symptoms and causes of homosexuality. Each chapter attempts to show the specificity of, and contradictions within, each field, whilst also exploring the ways in which they complemented each other and were associated with a range of places in, and debates about, the city. Together they illustrate some of the ways in which men who had sex with other men negotiated London and comprehended and took part in its culture of homosexuality.

CHAPTER I

London and the cities of the plain

The Introduction observed that late Victorian newspapers, court cases, science and fiction were important in the genesis and consolidation of modern ideas of 'homosexual' identity. In their work on these fields scholars have elaborated and modified Michel Foucault's famous assertion that the period saw the emergence of the homosexual as 'a species' and set in chain the binary heterosexual/homosexual logic of desire which maintains its power today.[1] However, whilst these years were marked by a crisis in, and discursive elaboration of, sexuality and sexual identification, identities and subcultural forms associated with homosexual acts can be seen well before, as can a strong connection with the city.[2]

In the Renaissance period, Alan Bray suggests, homosexual activity was associated with peripatetic theatre companies and the court, and most liaisons were opportunistic and associated with isolated acts rather than a wider subcultural identification.[3] Given differing understandings of selfhood, gender and sexual identity, people were not looking for homosexual activity in the same way as they were later. 'In general', Bray notes, '[it] went unrecognised or ignored, both by those immediately involved and by the communities in which they lived.'[4] In the late seventeenth and early eighteenth centuries, however, there seems to have been a conceptual shift in understandings of homosexual behaviour. Richard Davenport-Hines associates this with developing ideas of selfhood and individuality in the seventeenth century which allowed for the concept of a distinctive and potentially exclusive sexual identity.[5] Randolph Trumbach and Alan Sinfield note a concomitant change in understandings of gender categories, with ideas of masculinity and femininity becoming more fixed and increasingly related to who an individual had sex with. Masculinity was thus bound up with desiring women and femininity with desiring men. The corollary of this was that desire was understood to function across the gender divide. For a man to have sex with another man implicated effeminacy; he became 'like a woman'. This understanding was inherently problematic since a 'masculine' man would be necessary to satisfy the desires of an 'effeminate' one, spoiling, as Sinfield points out, 'the idea of effeminacy as the defining characteristic of same-sex passion'.[6] To complicate matters further the aristocratic fop was commonly described as effeminate, whether he had sex with men or not. In *Hell Upon Earth, or The Town in Uproar* (1729), a tract detailing vice in London, he was said to have a taste for fashion and affected manners, precisely the qualities ascribed to the 'Sodomite' a few pages later.[7] Effeminacy was thus a problematic and imprecise signifier of homosexuality at this time, and indeed for the centuries to come, but it was nevertheless used repeatedly in descriptions of men who had sex with other men. An oppositional understanding of sexual tastes had begun to emerge, which, though not as absolute as the homosexual/heterosexual division of the twentieth century, allowed for stereotypes and assumptions about exclusivity in sexual tastes to take hold. Men who contravened norms of masculine and sexual behaviour were increasingly seen as distinctive, and partly as a result their presence in the city was more evident and challenging.[8] In *Satyrical Reflections on Clubs* (1710) Ned Ward identified 'Mollies' clubs' attended by 'Sodomitical wretches' who were 'so far degenerated from all masculine deportment or manly exercises that they rather fancy themselves women'.[9] Twenty years later *Hell Upon Earth* referred to 'brutish creatures called Sodomites' in the city, adding to ideas of effeminacy the notion of animalism and also a paradoxical hyper-masculinity. A similar rhetoric ran through *The Phoenix of Sodom, or The Vere Street Coterie*, published in 1813, which also described a distinctive sub-group – 'a catamite brood, kneaded into human *shape, from the sweepings of Sodom, with the spawn of Gomorrah*'. They were the victims of 'damnable propensities' and 'a dreadful, malignant malady', already suggesting an association between pathology and particular sexual tastes.[10] The text also revealed marriage and birthing rituals at the White Swan pub in Vere Street, just off Oxford Street, which were similar to accounts of behaviour at Mother Clap's Molly House in Holborn almost a century earlier in 1726, indicating a lineage of subcultural activity in London.[11] The men involved in this subculture were apparently readily identifiable either by their general demeanor or their secret signals and presence in particular places. In 1781, for example, George Parker noted that men could be found 'around twilight' in Bird Cage Walk, St James's Park 'signalling' to each other:

If one of them sits on a bench, he pats the backs of his hands; if you follow them, they put a white handkerchief thro' the skirts of their coat, and wave it to and fro; but if they are met by you, their thumbs are stuck in the arm-pits of their waistcoats, and they play their fingers upon their breasts. By means of these signals they retire to satisfy a passion too horrible for description, too detestable for language.[12]

Earlier in 1726, Thomas Newton, working for the Society for the Reformation of Manners, used his knowledge of Moorfields as a cruising ground and of 'the methods they used in picking one another up' to entrap William Brown. Brown was subsequently pilloried, fined £6 13s and imprisoned for a year. He was unrepentant however, and told police that he thought there 'was no crime in making what use I please of my own body'.[13]

The insistence on the distinctive behaviour and habits of these men perhaps betrayed a concern about precisely the reverse. *Hell Upon Earth* drew attention to changing identifications, noting the 'strength and vigour' of condemned sodomites on the scaffold, but recalling their 'ridiculous affectations' in the clubs, 'assum[ing] the air and affect[ing] the name of Madam or Miss, Betty or Molly'.[14] They challenged the emergent stereotypes in court by citing their marital status and progeny by way of defence; they were worryingly 'normal' men. Later, in *The Phoenix of Sodom* (1813), Holloway pointed out the dual identities of the White Swan's clientele. He noted the 'generally received opinion' of effeminacy amongst these 'beings' but also observed that Fanny Murray, Lucy Cooper and Kitty Fisher, who were arrested at the pub, were 'personified by an athletic bargeman, an Herculean coalheaver, and deaf-tyre smith'.[15] In the pillories that followed the case it was precisely this lack of conformity to stereotype that attracted the most vitriol from the crowd. One newspaper noted that it was 'the apparently manly appearance [of one of the defendants which] drew down peculiar execrations on him'.[16]

The White Swan case demonstrated the scope for men to present themselves differently in different parts of the city: to be Fanny Murray at the Molly House and an athletic bargeman elsewhere. London had undergone massive expansion in the seventeenth century, and by 1700 had a population of around 600,000, twenty times more than the next largest town in England. By the time of the raid on the White Swan in 1813 one and a quarter million people lived in the city.[17] This meant that a greater degree of anonymity could be maintained as men moved between places and identities. The growth of the city also meant that there were increasing numbers of men who might take part in homosexual activities, allowing a subcultural network to become more organised and integrated into city life – and for a series of places to gain a reputation for their popularity with Mollies and sodomites. St James' Park and the area around it were mentioned especially frequently. In 1709 'a notorious gang of Sodomites' were arrested in a brandy shop on Jermyn Street, and the Royal Oak on the corner of St James' Square and Pall Mall was a Molly House in the 1720s, complete with private chapel for mock marriages.[18] The park itself was listed as a 'market' – a cruising ground – in *Hell Upon Earth* and was subsequently the focus of George Parker's account of the sodomite's secret signals.[19] The Little Theatre in the Haymarket and the Star and Crown in Broadway, just south of the park, were the scenes of scandals in the 1780s and 1790s,[20] and in 1791 the Grand Jury of Middlesex wrote to the Home Secretary urging that St James' Park should be locked at night to forestall 'that most detestable and abominable Crime'.[21] Seventeen years later the Home Secretary complained that many persons 'known to have unnatural propensities...have been found...loitering around St James' Park every evening after dark' with the intention of 'making assignations with each other'.[22]

Moorfields, just north of the City of London, had a similar reputation. It was well known to Thomas Newton in the 1720s, as was indicated earlier,[23] and the nearby Three Shoes pub was noted for serving ale to Mollies.[24] Further cases in Moorfields in 1810 indicate a long-standing notoriety.[25] Still in the City area, London Bridge and the Royal Exchange in Threadneedle Street featured in cases in 1707, and the latter was cited as a notorious meeting place in *Hell Upon Earth* just over twenty years later.[26] St Clements' Churchyard in King William Street and St Paul's Churchyard were also apparently popular with men looking for sex with other men in the 1720s,[27] as were the piazza at Covent Garden and Lincoln's Inn Fields 'bog-houses' further west.[28] Again there were accommodating pubs and houses nearby: Mother Clap's house in Field Lane, Holborn, was raided in 1726 and the Three Tobacco Rolls in Covent Garden was implicated in a case in the same year.[29] *The Phoenix of Sodom* mentions more pubs in the West End in the early nineteenth century, including the White Swan in Vere Street and others in St George's Fields, near what is now Marble Arch, and the Strand. These, Holloway suggested, were part of 'the vast geography of this moral blasting evil' in the city.[30] What is indicated is a range of indoor and outdoor spaces which provided opportunities for socialising, subcultural ritual and sex throughout the eighteenth and early nineteenth centuries.

Commentators were predictably indignant about these activities and the apparent tolerance of the authorities and the public at large. The extent of the latter is difficult to assess. The persistent use of cruising areas such as St James' Park and Moorfields suggests that there was no concerted crack-down and that periodic arrests and prosecutions did not comprehensively deter men from visiting these places. Some of the Molly Houses certainly seem to have been well known for long periods before they were raided and shut down. Witnesses in the trial of Gabriel Lawrence, who was hanged for his part in the Mother Clap case, testified that 'the house bore the public character of a place of rendezvous for sodomites' and that 'it was notorious for being a Molly House'.[31] Cook, the proprietor of the White Swan in Vere Street, had been in business for twelve years before being raided and was well enough known to attract customers from up to thirty miles away.[32] Policing of the capital was uneven and disorganised during the period, however, and the public vitriol once activities at the White Swan had been exposed is startling. The shops on the route of the procession from Newgate to the pillory in the Haymarket were closed and the streets lined with people. The cart carrying the prisoners was preceded by others loaded with offal, vegetables and excrement for the crowd to throw. By the time the men arrived at the pillory they looked like 'bears dipped in a stag-nant pool'.[33] The newspapers felt that the punishment was insufficient and that more action was needed to effect 'the annihilation of so detestable a race'.[34] Davenport-Hines accounts for the crowd's reaction partly through the continuing Napoleonic wars: the pillory was, he suggests, 'both pa-triotic and cathartic and offered a twisted form of social unity'.[35] The sodomite and Molly embodied a threat to the nation, not least by challeng-ing standards of masculinity and constituting a supposedly alien presence. They were, as we have seen, described as a 'race' apart, and indeed foreigners were consistently blamed for bringing the 'vice' to England. In *Satan's Harvest Home* (1749) and Parker's *A View of Society and Manners* (1781) Italians were said to have introduced it to England; Holloway's *Phoenix of Sodom* blamed foreign heretics arriving in 1315; and the *Morning Chronicle* at the time of the White Swan case suggested that the vice, which was 'horrible to the nature of Englishmen', had insinuated itself into the coun-try through the influence of foreign soldiers on our own troops.[36] The men involved were also seen to wreak havoc on putatively orderly notions of nation, gender and social hierarchy. *A View of the Town* (1735), for ex-ample, described an aristocrat looking for sex with an 'ingle', a servant or lower-class man:

He to St James's Park with rapture flies,
And roams in search of some vile ingle prize;
Courts the foul pathick in the fair one's place
And with unnatural lust defiles his race...
The great metropolis of England's isle
Had like to've been the nation's funeral pile.[37]

The danger to the race and nation here stemmed not just from the homosexual nature of the liaisons, but from the disregard of social boundaries. Similarly, in *The Phoenix of Sodom*, Holloway dwelt on the lack of social propriety at the White Swan, where 'men of rank and respectable station might be seen wallowing either in or on the beds with wretches of the lowest description'.[38]

Each of these texts uncovered a disgraceful subculture and implied by contrast the decency and propriety of the author and reader. They bolstered and helped to constitute prevailing ideas of normality and also suggested the need to control the sexual life of the growing city. The activities of the Society for the Reformation of Manners communicated similar messages. The society was founded by a group of puritanical Christians who used agents provocateurs to entrap men in places like Moorfields and the Royal Exchange in the early part of the 1700s and informers to indict Mother Clap, her clients and others in the 1720s.[39] These agents provocateurs and informers, together with the rhetoric of revelation and the tips for spotting sodomites and Mollies, brought the possibility of exposure, either of an isolated act or a set of subcultural practices, forcefully into the consciousness of those involved. Ideas of visibility and invisibility, of secrecy and exposure, were crucial to the genesis of ideas about homosexual identity in the city, not least in promoting the assumption that there was something, in addition to the genital acts themselves, to see, and in making people aware of the supposed tell-tale signs. Homosexual behaviour was thus incorporated into the visual economy of the city during the eighteenth century. Parks, churchyards, places of commercial exchange and the Molly 'clubs' were marked out as meeting places, and effeminacy and theatricality observed as defining characteristics of men seeking sex with other men.

The city's homosexual subculture continued to flourish in the nineteenth century. Rictor Norton notes that the area around Seven Dials was a productive cruising ground for William Beckford in the 1810s,[40] and in 1825 John Muirhead, a member of the Society for the Suppression of Vice, was arrested after picking up an apprentice outside a print shop in Sackville

Street, just off Piccadilly. In 1822 Percy Jocelyn, the Bishop of Clogher, was caught with a guardsman in the White Lion Tavern in the Haymarket. An ensuing condemnatory pamphlet asserted that 'there were various houses in the metropolis used by such wretches for their nefarious purposes, especially in the neighbourhood of St Mary-le-bone'.[41] Three years later twenty-five men were arrested in an upstairs room at the Barley Mow in the Strand, seven of whom were subsequently convicted of indecent assault.[42] A raid on the Bull in Bullen Court, just off the Strand, in 1830, revealed the use of an upstairs room by men who had picked up soldiers in Horse Guards Parade.[43] Other cases around this time involved soldiers at the Knightsbridge Barracks, and a canon of St Paul's, who was found in flagrante in a wharf off Upper Thames Street, just south of the cathedral.[44] Many of these cases were greeted with considerable public anger. Jocelyn and his guardsman lover had to be protected from angry crowds, whilst the men arrested at the Bull faced a mob of 500, who pelted them with mud.

Homosexual activity became more visible with the increasingly rigorous policing of the capital that followed the formation of the Metropolitan Police Force in 1829. H. G. Cocks' detailed analysis of arrests and prosecutions for homosexual sex shows a particular preponderance of offences in the area between St Paul's, Bishopsgate, the river and Finsbury Square in the City of London, and details the drag balls taking place regularly in the early 1850s at the Druid's Hall in Turnagain Lane, just to the north-west of the cathedral. These were publicly exposed when two men attending in women's clothes were arrested in 1854 for 'conducting themselves in a manner to excite others to commit an unnatural offence'.[45] Cocks notes further activity in the West End – in Hyde Park, Green Park, Piccadilly, Soho, Covent Garden and the Strand.

Yokel's Preceptor, or More Sprees in London (c.1855), a cheap, sensational guidebook to the capital's gin palaces and gaming houses, adds credence to Cocks' findings. It detailed the activities of 'Margeries' and 'pooffs' in London,[46] and, apart from indicating a new lexicon, offered advice on the 'way to know the beasts'. They could be recognised by their 'effeminate air and fashionable dress' and were to be found in the shopping area of the quadrant at the south end of Regent Street, completed in 1819, and on Fleet Street, the Strand and Charing Cross, where pubs had supposedly erected signs warning 'Beware of Sods'. These 'Sods' apparently also frequented the saloon bars of the theatres, coffee houses and West End picture shops. 'Will the reader credit it', the author wrote, 'that these monsters actually walk the streets the same as whores, looking out for a chance!'[47]

Explanatory notes in *Don Leon* (1866), a poem purporting to be by Lord Byron, detailed further cases, including the arrest of William Banks MP in 1841 for an offence in Green Park. The text is an early explicit call for legitimacy for homosexual relations; it attacked the use of agents provocateurs and noted by way of comparison the ease of homoerotic life in Turkey.[48] The poet nevertheless suggested that homosexual activity was endemic in London:

> Yes, London! All thy chastity is show;
> Be witness Vere Street and the Barley Mow.
> Lives there a man, what'er his rank may be,
> Who now can say my caste from stain is free?[49]

He went on to describe the places associated with homosexual activity: it took place opportunistically in barracks and schools; with more intent in Hyde Park and certain pubs. He traced a lineage of urban cases and observed that a distinctive subculture had become a durable and intractable part of city life.

The City of London was mentioned less and less from this time onwards and the West End became the main focus of reported activity. This coincided with what Erica Rappaport has identified as an increasing physical and ideological separation between shopping and other forms of commercial activity during, but especially in the second half of, the nineteenth century.[50] Regent Street and Oxford Street were by this time London's best-known shopping areas and it was mainly in and near these streets that department stores developed from the 1860s onwards. They advertised widely, stocked a baffling array of lavishly displayed products and became, Michael Miller suggests, the symbolic centres of consumer society, selling not just goods but the idea of consumption itself.[51] The City meanwhile became a more dour and serious financial district in the latter half of the century, and was figured as a masculine realm in opposition to the feminised and more overtly sexualised West End.[52] The Burlington Arcade (1817), just off Piccadilly, was 'the chief temple of frippery and frivolity',[53] and Alison Adburgham notes that a room above the bonnet shop in the arcade was regularly used by prostitutes.[54] Nearby Regent Street and the Haymarket were also notorious for prostitution and these streets came to represent both sexual and consumerist excess: places of frivolous purchase by day and unsanctioned sexual transaction by night. Men seeking sex and relationships with other men appear to have taken advantage of these developments and the West End became a popular cruising ground, apparently confirming the association of homosexual behaviour with fashion, effeminacy and monetary transaction.

This becom[es] [espec]ially clear in the case of Ernest Boulton and Frederick Park – also kno[wn as] Fanny and Stella – who were charged with 'conspiring and inciting pers[o]ns to commit an unnatural offence' after being arrested in women's clothes at the Strand Theatre in April 1870.[55] What emerged during the trial through the testimony of theatre managers, a Burlington Arcade beadle, a housekeeper and a hansom cab driver, was a circuit of West End spaces which Boulton and Park used with confidence to affirm and sustain their particular lifestyle and sense of identity. They had been known to John Reeves, Staff Superintendent of the Alhambra Theatre in Leicester Square, for two years. He had once thrown them out when, dressed as women, they gathered a crowd of men around them. He testified that on another occasion, this time out of women's clothes, the men leaned over the balcony 'making stupid noises, chirruping to each other with their lips [and] chucking each other on the chin and playing frivolous games'.[56] Their behaviour at the Strand Theatre in Blackfriars on another night was similar. *The Lives of Boulton and Park*, a broadsheet published just before the trial but after police court hearings, noted that 'these ladies leaned over their box, twirled their handkerchiefs, and lasciviously ogled the male occupants of the stalls'.[57] The prosecution also detailed their appearance in women's clothes at the Casino in Holborn, at the Oxford and Cambridge boat race and at fancy dress balls at Haxell's Hotel and the Royal Exeter Hotel, both on the Strand. *The Times* noted that they promenaded 'until late hours in the morning and made acquaintances' in Regent Street and the Haymarket, rather like the prostitutes who worked from these streets.[58] They shopped, again in make-up but sometimes not in women's clothes, in Regent Street and the Burlington Arcade, where they were ejected by the beadle after Stella was observed winking at a gentlemen and 'turning his head in a sly manner'.[59] Undeterred, the beadle testified, the pair returned several times.

On the day of their arrest one witness visited them at Bruton Street, Mayfair, where they 'talk[ed] constantly about performing and playing'.[60] They then took a cab to Chancery Lane Chambers on a visit before going back to Oxford Street to buy gloves, and Portland Place – the continuation of Regent Street to the north – to buy jewellery. When these and other items were displayed in court the *Telegraph* noted that 'it seemed...as though outcasts of one of the Monmouth Street [clothes shops] had been cast over the court of the Queen's bench'.[61]

This behaviour, together with over forty letters seized by the police, was taken as compelling evidence of homosexual activity by the prosecuting authorities. The Attorney General, H. James QC, for the prosecution, referred to the 'searching investigation', including a year of police surveillance,

Figure 1 'The Lives of Boulton and Park', 1870.

undertaken to ascertain whether 'the popular apprehension was correct'.[62] The committing magistrate refused the men bail and the author of *The Lives of Boulton and Park* saw 'the profligacy of the guilty cities of the plain' in their behaviour.[63] The defence, meanwhile, argued that sodomites would not advertise their condition so blatantly and that Boulton and Park were merely over-enthusiastic in their passion for the theatre. Both men had appeared as women in amateur theatricals in London, Scarborough and as part of a charity tour of village and town halls in Essex. But although in these contexts cross-dressing may have been seen as relatively benign, in the West End streets and theatres it was more suggestive, as Cocks points out.[64] In his summing-up the judge clearly associated effeminacy with homosexuality. He criticised James Paul, the police surgeon, for the unauthorised and inconclusive anal examination he conducted on Boulton and Park, but demurred from punishing him because they were 'two effeminate' rather than 'two strong' men.[65] The examination was apparently partially justifiable because of the defendants' effeminacy.

Given this popular apprehension Boulton and Park's public performance was a daring one: 'they used their frocks', Neil Bartlett argues, 'to create public space for themselves in London, in the separate but overlapping world of the actress, the prostitute and the *demimondaine*'.[66] They took on these roles self-consciously and convincingly; at the Strand Theatre some witnesses were sure, at least at first, that they were 'fast women' or 'fresh stars about to shine in the firmament of the *demimonde*'.[67] At other times they wore make-up but did not attempt to disguise themselves as women, yet were still allowed into the Burlington Arcade and tolerated at the Alhambra. Boulton and Park, as Bartlett suggests, played the city carefully, aware of where they could get away with particular outfits, and where adjustment or more comprehensive and convincing 'drag' was necessary.[68] In court they took on yet another role: they both wore suits, and Park, in a strategic use of contemporary ideas of masculinity, 'had grown stout' and sported a moustache.[69]

The Lives of Boulton and Park expressed outrage – a convenient vehicle for detailed revelation – at the men's behaviour and claimed that London now 'outvie[d] the Cities of the Plain and ancient Rome'. It suggested that Boulton and Park were part of a broader network of 'Margeries' who found the West End streets, pubs and theatres especially accommodating,[70] rather as *Don Leon* and *Satan's Harvest Home* had suggested. These men were 'poison[ing] society in our midst' and threatening those 'dearest to our heart and hearths'.[71] They were both anti-English – their activities took place to the indignation 'of every true Englishman' – and anti-domestic,[72] rather like the prostitutes being discussed by the Royal Commission on the Contagious Diseases Acts, sitting at the time as the trial.

Despite this threat, the public seem to have been entertained rather than appalled by the Boulton and Park case. The men faced little of the collective public outrage and dismay that greeted those arrested at the White Swan, even though the supposed connection between sodomy and effeminacy had been made more or less explicit during the trial. The *Telegraph* commented on the unstinting public interest and *Reynolds* noted a largely friendly crowd outside the court: 'some of the assembled mass cheered them, some hissed and some clapped their hands . . . Fairly seated in the cab, Boulton . . . put up his hands to his lips and kissed to his friends.'[73] Inside the court laughter accompanied much of the evidence and the outburst of applause which greeted the acquittal had to be suppressed by officials. Especially as there was no obvious victim in the case, the mens' performance was viewed as an intriguing and entertaining spectacle. There may have been wilful disbelief or genuine guilelessness in the interpretation of Boulton and Park's effeminacy and cross-dressing by some, as Bartlett and Sinfield have suggested,[74] but the absence of a complainant or any direct evidence that 'unnatural' practices had taken place were key both to the acquittal and the more general response to the case. When Wilde was prosecuted twenty-five years later his 'pose' was important, as with Boulton and Park, but so too was the testimony of the men he had had sex with. The stereotypes were well established by the 1870s even if they were not universally understood and it was this lack of evidence, together with what Cocks describes as 'an unusually sympathetic judge' and skilful defence team, which saved the men from prison.[75]

Sins of the Cities of the Plain, the pornographic novel published in 1881, a decade after Fanny and Stella's trial, indicated to a more limited audience the sexual possibilities London offered. A confident urban pose was again suggested and London's West End was shown accommodating performances like those of Fanny and Stella, as well as more explicit sexual antics for which the two men could certainly have been prosecuted. What the text usefully illuminates is the way in which prevailing class, gender and racial power dynamics were replicated in conceptualisations of homosexual behaviour during the period. It also outlines a fictionalised homoerotic geography of London which drew on real people and places and reproduced many of the images emerging from the courts, press and broadsheets. Crucially, though, it recapitulated these images and mappings outside the censorious juridical or journalistic context.

Two hundred and fifty copies of *Sins of the Cities of the Plain* were privately published in 1881 by William Lazenby, who had offices in Leicester Square. Peter Mendes suggests that it was a collaborative work by the publisher of erotica James Campbell Reddie and the painter Simeon Solomon, who, disgraced after his conviction for sex with a man in a Marylebone public toilet in 1873, was in desperate need of money.[76] The story takes the form of the memoirs of a young male prostitute, Jack Saul, who is paid to set down his experiences by a client, Mr Cambon of Cornwall Mansions, Baker Street – the address of a pornographer friend of Lazenby, William Potter. A male prostitute by the same name featured in the Cleveland Street male brothel scandal of 1889–90, and Fanny and Stella, whom Solomon had met during their trial, also appear in the text. Pisanus Fraxi – the scatological alias of Henry Spenser Ashbee, father of C. R. Ashbee – noted that 'they would almost appear to have been sketched from personal acquaintance'.[77] Real addresses, pubs and hotels are mentioned and it seems that the author/s not only knew London well, but had an intimate knowledge of its homosexual subculture. They aimed to arouse the reader through descriptions of sex in real places and with figures who were either well known generally, such as Fanny and Stella, or who might have had a subcultural reputation, like Saul. They deliberately presented sexual fantasies as documentary and consequently appeared to elaborate the dynamics of an actual urban subculture.

Saul recounts experiences on a farm in Sussex and at his public school, but it is at a London draper's, where he works from the age of sixteen, that his adventures really begin. He ministers to an aristocratic brother and sister in Piccadilly, to members of a secret club in Portland Place, owned by the suggestively named Mr Inslip, to another aristocrat living in Grosvenor Square and to a lawyer in his offices at the Temple. Saul also attends a cross-dressing ball with Fanny and Stella at Haxell's Hotel, has sex with them at a house in Eaton Square in Belgravia, and has further erotic adventures in the grounds of Hampton Court Palace during the Prince of Wales' garden party. Saul's friend, ex-guardsman Fred Jones, extends this geography in his embedded narrative and describes Mrs Truman's tobacconist's shop next door to the Albany Barracks, Regent's Park, from where guardsmen could be procured. He also notes six other brothels in central London 'where only soldiers are received and where gentlemen can sleep with them'.[78] In addition to these private and exclusive locales, Saul's client Mr Cambon notes that 'the Mary Annes of London ... were often to be seen sauntering in the neighbourhood of Regent Street or the Haymarket' and he himself picks Saul up in Leicester Square outside a picture shop, pinpointed twenty years earlier in *Yokel's Preceptor* as a particular haunt of 'Margeries'.[79]

Key dominant spaces of justice, aristocracy, defence and royalty all feature, as do the hotels, shopping areas, expensive private houses and streets notorious for prostitution. An outlawed set of practices and associated modes of behaviour gain substance in the novel through a dominant and widely understood geography. The significance of such mappings can be seen later in the diaries of Roger Casement and George Ives and in the memoirs of John Addington Symonds, who also visited a brothel near the Albany Barracks.[80] Each of these men carefully set down places with homoerotic associations. The individual who collected newspaper clippings and pasted them into the front of the copy of the *Phoenix of Sodom* held by the British Library may well have been attempting to give a similar geographical substance to his own desires, as Beckford and Ives did in their scrapbook collections.[81] However, in *Sins of the Cities of the Plain*, the element of danger which haunts Ives, the moral rectitude which hinders Symonds and the draconian laws apparent in the newspaper clippings are sidestepped because of the fictional, pornographic nature of the novel. In this way the text allowed for an imaginative leap beyond the limits of everyday life whilst remaining tantalisingly close to real people and places.[82]

Money is a crucial component of sexual relations in the novel. Saul, Jones and a further friend, George Brown, are paid for most of their exploits, and Saul's story is itself bought by the wealthy Mr Cambon. On their shopping rounds of the West End Cambon and the aristocratic siblings return home not with fabric or prints but with a teenage Mary-Ann they find in or outside the shops they visit. In this way the novel elaborates an existing association between commercial transaction and homosexual behaviour evident in the use of Covent Garden and the Royal Exchange as cruising grounds in the eighteenth century. Boulton and Park had earlier also indicated the connection, showing the West End to be an arena where acquisitive (homo)sexual desires might be indulged.

The relationship between homosexuality and prevailing social and economic structures in the city is suggested again in Saul's visit to Grosvenor Square. Saul is conducted into 'his Lordship's billiard room', where three youths from France, Italy and Africa emerge from 'what looked like a large bookcase'.[83] As well as employing aristocratic and domestic form and ritual, the episode trades on the supposed exoticism and pliancy of foreigners.[84] That these ideas emerged partly through an anthropological literature of exploration is wryly suggested by the youths' emergence from the library shelves, a detail which also indicated the potential to realise textual fantasies in the flesh. Their status as fantasy figures makes them pliable, and the aristocrat's power over, and difference from, his sexual objects charges the encounter. This power dynamic is evoked again in George Brown's embedded narrative. He employs a thirteen-year-old shoeshine boy from Whitechapel as his page, takes him to his apartment 'in a nice street in Camden Town' and forces him to have sex.[85] The pivot of Brown's abusive liaison is the social and corresponding geographical division of the city, which is reproduced and utilised in the text to homoerotic effect. Both the Grosvenor Square and Whitechapel encounters rely on apparently fixed positions of class, race and nationality, and the tendency of the city to throw extremes together.

Whilst the author/s used established social roles and dynamics, they also suggested that these might be disrupted within the city and amongst specifically urban players. Saul, Jones and Brown are differentiated from the other characters by being principally identified with the city and homosexual activity rather than with a particular class. As a result they are much more mobile than the men with whom they have sex and are able to occupy different power positions as they move around the city and assume different clothes and sexual roles. Before playing high class to the shoeshine boy, for example, Brown picks up and blackmails swells and 'a Jew from a city financial firm' as a working-class lad.[86] In his guardsman's uniform Jones is a recognisable working-class urban figure, one who features repeatedly in reports of homosexual activity during the period. At other points, however, he appears as a women and also in civilian clothes. Saul has a similarly flexible wardrobe, which includes a pair of 'pretty patent leather boots' and some 'tight fitting trousers'. Despite being the son of a wealthy Suffolk farmer and product of a minor public school, Saul easily casts off the dour middle-class fashion of the 1870s and opts for an outfit which indicates an affiliation to an urban sexual subculture instead.[87] This urban identification allows for an evasion of class proprieties and a wide-ranging exploration of sexual roles and partners.[88] In the city Saul, Brown and Jones relate to each other as apparent equals, without the subterfuge and acquisitiveness which marks their relations with those uninitiated into their milieu. They indicate a distinctive though flexible urban homosexual style which variously embraced, parodied and undermined prevailing social and cultural dynamics.

This pliancy is reflected in the depiction of the urban terrain in the novel, as each locale is carefully evoked but quickly abandoned in favour of another setting. After the appearance of the youths from the cupboard in the billiard room, for example, the aristocratic town house becomes an exotic eastern boudoir: the doors to an adjacent room are flung open to reveal the 'most seductive looking couches and ottomans [and] heavily curtained windows'.[89] Whereas the non-urban spaces that open the novel are fixed, London can reconfigure into one or both of the cities of the plain of the title.

The real and fictional paths Boulton, Park and Saul trod, together with those of the men discussed earlier, indicates an entrenched relationship between the city and homosexuality well before 1885. The notoriety of many of these cases and the continuing availability of some of these texts marked out a long lineage of homosexual activity. *Sins of the Cities of the Plain* continued to be available throughout the period and a new edition was published in 1902, probably by Smithers under the aegis of the Erotica Biblion Society of London. Fanny and Stella were the subject of an obscene limerick in the erotic journal *The Pearl* in 1879 and were also mentioned in newspaper coverage of the Wilde trials and again in 1910 after a spate of cross-dressing cases.[90] Those privy to Pisanus Fraxi's three-volume bibliography of erotica could read summaries of *Satan's Harvest Home*, *The Phoenix of Sodom*, *Yokel's Preceptor*, *The Sins of the Cities of the Plain* and *Don Leon*.[91] Case studies in Henry Havelock Ellis' *Sexual Inversion* (1897) and Xavier Mayne's *The Intersexes* (1908) likewise included details of homosexual exploits in London's parks, theatres and streets in the 1860s, 1870s and 1880s. Gossip and personal testimony doubtless marked out other places in the city which had been used in previous years. These various accounts exposed the risks of homosexual activity in London but also inculcated a sense of permanence and belonging. They indicated a series of places in which prevailing conventions and ideologies might be exploited, adapted or resisted.

'REBUILDING THE CITIES OF THE PLAIN': LONDON, 1885–1914

As the West End changed physically in the 1880s so its reputation for cosmopolitanism, entertainment and consumption was further extended. Piccadilly Circus trebled in size in the late 1880s when the eastern quadrant was demolished to make way for Shaftesbury Avenue. Charing Cross Road was constructed around the same time, connecting the eastern side of Leicester Square directly to Oxford Street and the Strand, the key entertainment and shopping area to the south. New theatres were quickly built on both streets: six on Shaftesbury Avenue, two on Charing Cross Road. On Leicester Square the vast Empire Theatre opened in 1881 and was joined in 1884 by the refurbished and restyled Alhambra. Fashionable cafés, restaurants and hotels appeared across the West End and between 1885 and 1911 the size of the listings section in Baedeker's successive guides to the city increased by a third.[92] These listings included details of lavish new hotels like the Savoy and the Ritz, cheaper cafés like Locklands, Lyons and Flemmings, and continental-style restaurants such as the Tivoli in the Strand, Café Monaco in Shaftesbury Avenue and the Criterion on Piccadilly Circus. These developments drew more visitors to the area and promised new experiences and excitement. They also caused considerable anxiety. Because of their luxury and cosmopolitanism the new hotels were considered anti-domestic and even inappropriate for families,[93] whilst the police and the fledgling London County Council, which was founded in 1888, voiced concern about the swelling West End crowds, risqué entertainments and an increase in prostitution on the main shopping streets.[94] The area was increasingly seen, Judith Walkowitz argues, as 'the site of exchange and erotic activity, a place symbolically opposed to orderly domestic life'.[95] The journalist George Sims noted 'a babel of strange sounds, a clash of unfamiliar accents, a busy crowd of men and women of alien types and un-English bearing' in the Soho streets, and it was here that the illustrator Arthur Ransome later felt himself transformed into a Parisian 'in a moment'.[96] To visit the Moorish café on Soho Street, Ransome went on, was 'to hear strange Moorish melodies, to dream of white buildings with green-painted porticoes'.[97] Piccadilly Circus was similarly slippery. In Oscar Wilde's *The Decay of Lying* (1889) it becomes Japanese in Vivian's aesthetic imagination,[98] whilst in Fergus Hume's murder mystery *The Piccadilly Puzzle* (1889) fog transforms it 'as if by magic ... into a vague immensity resembling the Steppes of Russia', out of which 'ragged figures with sinister faces would loom suddenly'.[99] The area was repeatedly described eluding its geographical position, and whilst the East End had become 'darkest' Africa, parts of the West End shifted between Paris, the Far East, North Africa and even the Russian Steppes. It was cast as a fantastical and sensual realm and appeared to invite reinvention. At the Café de l'Europe in Leicester Square Ransome observed 'office boys trying to be men, and worn-out men trying to be boys'; the social purity tract *Tempted London* (1889) meanwhile baulked at the improprieties of theatre-land, where lower class men 'assum[ed] the feathers to become counterpart to the bird'.[100] In the West End crowd the middle-class Nancy in George Gissing's *In The Year of Jubilee* (1894) 'forgot her identity ... and her emotions differed little from those of any shop-girl let loose'.[101] These depictions suggested the disruption of the urban typology as identifiers of class and nationality

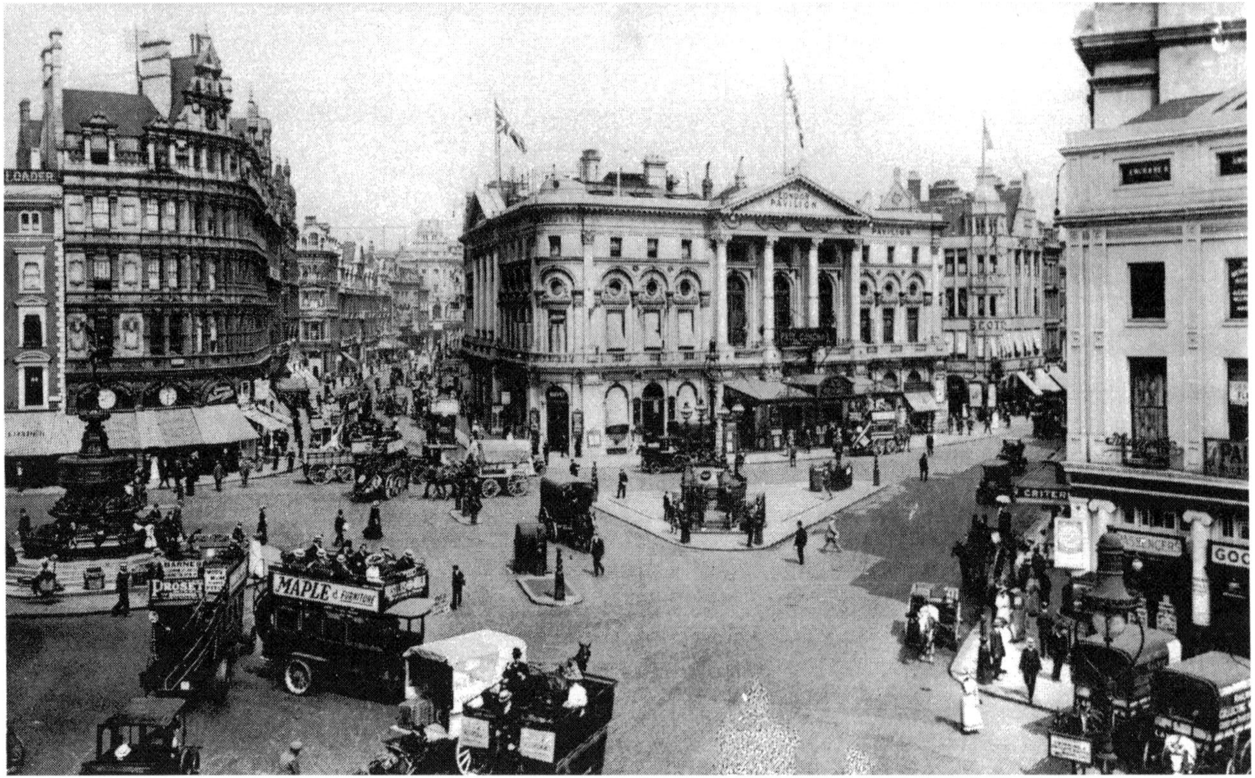

Figure 2 Picadilly Circus, *c*.1901.

were momentarily lost or deliberately eluded. The West End was an obvious area for sensual experimentation and adventuring.[102] The author of *Tempted London* concluded that it 'must have the very worst effects on youth'.[103]

Piccadilly Circus had a subcultural and more general notoriety for renters and homosexual cruising.[104] It was here in 1889 that a real-life Jack Saul, represented as a cross-dressing 'Piccadilly vulture' in the *Illustrated Police News* (see fig. 8, p. 56), handed out cards referring men to the Cleveland Street brothel. Oxford Street had a similar reputation. By this time it was famous for vast drapers and clothing outlets, and it was perhaps no coincidence that the street was mentioned in a number of cross-dressing cases during the period. These included the case of Henry Müller, a French 'alien', who was jailed for three months with hard labour for trying to solicit men near Oxford Circus whilst dressed as a woman in 1906.[105] Roger Casement reported meeting men at both Oxford Circus and Piccadilly Circus, and also on other West End streets, including the Strand, Marble Arch, Tottenham Court Road, the Mall and Victoria Street.[106] Casement was meticulous in his record-keeping. Alongside the meeting place, he noted the age, penis size and nationality – he had a particular penchant for French, Italian and Irish men – of his pick-ups. If he had paid for sex the amount was added to a right-hand column of other expenditure for the day, a pragmatism which indicates the habitual nature of this kind of encounter for him. His record conflated the bodies and genitalia of his anonymous sexual partners with monetary exchange and with particular places in the capital, overlaying the principal streets and intersections with his own homoerotic associations. Such casual encounters were also facilitated by the new iron urinals which appeared across the area from the 1860s. Those at Great Castle Street and Woodstock Street, near Oxford Circus, and in Danbury Place, off Wardour Street in Soho, had a particular reputation, and the new public toilets which came with the expansion of Piccadilly Circus also appear to have been in frequent use.[107] Hyde notes that 'gents' were sometimes collared and threatened in urinals in Berkeley Square.[108]

Knightsbridge Skating Rink and Earls Court Exhibition Hall, opened in 1887 by J. R. Whiteley, were popular meeting places,[109] though on one of his frequent visits to Earls Court in 1901 a disappointed Ives noted that there had been 'many pretty things all around, but no adventures'.[110] The notoriety of the central London parks was ongoing and Hyde Park was well known for the soldier prostitutes who picked up clients there.[111] In 1903, in recognition of the problem, the army issued an order forbidding uniformed soldiers from 'loiter[ing] without lawful purpose in the parks after dusk'.[112] Soldiers were nevertheless implicated in a number of gross indecency cases throughout the period and well into the new century,[113] and they were figures of erotic fantasy for John Addington Symonds, Roger Casement, George Ives, the poet A. E. Housman and many others.[114]

The trains and grand new stations allowed for chance meetings and anonymous sex, as was noted in the Introduction, and the buses and trams presented similar opportunities. The aesthetic occultist Count Stenbock met a sixteen-year-old boy on top of a Piccadilly horse bus in the late 1880s; Casement encountered a 'lovely Italian' on a Clerkenwell tram in 1911; and Ives catalogued a number of arrests on buses as well as trains in his scrapbooks.[115] At the culmination of a poem about the working-class lads it was possible to meet in London's streets – including the newspaper and bootshine boys, the barber's apprentices, the bookstall clerks, the guardsmen and the telegraph boys – 'Uranian' poet John Gambril Nicholson noted with relish the sustained proximity the buses and trams facilitated: 'When travelling home by 'bus or tram / I meet a hundred boys again / Behind them on the 'bus I ride / Or pace the platform by their side.'[116] These new modes of transport changed the nature of urban encounter and it was possible to meet other men waiting at tram stops and stations as well as on the buses, trams and trains themselves. The infrastructure also opened up new areas and made the West End and its streets, theatres and eateries more accessible than before.

The opportunities provided by the crowded streets, toilets, parks, stations and trams could be taken up casually by men not initiated into a subculture. Despite Casement's prolific sexual adventuring in the area, for example, he seems to have been entirely unaware of the associations of particular pubs, hotels and theatres, which formed an indoor social and sexual network in the city.[117] These included the Crown in Charing Cross Road, the Windsor Castle in the Strand, and the Packenham and Swan in Knightsbridge.[118] Wilde was famously associated with the Café Royale, at the south end of Regent Street, and Kettners, one of the first foreign restaurants in Soho, both of which opened in the 1860s. Ives noted that the Criterion Bar on Piccadilly Circus was 'a great centre for inverts' (see Figure 3; the exterior signage is visible to the right of Figure 2).[119] Sims observed in 1902 that it attracted 'men in evening dress, and men in mufti, guardsmen and garrulous music hall artists . . . all sorts and conditions of men'.[120] Ives himself favoured the Trocadero and later Lyons Corner House just across the road.

Figure 3 The Criterion Bar (*c*.1902).

The new hotels were also used for homosexual liaisons. In the early 1890s the blackmailing duo Freddie Atkins and James Burton made use of the Victoria Hotel in Northumberland Avenue – another new West End thoroughfare – and the smaller Anderton's Hotel in Fleet Street. Atkins would pick up men in the Alhambra, public toilets and at the Knightsbridge skating rink, and take them back to the hotel, where 'uncle' James would burst in and extort money.[121] The Albermarle and Savoy Hotels were both named in the Wilde trials, and Ives ate with Wilde and other friends at the latter on a number of occasions.[122] The journalist Robert Machray noted in 1902 that guides to 'the worst and most devilish features of the night side of London' could be found 'lurking near the entrances of the great hotels of London – just as in Paris'.[123]

Bookshops around Soho had a certain notoriety. Charles Hirsch claimed to have sold 'Socratic' material, including *Sins of the City of the Plain*, to Wilde and his friends from the bookshop he ran between 1890 and 1900 in Coventry Street, just off Leicester Square, and it was also from here that the growing manuscript of the homoerotic pornographic novel *Teleny* was dropped off and picked up in the course of 1890.[124] Leonard Smithers, who eventually published *Teleny* in 1893 and also championed the work of both Wilde and decadent illustrator Aubrey Beardsley, had offices at number 3 Soho Square, whilst his business partner, pornographer Harry Nicholls, had bookshops first in Wardour Street and then, from 1894, in the same building as Smithers. Their associate Edward Avery operated from a shop in Greek Street.[125] Whilst these booksellers and pornographers were not dealing exclusively in homosexual material, it seems likely that they were known sources, supplementing the additional outlets further east in Holywell Street, off the Strand.[126] Soho also figured in the Cleveland Street male brothel scandal of 1889–90: the real Jack Saul – now aged thirty-eight – was first interviewed by police at 150 Old Compton Street and he seems to have lived in the area for some time, along, Morris B. Kaplan notes, with a series of 'female prostitutes, men with women's names, theatre people and blackmailers'.[127] Soho was conveniently located between Cleveland Street, just north of Oxford Street, and Piccadilly Circus, where Saul solicited for custom. The telegraph boys operating from the Cleveland Street house had further to travel: when they appeared there in their uniforms they had probably cycled or walked straight from the imposing Post Office headquarters in St Martin-le-Grand in the City.

The theatre had long-standing associations with homosexuality and offered an additional space for men to cruise and socialise with each other. *Yokel's Preceptor* had noted that actors were commonly 'pooffs' and Fanny and Stella's on and off stage performances and visits to the theatre were infamous. This association developed further with the expansion of theatreland. The Alhambra was a particularly well-known meeting place and other theatres also presented opportunities, including the Pavilion in Piccadilly, the gallery at the Empire on Leicester Square and the bar at the St James' Theatre in King Street, just south of Piccadilly.[128] Alfred Taylor met Sidney Mavor – with whom Wilde slept at the Albemarle Hotel – at the Gaiety, one of the new theatres in Shaftesbury Avenue,[129] and Hirsch described seeing Wilde and Lord Alfred Douglas sitting in front of him at the Empire in an intimate embrace: '[Wilde] had his arm around the neck of the Ephebe who was pressed against him, in a gesture which would have been considered improper even in a less strait-laced *milieu*.'[130] The playwright notoriously attended the premiere of *Lady Windemere's Fan* at the St James' with a group of young men, all wearing green carnations, supposedly the symbol of homosexual desire in Paris.[131] Later, Arthur Mellors, an actor himself, took several lovers to West End theatres according to police surveillance reports cited in the 1906 case against him.[132]

More broadly, the theatre was frequently represented as a liberal and radical arena, where sexual hypocrisy might be challenged and difference affirmed. The 'new theatre' of the 1890s heightened this reputation, lending the London theatre what Kerry Powell calls 'an intellectual and aesthetic excitement'.[133] J. T. Grein's Independent Theatre Club, launched with a production of Ibsen's *Ghosts* at the Royalty Theatre in 1891, provided a means of sidestepping the Lord Chamberlain's censorship and allowed for more avant-garde productions. Other theatre clubs and societies followed, including the Stage Society, which fostered George Bernard Shaw's work at the Royal Court Theatre in the early 1900s.[134] These societies provided a space, albeit limited, in which prevailing norms and prescriptive roles could be questioned. Wilde's plays mounted some similar challenges, though they were sufficiently oblique to be performed on the West End stage before large audiences who were simultaneously entertained and parodied.[135]

The cross-dressing and gender ambiguity of music-hall acts toyed with convention in different ways. The conservatism and self-censorship of the halls by this time has been well documented,[136] but the various turns suggested the mutability of gendered and sexual roles, and the possibility of – to use Martha Vicinus – 'rewrit[ing] and partially control[ling] pre-existing sexual scripts'.[137] The audiences themselves sometimes played with conventions and propriety, as we have seen, dressing up or down for a night out, and entering into the bohemianism associated with the West End. The theatricality and general tenor of the area seemed to endorse sensual experimentation, and related closely to the performativity which clung to prevailing conceptions of homosexual behaviour and identity.[138]

For many upper and upper-middle class men the opportunities offered by the cosmopolitan West End were supplemented by a tradition of homosociality which often protected them in their sexual exploits. The clubs and bachelor chambers in Pall Mall and St James' developed from the 1830s and formed a continuation of the homosocial worlds of public school and

Figure 4 Backstage at the Royal Holborn music hall (*c.*1902).

university. Hyde suggests that the men in this exclusive milieu were linked by a tacit knowledge of the extent of homosexual relations in the all-male establishments from which they had emerged.[139] The Earl of Euston and Lord Somerset, who were implicated in the Cleveland Street scandal, Wilde, Lord Alfred Douglas, Wilde's literary executor Robert Ross and George Ives were all club members. After Robert Ross' inconclusive libel action against Lord Alfred Douglas in 1914, in which his homosexuality had been at issue, a suggestion that Ross be expelled from the Reform Club was turned down by the membership. Support was similarly forthcoming for Lord Somerset at the Turf and Marlborough Clubs.[140] Following the arrest of Prince Francis Joseph of Braganza for gross indecency during his visit to London for the coronation of 1902, Ives found Royal Society Club members, including George Sims, broadly sympathetic. 'I was pleased', he noted, 'to see that [Sims] was not spiteful about the cult.'[141] Ives also shared gossip at the

Authors' Club about an 'Asiatic' dignitary who brought his male lovers to London with him at the time of the Wilde trials.[142] Earlier, a man Ives met on the street took him to the Army and Navy Club in Pall Mall. It was clearly a comfortable place for the man to retreat to with his new-found friend, whilst his club membership served to ease Ives' usual suspicion of casual meetings.[143]

City centre bachelor chambers were similarly part of a homosocial circuit. C. R. Ashbee's biographer Alan Crawford notes that it was 'a normal part of Victorian respectability for [an upper-middle and upper-class man to] have had rooms and habits of life that were separate from, and not to be questioned by, his household and family',[144] and such a convention made Wilde's chambers in St James' uncontroversial, at least until the trial. In 1894 Ives took chambers at The Albany (Flat E4), off Piccadilly,[145] an address used by Wilde for Jack Worthing in the original four-act version of *The Importance of Being Earnest* (1895). It was removed from the performed play, along with a comment by Miss Prism that the 'wicked' Ernest must be 'as bad as any young man who had chambers in The Albany, or indeed in the vicinity of Piccadilly can possibly be'.[146] Tubby, the effete protagonist of G. S. Street's novel *Autobiography of a Boy* (1894), has chambers in Jermyn Street, St James' – the 'inner sanctum of the masculine city', according to Roy Porter – and he travels by sedan chair to the London and Provincial Turkish Baths at number 76, another important homosocial West End space (see Figure 5).[147] In Vernon Lee's short story 'Lady Tal' (1896) the 'dainty but frugal bachelor' Jervase Marion, supposedly a parody of Henry James, has a flat in Westminster, just across St James' Park.[148] Throughout Jervase is referred to by his feminised surname, which Lady Tal's companion, Christina, pronounces 'Mary Anne, with unfailing relish of the joke'.[149] Bachelors living in city centre flats featured frequently in court cases involving homosexual activity, and this familiar and largely respectable figure became loosely linked to dissident sexuality during the period. The narrator of 'Lady Tal', for example, protests that Marion was 'a manly man' 'for all his bachelor ways'.[150] Later *The Modern Man*, a weekly male 'lifestyle' magazine, published between 1908 and 1911, gave tips on proper behaviour for the single male, suggesting again certain unwanted associations of this status.

The single bohemian and dandy similarly attracted suspicion, especially after the Wilde trials. Ellen Moers argues that the dandy became increasingly associated with the aesthetic fringe rather than the ruling aristocracy in the 1890s, and Wilde affiliated himself closely to this quintessentially urban figure.[151] The adjective 'bohemian' cropped up repeatedly during his trials.

Figure 5 'The Turkish Bath in Jermyn Street' (*c.*1906).

Alfred Taylor's flat was described as bohemian, and one of the witnesses professed himself unsurprised when Wilde kissed the waiter at Kettners on account of the playwright's bohemianism.[152] In 1906 the murder of the artist Archibald Wakley in his Kensington studio – apparently by a soldier he had picked up in Hyde Park – again drew a connection between homosexual activity in the West End and the bachelor and bohemian life.[153] However, although there were increasing suspicions about these figures and domestic arrangements during the period, they continued to provide a relatively secure screen for the sexual and social lives of wealthy men in London. Ives slept with Lord Alfred Douglas at the Albany, and he also enjoyed uninterrupted meals there, at his former chambers in St James', and at nearby clubs with Wilde, Edward Carpenter, Robert Ross, Oscar Browning and others.[154] The privileges of masculinity and the embedded traditions of homosociality protected his lifestyle.

Other groups in the city provided tacit and sometimes explicit support for same-sex relationships and desires. In the early 1890s Ives formed the Order of the Chaerona, an exclusive and secretive support and pressure group composed of men who drew on Hellenism to understand and legitimise their desires. The affiliation and the ritual that cemented it constituted a protective and quasi-Masonic bond based specifically on sexual preference. It formed an invisible boundary between 'them' and 'Us' and sustained an exclusive fraternity and virtual safe space in the city for Ives and his fellow members. They were fortified through the invocation of more heroic times and places and were protected by Ives' obsessive secrecy. The codes and initials in his diary still make the membership difficult to discern. There are nevertheless regular references to new members joining and to meetings with others, suggesting a fairly substantial grouping. It probably included the architect C. R. Ashbee, poets Montague Summers and John Gambril Nicholson, and Charles Kains Jackson, who edited *The Artist and Journal of Home Culture* between 1888 and 1894.[155] The journal itself served what Laurel Brake describes as 'a community of self-identifying "gay" readers and writers',[156] and during Jackson's tenure it published homoerotic verse and features, often in Hellenic vein, as well as an explicit call for the legitimisation of homosexual relations.[157] The journal consolidated a social and cultural link between a group of privileged but sexually dissident men who were, by and large, based in London. Later the Bloomsbury group of artists provided a less specifically homosexual support structure for artists and writers exploring different sexual possibilities – to the point, it seems, of boredom: Lytton Strachey noted in his diary of 1910: 'dinner at Gordon Square. Clive very fat. Discussion as to whether sods were *a priori* better than womanisers. Very dull.'[158]

The importance of Hellenism in contemporary discourse on homosexuality made the British Museum, and especially the statue galleries, an important site in the city for many men (see Figure 6). It was a place where it was legitimate to look at sculptures of naked men: they were associated with an Hellenic ethos of self-realisation and control rather than 'modern' urban debauchery. *The Artist* was especially enthusiastic about the neo-classical façade of 1842 and enthusiastically reported developments in the display of the Parthenon sculptures, the most dramatic implantation of ancient Greece in modern London: 'They are set forth in a hall of magnificent dimensions, and especially constructed for their reception, where they can be seen and studied and admired, at leisure and at ease, from every point of view.'[159] Walter Pater had already undertaken just such a close study, teasing out the muscular sensuality of the exhibit. In *The Renaissance* he offered an almost sadomasochistic description of the Parthenon frieze, with its 'line of youths on horseback, with their level glances, their proud patient lips, their chastened reins, their whole bodies in exquisite service'.[160] In 'The Age of Athletic Prizemen' he relished 'the face of the young man as you see him in the British Museum': 'look into, look at the

Figure 6 The Phigaleian Room at the British Museum, with the Elgin Room beyond
(*c*.1875).

curves of the blossom-like cavity of the opened mouth', he instructed.[161] E. M. Forster's imagination was caught by the 'wonderful boy with the broken arm': 'right across the Assyrian transept he throbs like something under the sea', he wrote.[162] 'Loitering with a vacant eye / Along the Grecian gallery' the poet A. E. Housman similarly felt drawn to a statue: 'still in marble stone stood he / And steadfastly he looked at me'.[163] The scenario is redolent of fleeting urban encounters: the narrator 'loiters' in the museum and 'meets' the statue, which seems almost to be hanging around for just such contact and exchanged gazes. As with Pater and Forster's descriptions of 'a young man' and 'a wonderful boy', there are also echoes of the popular Pygmalion myth in the poem, as stone turns into flesh.[164] Forster, who registers a series of urban spaces for potential homoerotic encounter in his 1914 novel *Maurice*, including the commuter train and bachelor flat, has the eponymous hero arranging to meet his working-class lover, Alec Scudder, at the British Museum. It is, Maurice feels, an anonymous space, but he nevertheless thinks he is being blackmailed there by Alec. It is a less idealised and comforting depiction of the museum galleries; 'the rows of old statues tottered', seeming to indicate the inadequacy and fragility of the Hellenic ideal of same-sex love in the sustenance of this contemporary relationship between two men of different classes.[165]

The British Museum was free and open to all, but the Hellenic ideals which informed the gaze of these Oxbridge-educated observers was less likely to be available to those who had not been through the public school and university system. Similarly the Order of the Chaerona, the clique around *The Artist and Journal of Home Culture*, and the Bloomsbury group, were exclusive and restricted chiefly to an educated elite. There were, however, other groupings in the city which were somewhat more accessible. The despairing author of *Tempted London* noted the growing number of amateur theatre groups and – as with the music halls and theatre-land more broadly – suggested that they resulted in both class and sexual transgression. A group in Hammersmith apparently included in its membership 'young men of the shopkeeper class' who 'are terribly clean shaven, let their hair grow as it will, wear long coats, and in many instances white hats'.[166] The men had become dandified and bohemian and their class origins obscured. They also followed the fashion for shaving, which, though certainly not a definitive indication of sexual deviance, was a commonly noted feature of defendants in cases of gross indecency between men. One of Ives' housemates, Frederick Smith, was closely involved in a theatre group around 1905 and took part in a production of Wilde's banned play *Salome*.[167] A friend of Robert Ross was a member of an another group in the 1910s and was fond of 'painting and powdering his face'.[168] These groups appear to have allowed men to experiment with different roles and may have provided some informal support for their male–male sexual relationships.

Sports clubs and swimming pools were other possible forums. The inception of the London County Council in 1888 brought with it a progressive improvement in sporting facilities in the city. Many of the new tennis courts and football and cricket pitches had to be reserved in advance and this encouraged the formation of groups of men dedicated to physical exertion, health and self development. These ideals related both to the drive by the LCC to reinvigorate the putatively degenerating urban populace, and, for the classically educated, to a Hellenic ethos of bodily vigour and perfection.[169] Ives was a dedicated cricketer, and although his teammates at Lords teased him – calling him Lady Ives, for example – he noted that 'it is all meant to be friendly enough and I feel no resentment'.[170] His long-running membership suggests that his club provided a congenial and supportive environment. At the Serpentine in Hyde Park there was scope for cross-class fraternization, and working-class men could be observed bathing in an idyllic pastoral setting. Sims included a photograph and description in *Living London* (1901) (Figure 7), and Baedeker's guide commented on this 'scene of unsophisticated character' with evident relish: 'when a flag

Figure 7 'Early Morning Bathers at the Serpentine' (c.1902).

is hoisted, a crowd of men and boys, most of them in very homely attire, are to be seen undressing and plunging into the waters, where their lusty shouts and hearty laughter testify their enjoyment'.[171] John Addington Symonds was more personally and erotically engaged but his language was similar: 'Early in the morning', he wrote in his *Memoirs*, 'I used to rise from a sleepless bed, walk across the park, and feed my eyes on the naked men and boys bathing in the Serpentine. The homeliest of them would have satisfied me'.[172] Ives swam there, meeting, in the summer of 1894, 'a jolly youth ... evidently a worker ... and so frank and unsophisticated as to be quite a study'.[173] He was also a regular at various swimming baths he knew to be popular with working-class men, including Whitechapel, Rugby House settlement in Notting Hill and Hampstead outdoor ponds. He enjoyed watching the naked men at these venues: 'a superb figure ... with the limbs of a classic Bachus' at Rugby House and 'the lads [who]sit and lie about ... in the altogether' in the undressing sheds at Hampstead.[174] Activities at the university settlements, involving Oxbridge undergraduates and local working-class men, were frequently based around sport and games. Ives, for example, 'played chess and draughts with ... ragged, unkempt urchins' at Rugby House. Forster's Maurice coaches at an East End club and C. R. Ashbee took the men working for his Guild of Handicraft in Mile End Road for regular work-outs at the nearby People's Palace gymnasium, which was completed in 1888.[175]

The settlement movement had begun in the 1880s in response to the perception of a widening gulf between the classes and the growing consciousness of the city's desperate poverty. This had been described in horrifying detail by Henry Mayhew and Charles Dickens in the mid-century, but there was a fresh wave of fictional, journalistic and survey material centring on London's poverty in the 1880s and 1890s.[176] These works countered the arrogant architectural rhetoric of commerce and empire and the frivolous consumption associated with the West End. They also stoked fears about revolt, violence, sexual dissipation and racial degeneration, especially during the economic and housing crises of the 1880s.[177] Fostering understanding between classes was seen to be one way of ameliorating the crises; Ashbee, for example, argued that cross-class contact was 'one of the motors for social reconstruction'.[178] The settlements set up by various Oxford and Cambridge colleges facilitated such contact and incidentally, Judith Walkowitz points out, gave middle-class men temporary respite from 'bourgeois culture'.[179] Edward Carpenter felt that it was in such places that the value of 'the intermediate sex' might especially be felt and demonstrated. He envisaged middle-class men, motivated by feelings 'personal and close' and with inborn skills as intermediaries between both sexes and classes, fulfilling a psuedo-social work role. He noted that one man 'saved a boy from drunken parents, [took] him from the slums and by means of a club helped him out into the world. Many other boys he had rescued in the same way.'[180] His epic prose poem *Towards Democracy* includes a vignette about a 'young man who organises his boys from the slums' and who is inspired by 'something more, more personal and close, than philanthropy'.[181]

Although their paternalism complicates their claims, Ives, Ashbee and Carpenter were doubtless sincere in their conception of the value of cross-class relationships, but these liaisons were commonly viewed with suspicion. In the wake of the Wilde trials a correspondent in *Reynolds* drew attention to the 'Mary-Anns' 'who plied their beastly trade' in Piccadilly and noted a connection between them and the men working in the university settlements. He alluded to the cover-up of a 'grave scandal' at 'a certain philanthropic institution' where there was 'the gravest suspicion that the club was a place of assignation for some few of the philanthropic undergraduates'. He went on to question any cross-class friendships: they could not 'be readily explained', he claimed, 'except by a theory of unnatural sexual relations'.[182]

Such cross-class transgression was a key component of homosexual scandal – and indeed sexual scandal more generally – in the 1880s and 1890s,[183] and working-class soldiers and telegraph boys featured with middle- and upper-class men in a number of cases during the period.[184] Whilst 'rough lads' and uniformed men were reported 'ministering' to higher class men in the West End, however, there were relatively few reports of middle- and upper-class men travelling to the poorer areas to find them, except as part of sanctioned settlement or other philanthropic work. Casement went cruising in the docks a number of times and he could not have been unique,[185] but in general it seems that men of his class preferred to pick up their working-class partners in the less threatening and more convenient West End. This was where soldiers were stationed, telegraph boys did much of their work and where there was considerable class cross-over. The area was still associated with privilege and wealth, however, and it was certainly not a levelled or neutral terrain. Power in the relationships forged there usually resided with the men who had the money to buy sex and rent hotel rooms, and – newspapers during the Cleveland Street scandal suggested – the privilege to evade prosecution. Eve Sedgwick points out that most men did not have 'easy access to the alternative subculture, the stylised discourse or the sense of immunity of the aristocratic/bohemian minority'.[186] It was the wealthy who appeared to create the norms of homosexual behaviour during this period as before.[187] Sinfield shows how the Molly House subculture of the eighteenth century mimicked the affected manners of the aristocracy, and in the 1890s it was fashion and extravagance, the high life of the capital, that came to be associated with London's culture of homosexuality.[188] After the trials of 1895 the *Evening News* rebuked the working-class men who had crossed social boundaries: 'The conviction of Wilde for these abominable vices, which were the natural outcome of his diseased intellectual condition, will be a salutary warning to the unhealthy boys who posed as sharers in his culture'.[189] The homosexual subculture and condition was cast as decadent; one in which the working class could only 'pose' as 'sharers'. When they appeared in reports of homosexual activity it was as sexually pliant adjuncts, underscoring prevailing assumptions about a sexually dissipated aristocracy and a working class who were either grasping or vulnerable to corruption on account of their lack of moral agency. Working-class men were apparently unable to shape their own sexual lives in London except as renters or blackmailers. They were hidebound by this rhetoric and by their socio-economic and cultural position – by enforced working hours, the frequent absence of privacy and the lack of sustaining groupings, for example. Though they obviously did have erotic and emotional relationships with other working-class men, accounts of these were rare, and it was their scandalous encounters with middle- and upper-class men which were trumpeted most loudly.[190] As Sedgwick suggests, there was less to support the choices these men made than for those who had passed through Oxford and Cambridge and who had an inbuilt homosocial support network in the city as well as ready access to proliferating stories about themselves and their milieu in sexology, literature and other writing of the period.

Homosexuality was woven into the fabric of urban culture. Depictions of homosexual activity involved the centres of leisure and entertainment, spaces of masculine privilege and social reform, and symbols of urban innovation, like the stations, trains and trams. The appearance of many of these places in Sims' survey of the city, *Living London*, underscores the overlap between prevailing representations of 'modern' London and spaces which had at least a subcultural reputation for homosexual activity (see Figures 3, 4, 5, and 7). Class dynamics familiar from the literature of urban exploration, together with a series of wider concerns about city living, were frequently shown bracing homosexual lives and relationships, as subsequent chapters will show. Finally, reports of homosexual activity implicated a series of well-known urban types: the bachelor, bohemian, theatregoer, actor, dandy, settlement worker, soldier and telegraph boy.

The overlap between recognisable urban figures and homosexual behaviour belied ideas about the distinctiveness of the sodomite, invert or Mary-Ann, and, as in earlier periods, there was concern about misrecognition and a perceived need to distinguish suspect types, fashions and activities. This was especially apparent in *Modern Man*, aimed as it was at the urban bachelor. An early issue appeared under the by-line 'Full-blooded, Vigorous, and Clean', echoing the rhetoric of muscular Christianity and social purity. It included a piece ridiculing the dandy and his fake tan, powder and rouge. 'These call themselves men?', the writer declared.[191] Other issues asked: 'Should Men Wear Corsets?' – yes: as many army men wear them –; and 'Should Men Wear Scent?' – no: 'a man who smells of scent is a ridiculous person, and to call him effeminate is to put things in their mildest form'.[192] A subsequent piece by C. D. Witton bemoaned the damage done to the fashion for buttonholes by Wilde's penchant for green carnations.[193]

The first eleven issues included a series entitled 'London Hell', which dealt with the perils of London living, and described suspect male figures such as 'the blackmailer' and 'the vampire'. Vampires were thieves who gained money by striking up friendships with unsuspecting men. Their homosexuality was strongly suggested: they were 'the black sheep' of their families and 'specialists in sin', who, 'dressed in purple and fine linen', haunted 'the restaurants, cafes and bars of Piccadilly and its vicinity' on the lookout for 'undergraduates ... green subalterns [and] young naval officers'.[194] With the blackmailer the reader was warned to be particularly wary in the music halls, where he 'commences his operations' by 'striking up acquaintance' with young men.[195] Readers needed to negotiate the West End streets, cafés and music halls with care, and a 'masculine' acumen was necessary to forestall trouble. Despite the magazine's efforts to indicate suspect fashions and to outline these troublesome figures, its concern was associated with the indistinctness of homosexuality in the city and the cross-over of respectable and dissident identities. There was neither an entirely discernible figure nor a separate territory and we begin to see the ideological threat 'homosexual' men posed by using the same city spaces and appearing indistinguishable from the 'normal', middle-class, 'modern man'.[196]

These journalistic prescriptions, along with the expanding metropolitan police and detective force, the preoccupation with urban types and the proliferating accounts of London past and present,[197] signalled an impulse to order and understand the metropolis. There were, however, too many people, too many different kinds of spaces and too many contradictory understandings of urban life to quell the enduring sense of chaos. The orderly conceptual division between public and private, for example, was compromised by places which seemed to fall between the two – the West End hotels and restaurants, for instance – and by behaviour deemed inappropriate to either realm. The city's scale and complexity offered the possibility of evasion, of personal transformation and anonymity, and of encountering others who might not conform to the projected 'norm'. Such indeterminacy surrounding places, identities and behaviour provided a range of possibilities for men looking for sexual and social relationships with other men. Wilde was husband, father, bohemian, dandy, aesthete and man-about-town; identities which were not necessarily incompatible but which came into focus at different times and in different parts of the city. He relished the West End cafés and restaurants, the theatres and hotels, and found ample scope to cultivate relationships and a social circle there. These arenas provided an alternative to the domestic home base in which he nevertheless had a stake. Ives was friends with Wilde and took in elements of his West End circuit, especially in the early 1890s, but he also visited the parks, university settlements and swimming pools, and went on midnight bicycle rides through the city. He self-consciously played the social radical and the confirmed and in some ways conservative bachelor. Ashbee lived near Wilde in Cheyne Walk in fashionable Chelsea but cycled daily to work at the Guild of Handicraft in the East End. He seems to have engaged little with the West End but met his lover George Robson outside Charing Cross, which he probably passed most days on his bike. Casement, finally, cruised the parks, docks and the West End streets extensively, but seems to have remained unaware of the strong community bonds which Wilde, Ives and Ashbee felt in different ways. Though there was significant overlap and a shared knowledge of London, each of these men had his own map of the city and his own way of understanding his desires there. These were shaped variously by the privileges associated with their class status and masculinity, by fleeting personal encounters, subcultural histories, gossip and a communal 'knowingness' (to use Peter Bailey),[198] by circulating ideas about the city and what was possible there – and by a series of contemporary accounts of, and debates about, homosexuality.

CHAPTER 2

The grossly indecent city

THE LAW AND THE PRESS

Legislation against sodomy was in place and enforced well before the Criminal Law Amendment Act was passed in 1885. The pre-existing legislation was based on the 1533 statute against sodomy 'with mankind or beast' and had been modified in the course of the nineteenth century. In 1828 it was re-enacted in the Offences Against the Person Act, a piece of legislation which covered murder, abortion, rape and sex with girls under twelve. Further offences were added to the Act in 1861 and sodomy was dealt with in a new 'unnatural offences' subsection. The death penalty was replaced with imprisonment for between ten years and life, whilst attempted sodomy or 'any indecent assault upon any male person' carried a sentence of between three and ten years' imprisonment or up to two years with hard labour.[1] When the Criminal Law Amendment Act was added to the statute books in 1885 these existing measures remained in place and section 11 – the so-called Labouchere Amendment – came as an ill-defined addendum. It read:

Any male person who, in public or private, commits, or is party to the commission of, or procures the commission by any male person of, any act of gross indecency with another male person, shall be guilty of a misdemeanour, and being convicted thereof shall be liable at the discretion of the court to be imprisoned for any term not exceeding two years, with or without hard labour.[2]

 Change in law

Ed Cohen and Jeffrey Weeks have suggested that this provision marked a departure in the legal status of homosexuality in that it was directed specifically at sexual relations between men; sodomy, on the other hand, could occur with man, woman or beast. However, given that the attempted sodomy and indecent assault clause of the 1861 Act referred specifically to 'male persons' it was in fact less of a decisive shift than they suggest.[3] It nevertheless came as a direct reiteration of concern about sexual relations tween men and about unbridled male lust in general. The provision against 'acts of gross indecency' acknowledged a diversity in the possible expressions of homosexual desire, and since any indecent assault against a male person was already a criminal offence, the Amendment tacitly moved the emphasis from unwanted advances to consensual sexual relations. Such behaviour was prosecuted before – under the provisions against attempted sodomy, for example – but the new clause re-emphasised that any sexual act between men, whether or not it was intended to lead to sodomy, was beyond the pale. The spaces in which these acts were illegal were also carefully spelt out and the coda 'in public or private' appeared before gross indecency was even mentioned. The detail was strictly speaking irrelevant: if these acts were illegal then they were illegal everywhere, as sodomy was, and there was no mention of place in the 1861 Act. However, the specification indicates the importance of the conceptual division between public and private at this time and the way in which the Labouchere Amendment sought to override it. Lucia Zedner argues that by the late nineteenth century the private or rather the domestic sphere was conceived as a zone regulated by the conventions of the family rather than the strictures of the state.[4] The provision thus reclaimed the private as a province for the law in respect of homosexual activity and these dissident acts were determinedly cast as an offence to state and morality wherever they occurred. At the time of the Cleveland Street scandal of 1889, Henry Labouchere, who drafted section 11, wrote in *Truth*, the weekly crusading journal he edited, that the offences 'put those who commit them beyond the pale of privacy'.[5]

Activity on the streets continued to be of particular concern, however, and in 1898 the Vagrancy Law Amendment Act was passed with a clause against men who 'in any public place persistently solicit or importune for immoral purposes'.[6] The crime carried a one-month prison sentence, with hard labour, in line with the 1824 Vagrancy Act, but this was increased to six months with discretionary whipping for a second offence under the Criminal Law Amendment Act (White Slave Traffic Act) of 1912.[7] Like the Labouchere Amendment, the provision directed attention to the scene of the crime before the crime itself was mentioned. The criminal act, as with 'gross indecency', remained vague. Although the police had previously used nuisance legislation to prosecute supposed homosexual behaviour, this provision again directed attention specifically towards it. It also broadened the possibilities for arrest and allowed police to act upon their assumptions about places and forms of non-sexual behaviour. Ives complained in *The Continued Extension of the Criminal Law* (1922) that with this legislation 'an alleged smile or wink or look may cause an arrest'.[8] Thus in 1902

Lawrence Salt appeared before magistrates for 'persistently soliciting' after being observed in Piccadilly Circus talking to a man who was known to be 'an associate of bad characters'. The magistrate dismissed the case, but excused the policeman's seemingly excessive rigour on account of Piccadilly's reputation.[9] In 1912 John Hill and Robert Freeman were jailed under the 1898 statute after attempting to engage men in conversation on Charing Cross Road.[10] In the same year an actor, Alan Horton, was sentenced to ten weeks with hard labour after he was observed by plainclothes police officers entering the public toilets in Piccadilly Circus and Leicester Square around midnight. He did not make contact with any one during this time but according to police evidence 'while in said lavatories and also while in the street he smiled in the faces of gentlemen, pursed his lips and wiggled his body'.[11] The police also cited his use of make-up. No one apart from the police complained or appeared to notice his behaviour but the conjunction of time, place and his effeminacy were sufficient to effect arrest and imprisonment.

In many ways this section of the Vagrancy Law Amendment Act did more to criminalise a putative homosexual identity than the Labouchere Amendment. The latter, whilst broadening the remit from sodomy, maintained the focus on sexual acts. What the 1898 provision did was to heighten the significance of behaviour that was not explicitly sexual – Horton's make-up and 'wiggle', for example – and of places that had a reputation, such as Piccadilly Circus, Oxford Street and Charing Cross Road. The police did not arrest because sexual acts had actually been committed but on the basis of a judgement they had made about the propensity of an individual to commit them. The measure, to Ives, meant that London suffered 'more public tyranny than most cities on the continent'. 'Think', he went on, 'how boys are convicted for soliciting and importuning who are not even alleged to have touched or spoken to anyone.'[12]

These legal developments in the last years of the nineteenth century sent out powerful messages about expectations of private conduct and public behaviour.[13] They also gave a focus for protest which the long-standing and less gender-specific measures against sodomy had not. Henry Havelock Ellis attacked the 1885 Act as 'exceptionally severe' in *Sexual Inversion* (1897) and saw it as a symptom of a wider cultural refusal to accept the biological realities of sexual life.[14] Ives saw it as 'a piece of panic Puritanism', producing 'its yearly crop of victims', whilst the 1898 provision he described as 'poisonous'.[15] The Order of Chaerona was in part a response to the tightening of the law and its apparently more rigorous implementation.

Although the bare bones of the Labouchere Amendment made certain behaviour illegal everywhere – in public and private, in country and city – this
apparent ubiquity was in fact richly textured and contingent. The circumstances in which legislation was discussed and passed, and the individuals
involved in promoting it, framed the words on the statute books. In this
case, the provisions related specifically to London rather than the nation,
even though this was not explicit in the wording of the Amendment itself. It
was part of a bill raising the age of consent for girls and regulating brothels,
and was driven through parliament in response to the Maiden Tribute child
prostitution scandal which erupted in London in July 1885.[16] It thus came
as a direct response to abusive and predatory sexual activity in the city.
The incorporation of Labouchere's Amendment into the Act connected
homosexuality not only with child prostitution but once again with the
city. Labouchere later claimed that he had drafted section 11 in response to
what he perceived as the growth of homosexual activity in the capital.[17] The
genesis of the 1898 provision against soliciting is less clear and parliamentary debate was limited largely to discussion of appropriate punishment
rather than of the offences themselves.[18] It was part of an Act dealing with
prostitution, which was causing increasing concern to the metropolitan
police as the West End drew more and more people to its new theatres,
cafés and restaurants. In the 1888 report to parliament by the metropolitan
police commissioner, the last to include comments from each divisional
superintendent, Superintendent W. G Hume complained about the additional crowds drawn by the new theatres on Shaftesbury Avenue. Many of
the estimated 20,000 people leaving the theatres each night went straight
home, he said, but increasing numbers of young men lingered, attracting
more prostitutes to the area.[19] Convictions of prostitutes increased in the
1890s and were especially high in the year the Vagrancy Law Amendment
Act was passed. In 1895 498 women were convicted, rising only slightly in
the following year to 523. In 1897 and 1898, however, convictions reached
968 and 1,326 respectively.[20] Once again it seems that parliament had an
urban problem in view when they passed the Vagrancy Law Amendment
Act, indicating prevailing concerns about sexual profligacy and its visibility
in London's streets. The problem worsened in the years that followed and
conviction figures grew further, reaching 3,443 in 1912, the year in which
punishment for soliciting was extended.[21]

Other legislation was also used to regulate homosexual behaviour. Measures relating to nuisance, intent and disorderly conduct were regularly
evoked, as they had been in the years before 1885. Arthur Marley, a music
hall female impersonator, and John Severs, a tobacconist's assistant, who

were both dressed in women's clothes when they arrived at a party in Fitzroy Square in August 1894, were prosecuted and fined for idle and disorderly conduct, for example.[22] Later William Ryan and Thomas Riley were arrested but acquitted for loitering with intent on the Embankment in 1905.[23] The following year twenty-year-old Albert Smith received twelve months with hard labour and thirty lashes for the same offence after being seen 'loitering outside White's Club in Piccadilly and trying to engage men in conversation'.[24] A range of laws could be used to arrest men supposedly involved in homosexual activity and this also gave flexibility in terms of punishment. A man arrested and prosecuted for intent could receive a more severe sentence than a man arrested for soliciting, for example. Likewise, the crimes of 'attempted sodomy' and 'indecent assault on a male' carried a longer prison term than 'acts of gross indecency' with another man. Different sorts of evidence were required for each crime and the prosecuting authorities could decide which charge was most likely to stick.

Partly because many cases were hidden within these other crime categories it is difficult to discern levels of arrest and conviction for homosexual behaviour in London. Figures for men arrested for soliciting under the 1898 Act, for example, were not separated from other Vagrancy Act infringements in the statistics presented annually to parliament. Likewise, before the inception of gross indecency legislation in 1885, arrests for homosexual behaviour, other than sodomy or attempted sodomy, were disguised in figures for broader crime categories, making comparisons with the post-1885 period difficult. An examination of figures for gross indecency, sodomy and attempted sodomy nevertheless indicates a gradual increase in arrests and prosecutions over the period, as the Appendix shows. Between 1885 and 1889 arrests and prosecutions in London were low. Sodomy and attempted sodomy cases in fact fell slightly on the preceding five years. Arrests for gross indecency, meanwhile, stood at approximately 11 per year, much lower than in the 1890s and 1900s. This may have been because police were still working out when and how to use the new provision. Between 1890 and 1894 arrests under the gross indecency measure grew sharply, with an average of 29.6 per year, and arrests for sodomy and attempted sodomy more than doubled to an average of 12.4 per year. In the five years following the Wilde trials there was a further, though much less dramatic, increase. Combined total annual arrests for the three offences – sodomy, attempted sodomy and gross indecency – went from an average of 42 per year between 1890 and 1894 to 51 per year in the five years that followed. The figures continued to increase slightly between 1900 and 1909, before jumping significantly in the final five years of the period. Whilst between 1910 and 1914 arrests and prosecutions for sodomy fell slightly and those for gross indecency continued their gradual increase, arrests for attempted sodomy more than doubled, from an average of 13.2 per year to 30.4 per year. The average total number of arrests for all three crimes in London thus grew from 58.6 per year between 1905 and 1909 to 76 per year between 1910 and 1914.

With no accompanying commentary on these figures in the police commissioner's reports it is hard to discern police policy and practice with regard to homosexual behaviour or to account conclusively for the fluctuation in the numbers of arrests and prosecutions.[25] H. G. Cocks nonetheless demonstrates a frequent reticence on the part of the police and others to pursue prosecution. This was firstly because of the perceived dangers to public morals of extensive exposure of dissident sexual activity and secondly because of the frequent difficulty in obtaining adequate proof, especially in cases of consensual sex in private.[26] During this period there is certainly little evidence of a concerted purge, though there are years when arrests and prosecutions were significantly higher than others. This may indicate a greater sensitivity and intolerance on the part of the police or alternatively a greater visibility of homosexual behaviour in the city. 1890, 1898, 1899, 1906 and the period 1910–14 are notable in this respect and each of these years was marked by newspaper or parliamentary discussion of homosexuality in the city which may have prompted, or been prompted by, police activity. In the Cleveland Street scandal of 1889–90 the police and courts faced criticism for their handling of suspects, as will be shown later, and there was a lengthy exchange in parliament about the case which drew attention to an apparent increase in homosexual activity in the city. 1890 also saw a change in police commissioner: James Munro resigned from the post after only two years following criticism of his handling of the Cleveland Street case and his failure to solve the Jack the Ripper murders, for which his predecessor Charles Warren had also left the force. It is possible that his replacement, Colonel E. R. C. Bradford, sought a more rigorous approach to the policing of sexual crime in the city.[27] In 1898 various members of a West End blackmailing gang were sensationally bought to trial and the Vagrancy Law Amendment Act was debated in parliament. In 1906 the prosecution of the actor Arthur Mellors and the murder of artist Archibald Wakley, apparently by a soldier he picked up in Hyde Park, received widespread newspaper coverage. Homosexual activity in the city was again highlighted, possibly encouraging increased police vigilance. In May 1912, finally, the Metropolitan Police were stung by criticism from Liberal MP Handal Booth that they turned a blind eye to West End sexual profligacy in return for financial recompense. 'How is it that you see the women parading up and down the West End each night, and stepping into cabs with men under the noses of the police if they haven't paid a toll?', he asked in parliament. *Reynolds* reported that 'a wave of indignation has swept over the police force'.[28] The police response could well have included action against homosexual activity, especially as it was repeatedly bracketed with prostitution. Later in the same year, parliament again discussed the apparent rise in homosexual crime in London, and as part of the Criminal Law Amendment Act (White Slave Traffic Act) punishment for male soliciting was increased. The two years that followed saw particularly high levels of arrests for attempted sodomy, which potentially carried longer sentences than gross indecency. This suggested a greater desire for heavy punitive action against sexual dissidence at a time of increasing international tension.

Whilst suppositions can be made about fluctuations, the figures remain unpredictable. In the aftermath of the Wilde trial there is no evidence of a newly sensitised constabulary patrolling the streets. Arrests remained steady and prosecutions in fact fell in the two years following the case. Indeed, whilst the ratio of prosecutions to arrests was particularly high in 1895 (32:44), suggesting a willingness to convict on the part of the courts and/or especially compelling evidence being submitted by the police, in 1896 there appears to have been a greater reluctance to prosecute, with only 17 out of 42 cases involving sodomy, attempted sodomy and gross indecency resulting in prosecution.

Whatever the specific reasons for peaks and troughs at different times, arrests and prosecutions under these provisions became more frequent over the course of the period. As a result, details of homosexual crime appeared more frequently in the newspapers, particularly as the majority of cases passed through both police and crown courts, significantly increasing exposure. In the Wilde case, for example, in addition to the three major trials, there were four police court committal appearances by Lord Queensberry, Wilde and Alfred Taylor, Wilde's co-defendant. The homosexual life of the city was rarely out of the public eye and the newspaper-reading public had consistent reminders of it, especially as many other cases came to court under statutes other than the three for which figures are available.

These statutes and statistics tell us only so much about homosexuality. Whilst the importance of the legislation of 1885 and 1898 and the circumstances in which it was passed should not be underestimated, the specific provision against homosexual activity contained in the Criminal Law Amendment Act and the Vagrancy Law Amendment Act were secondary to their central focus on under-age sex and prostitution. Newspaper reports on the passage of the Acts included barely any reference to the clauses relating to homosexual activity. Moreover, the statistics relating to gross indecency, sodomy and attempted sodomy indicate levels of arrest and prosecution for these particular crimes, but tell us nothing about the often compelling and memorable details of individual cases. Such details often appeared in the newspapers, supplying potent images of the sexualised spaces of the city and of the men that used them, as we will see.

The second half of the nineteenth century saw significant changes in the newspaper press. Technological advances meant newspapers could be produced more quickly than before, whilst the earlier abolition of advertisement, stamp and paper duties – in 1853, 1855 and 1862 respectively – and improved national and local transport infrastructures meant that more newspapers were on the market and were more widely available. In 1846 there were six morning and four evening daily newspapers published in London; by 1885 this had risen to fourteen and seven respectively. In 1914, whilst the evening press remained stable, the number of morning papers published in the capital had risen to twenty-five.[29] Most sold for one penny or more, but the *Echo* (1868), the *Star* (1888) and the *Evening News* (1889) were all just half a penny, a pricing policy which increased the potential readership significantly. All three were particularly popular during major trials as they came out in the evening and so gave the latest details. The weekend papers, like the radical *Reynolds* (1850), were also popular for providing a digest of the week's events.

Accompanying the quantitative change was a shift in style. In the 1880s W. T. Stead at the *Pall Mall Gazette* and T. P. O'Connor at the *Star* altered their approach to editing, precipitating a wider change in newspaper content and style. Whilst there were significant continuities with previous journalistic styles, the 'new journalism' radically altered the way news was consumed.[30] Investigative reports, campaigns – such as the *Star*'s backing of the striking dockers in 1889 – , and 'stop-press' were incorporated, and editorial comment foregrounded. The articles themselves were more direct and headlines and sub-headings became more descriptive, delivering mini-narratives at a glance. T. P. O'Connor compared the new style to the intimate personal histories of Thomas Macaulay and suggested that 'to get your ideas through the hurried eyes of the whirling brains that are employed in the reading of a newspaper there must be no mistake about your meaning...you must strike your reader between the eyes'.[31] The papers were catering for the supposed quickening pace of city life. They competed for detail during the major scandals and communicated cogent moral messages to a massive readership.[32] The new style press often took on a crusading mantle; they did not merely report on parliamentary, police and court action but also highlighted inaction and corruption, and pressed for and prompted change. This is apparent with Stead and his 'Maiden Tribute of Modern Babylon' articles about child prostitution in London which precipitated the swift passage of the Criminal Law Amendment Act, whilst during the Ripper murders the newspapers arguably shaped the police response through their coverage and criticism. In neither case were the perpetrators arrested, and the only conviction was of Stead himself for procuring a young girl as part of his investigations. The impression given by the press was of a city which the police and the courts were either unable or unwilling to control. The newspapers also highlighted particular places in the sexualised city, such as Piccadilly Circus, the Haymarket and Regent Street, and familiar urban dynamics, of the east versus the west, for example. They were instrumental in shaping images of deviance in London and so in controlling and regulating it. The press, Wilde claimed in 1891, 'monopolis[ed] the seat of judgement'.[33]

Coverage of cases involving homosexuality ranged from the large-scale scandals involving Cleveland Street and Wilde to low and medium-scale reports of other cases. The Cleveland Street scandal was a protracted affair, involving three trials and heated exchanges in parliament. It began in July 1889 when Charles Swinscow, a fifteen-year-old telegraph boy working from the General Post Office headquarters in St Martin-le-Grand, admitted being paid for sex with men at 19 Cleveland Street, just north of Oxford Street. Charles Hammond, the proprietor of the Cleveland Street house, fled abroad once he had been implicated by Swinscow, but his accomplice Charles Veck and the supposed ringleader at the GPO, Henry Newlove, were tried at the Old Bailey on 18 September 1889, under the Labouchere Amendment. They were sentenced to nine and four months with hard labour respectively, but the case went unreported. Rumours circulated about the men who had used the brothel, including army bachelor Lord Arthur Somerset, the divorcee Henry James Fitzroy, Earl of Euston, and Prince Albert Victor, the Prince of Wales' eldest son and heir. Ernest Parke, the editor of the new radical weekly the *North London Press*, decided to go public with the speculation and in November published Somerset and Euston's names in connection with the Cleveland Street house.[34] Euston sued for libel. After widely reported committal proceedings in November and December, the case was heard on 15 and 16 January 1890. The trial included sensational and detailed testimony from Jack Saul, who supposedly handed a card advertising the Cleveland Street house to Lord Euston at

Piccadilly Circus, and Ann Morgan, who lived at 22 Cleveland Steet and claimed to have seen Euston visit on several occasions. Parke was nevertheless found guilty of libel and jailed for a year.[35]

After the case *Reynolds*, the *Pall Mall Gazette*, the *Star* and *Truth* all reiterated concerns that the authorities had orchestrated a cover-up, and Henry Labouchere took the matter up in parliament on 28 February 1890, in a debate lasting several hours. The Prime Minister, Lord Salisbury, rebutted Labouchere's accusations of dishonesty in a statement to the Lords. Just over two weeks later, on 12 March 1890, the third case associated with the scandal finally came to court. This involved Lord Somerset's solicitor Arthur Newton, who was charged with conspiracy to pervert the course of justice. Newton pleaded guilty to one count of attempting to prevent prosecution and was sentenced to six weeks in prison. Citing the 'mischief' done by witness revelations in open court, the prosecution offered no evidence for the other five counts.[36] Somerset himself had by this time left the country.

The three infamous Wilde trials five years later ran from 3 April to 25 May 1895. The first was a libel action taken by Wilde against the Marquis of Queensberry, who had left a card with the words 'posing as a somdomite [*sic*]' for Wilde at his club, the Albemarle. During the trial Queensberry and his team set out to substantiate their plea of justification, prompting Wilde to withdraw. As a result of the revelations in the libel case Wilde was arrested, along with Alfred Taylor, one of his associates, and charged under the Labouchere Amendment. The two men were tried together between 29 April and 1 May, but the jury could not agree on a verdict and the judge ordered a retrial. This time Wilde and Taylor were tried separately, with Taylor's case heard first. The Solicitor General, Sir Frank Lockwood, took up the case for the prosecution and the two men were found guilty and sentenced to the maximum term of two years' imprisonment with hard labour.

Both the Cleveland Street and Wilde cases dominated the news for months and other cases reported during the period worked cumulatively to elaborate images emanating from these larger scandals. The choices editors made in terms of curtailing coverage or highlighting one case at the expense of others drew attention to particular networks of places and modes of behaviour. This is perhaps most obvious during the Wilde trials when five other cases were covered by *Reynolds*, reiterating on a weekly basis the images emerging from the more major sensation. Two received front page coverage alongside details of the Wilde case, under the headlines 'Other Serious Charges' (14 April) and 'Other Cases – Horrible Condition of London' (28 April). The case of John Goodchild, a chemist's assistant from the East End, was the focus of both reports, and a further item on 5 May. Goodchild was charged with inciting a fourteen-year-old Jewish match boy, Jon Abrahams 'to commit an unnamable crime'. He had apparently approached Abrahams on Old Broad Street, near Liverpool Street Station, and tempted him with treats to a bedroom above Pearce's Dining Room (also on Old Broad Street) where 'acts of gross indecency' were allegedly committed.[37] A search of Goodchild's room yielded a collection of photographs and a diary, which suggested involvement in the Cleveland Street scandal and relationships with a number of teenagers, including some who had subsequently been imprisoned for blackmail. The Goodchild case was given precedence over the committal of Walter Woolverton, a respected YMCA member, for indecency in a boat race crowd, which was detailed in a paragraph at the end of the Goodchild story of 14 April. The case of James Munro, a seventeen-year-old charged with indecency with a number of other teenagers, was mentioned in a single sentence on 5 May.[38] In highlighting the Goodchild case a particular territory was again outlined alongside a form of predatory sexual behaviour. The case echoed aspects of the Wilde trials which dominated the front pages, most significantly in its depiction of relationships between older men and teenagers or young men. Similar high-profile coverage during the Wilde trials accompanied a blackmailing case centring on a public toilet off Oxford Street (which is discussed later), and the story of Wilhelm Julius, who was bound over for three months after being arrested in women's clothes in Waterloo Place just off Pall Mall.[39]

Taken together, these five cases underscored the debauchery of the capital indicated by the Wilde trials. The suggestion was that the offences relating to homosexuality had increased significantly, that it was particularly prevalent in certain areas, and that London was being more vigorously policed. This did not necessarily reflect the reality of the situation, and in fact, as was indicated earlier, the total number of arrests for sodomy, attempted sodomy and gross indecency for 1895 was only two above the average for the preceding five years (forty-two) and was seven below the average for the period 1895–9 (fifty-one). Editorial decisions were shaping perceptions of sexual offences in the city and sketching out patterns of criminal sexual behaviour which were not necessarily borne out by the range of cases before the courts. The decisions to stress these cases nevertheless starkly redrew the boundary between sexual dissidence and normality.[40]

At less sensitive times more minor cases were relegated to two or three paragraphs on the inside pages, and many were not covered at all. In 1891

Hamilton de Tatha, a retired army medical officer living in St James', wrote to *Reynolds* to register his acquittal on charges of gross indecency with 'lads' at the Junior United Service Club in Pall Mall. The paper, having reported the initial hearing, had failed to note the result of the subsequent case.[41] Earlier, in 1886, *Reynolds* was similarly inattentive in the case of Arthur Brown, which was discussed in the Introduction. They did not report his prosecution for an act of gross indecency in Victoria Station toilets in February 1886, one of the first Labouchere amendment cases, and covered only part of the appeal process in May of the same year under the unprepossessing headline 'Middlesex Sessions Appeals'.[42] The result of the appeal, like the earlier trial, went unreported. Brown's behaviour was considered worthy of prosecution and the maximum possible sentence, two years with hard labour, but the story – involving a classic tryst between 'a gentleman of means' and a guardsman – was not published in *Reynolds*. At other times – during the Cleveland Street or Wilde scandals, for example – the cases would probably have been given a much higher profile.

More generally, newspaper coverage of the central London courts, as opposed to those in suburban areas or the provinces, suggested a particular concentration of homosexual activity in the city. Though the London press was increasingly catering for a national readership in this period, it lacked regional correspondents.[43] Consequently even *The Times*, the newspaper perhaps most identified with the nation rather than the city where it was produced, principally covered London police and crown court cases, masking, as Cocks has argued, the substantial levels of convictions elsewhere.[44] Thus when the Liberal MP and *Star* editor T. P. O'Connor suggested in the parliamentary debate on the Cleveland Street scandal that there was a high level of cases involving homosexual activity before the rural assize courts, Colonel Kenyan Slaney, MP for Newport Shropshire, furiously rebutted his claims: in Shropshire labourers did not 'bear this character' he insisted.[45] He and the press conceived of a determinedly urban vice.

If an uneven territory of criminality was suggested by the cases and courts editors decided to cover, the press was itself keen to indicate parallel inconsistencies in the application of the law. The Cleveland Street scandal is the most obvious example. Editorials proclaimed their duty to expose the inconsistencies in policing and sentencing and to force appropriate redress. The *Star*'s front page editorial declared 'we must probe this hideous evil down to its lowest root' and added: 'will not a large section of the public say that if the police authorities will not do their duty, the press must not be prosecuted for trying to compel them?'[46] Towards the end of the affair, and after his affray in parliament, Labouchere published two articles in *Truth* exposing the double standards in the application of justice and the direct results this had for morality in London:

> The offence has increased in London to a fearful extent owing to the practical immunity that is extended to it. Every person connected with the administration of the criminal law in the home office and the treasury, from the highest to the lowest, is steeped in the illusion that this immunity ought to continue ... every constable knows that he does not consult his own interests, but very much the reverse, by putting himself in conflict with this official doctrine.[47]

The press drew attention to this supposed laxity and suggested a cosseted subculture which was protected at the highest levels. They foregrounded Saul's comment in the Euston libel trial that the police 'had been kind to him' and turned a blind eye 'to more than him'.[48] Wide coverage also attended T. P. O'Connor's observation in the Commons that whilst detectives 'dogged' Irish MPs, none could be found 'to dog the footsteps of a ruffian who, for upwards of a year, has kept a house in the city which has brought disgrace on the character of the city'.[49]

At other times, however, the police appeared draconian. In June and July 1912, for example, Alan Horton, John Hill and Robert Freeman, whose cases were mentioned earlier, were arrested and convicted for intent and soliciting, despite there being no complaints about their behaviour. Ives commented in July 1912 that there had been 'many tragedies' and that 'persecutions' had been 'falling upon many people'.[50] The ratio of arrests to prosecutions for this year suggests that the police were arresting more people with less compelling evidence than before, or else magistrates and jurors were becoming more lenient. Between 1890 and 1909 an average of 47 per cent of men arrested for sodomy, attempted sodomy or gross indecency were convicted, but in 1912 the figure was only 36 per cent. In 1913 and 1914 the figure fell further, to 34 per cent and 32 per cent respectively.

This lack of consistency meant continual uncertainty for men involved in homosexual activity in the city. The blind eye turned to Jack Saul's behaviour by police or the warnings given to the actor Arthur Mellors before his eventual arrest and prosecution in 1906 were not always forthcoming.[51] The reputation of particular places, moreover, seems to have influenced the police in terms of the men they arrested. They knew a man apprehended in Piccadilly Circus might be convicted with less evidence than someone caught elsewhere. Prevailing stereotypes of homosexual behaviour, like that exhibited in the case of Horton, also influenced arrest patterns, particularly with regard to solicitation. A man with similar intent to Horton but without the make-up or effeminate wiggle was clearly more likely to evade arrest. The press, meanwhile, shaped some of these ideas about places and deviant types through selective and sometimes sensational reporting. Men wanting sex with other men had carefully to negotiate these assumptions about bodies, behaviour and territories if they were to go unprosecuted in London. They also had to remain sensitive to the shifting frontiers of criminality in the city, which meant that some places were more permissive than others and some periods more liberal. In 1871 Fanny and Stella could get away with winking at the Burlington Arcade beadle and wearing make-up in public. In 1912 similar behaviour led to prosecution and imprisonment for Horton.

BODIES, STREETS AND PERFUMED ROOMS

In large-scale and more minor cases police assumptions, court proceedings and press reporting helped to cultivate ideas about a 'homosexual' body and territory. The succession of newspaper reports of court cases Ives pasted into his scrapbook together suggest where men could be found and outlined what they looked like. Perhaps most significantly, the courts and the newspapers bracketed this distinctive figure and these spaces together. Within this juridical/journalistic framework men who had sex with other men were largely defined by space and described as creatures of their environment. The emphasis was on acts and where they were committed: the Labouchere Amendment had specifically emphasised 'public and private' spaces and the suspect's presence in certain parts of the West End, in public toilets or in the parks at certain times enabled particular conclusions to be drawn. Arrests came after 'dens' had been searched and movements through the city had been tracked; prosecution was usually followed by removal to the punitive space of the prison. Newspapers emphasised this connection. Headlines from the period announced: 'The Cleveland Street Case'; 'The West End Scandals' and 'Another London Scandal' (1890), 'Fitzroy Square Raid' (1894); 'The West End Blackmailing Case' (1895); 'West End Blackmailers' (1898); 'West End Flat Scandal' and 'The Studio Murder' (1906); and 'Met In Hyde Park' (1908).[52]

The places mentioned in the court cases and newspaper reports were characterised in two main ways. On the one hand they were utterly separate from the middle-class domestic sphere and deemed somehow appropriate for such unspeakable sexual crimes. On the other they were well-known and 'respectable' sites which were hideously compromised by the homosexual activity which took place there. These conceptions figure homosexuality as both outside but also dangerously within mainstream urban culture. During the Cleveland Street scandal, for example, the *Star* described the

Figure 8   The Cleveland Street Scandal, *Illustrated Police News*, 25 January 1890.

house as 'a hideous cesspool of wickedness and foulness'[53] and *Reynolds* referred to 'a horrible den of vice', 'a hideous place,' 'a den of infamy' and an 'abominable institution'. The paper also referred to 'the infamous Cleveland street inferno' and 'the abominable orgies of Cleveland Street'.[54] This, however, was set against the location of the house. Labouchere was widely quoted in the press when he commented in parliament that 'the house is in no obscure thoroughfare, but nearly opposite the Middlesex Hospital', and the *Illustrated Police News* showed it to be like most other town houses in the area (see fig. 8).[55] The papers of course also mentioned the involvement of telegraph boys from the GPO headquarters. The 'den of infamy' was not in a – presumably more fitting – 'obscure' street and involved not common street boys but post office employees in uniform.

In the Wilde case, Alfred Taylor's darkened, perfumed rooms were repeatedly evoked in court and described by the press. In his summing-up for Lord Queensberry at the first trial, Edward Carson talked of the 'shameful' and later 'extraordinary' 'den'.[56] In the second trial Taylor's landlady at 13 Little College Street testified that: 'The windows of his rooms were covered with stained art muslin and dark curtains and lace curtains. They were furnished sumptuously, and were lighted by different coloured lamps and candles . . . the windows were never opened and the daylight was never admitted.'[57] The description recalls the home of Des Esseintes in J.-K. Huysmans' French decadent classic *A Rebours* (*Against Nature*)(1884), in which 'natural order' was inverted to cast a shadowy darkness during daylight. The press foregrounded these details as they were repeated in the three trials. Each time the heady perfumes, artificial light and sumptuous furnishings were evoked. Fresh air and light, the conduits of Victorian heath and vitality, were absent, and the public gaze was shut out, as in the Fitzroy Square case of 1894, in which all the curtains were reportedly drawn. It was the antithesis of rooms described in a piece on Piccadilly in *Chamber's Journal* in 1892: 'Through the French windows travellers outside in the omnibus can catch a rapid sight of statuettes, a neat white bookcase well filled with bright volumes, a few pieces of choice French furniture – nothing approaching the palatial; but neat, tasteful and orderly, like the house of any English gentleman.'[58] Here was a general standard to which the respectable Englishman should conform. It was orderly and neat, with nothing too lavish, and was, perhaps most significantly, unashamed of the public gaze. The Little College Street chambers disrupted these ideas of English propriety and were envisaged as the natural habitat for the sexual deviant, who shaped his domestic space on degenerate foreign ideas of home. The *Evening News* editorial observed on the day of Wilde's conviction that 'such people find their fitting environment in the artificial light and the incense-laden air of secret chambers curtained from the light of day'.[59] As Ed Cohen argues, Taylor's rooms become a 'liminal space whose decorative perversions of bourgeois domesticity came to signify larger violations of the sexual/moral codes that such domesticity (re)produced and reflected'.[60]

The location of these rooms was also stressed. Charles Gill, prosecuting in the second trial, suggested to Wilde that it was 'rather a rough neighbourhood' and 'not the sort of place you would usually visit'.[61] In the final trial the solicitor general, Sir Frank Lockwood, characterised the area as a 'place where debased persons congregated'.[62] He later commented that it was 'not a very cheerful street'.[63] The apartment and street were marked out as distinct and somehow suitable for the alleged sexual activity that occurred there. Wilde attempted to disarm this rhetoric, suggesting instead that it was part of, and not separate from, the dominant urban terrain. In the first trial Wilde said he did not find the rooms strange, only 'bohemian'.[64] In the second he said that it 'was merely a bachelor's place' and that he did not know about it being a rough area, but only that it was near the Houses of Parliament.[65] When Lockwood asked Wilde if he liked the situation of the apartment, he replied that he thought it 'was a particularly nice one – close to Westminster Abbey'.[66] According to the *Star*, Taylor's council, J. A. Grein, was 'anxious to show that the darkening of Taylor's windows at Little College Street was only the draperies usual in continental cities and the modern flat' – the noted anxiety subtly undermining Grein's claims.[67] The defence repeatedly returned to the 'normal' and the 'usual', and Wilde to the 'bachelor' and 'bohemian', to counter prosecution depictions of luxury, elaborate furnishing and exotic perfumes. The nature of the flat and its location were perceived to be important in discerning the desires of the defendants. If they could be proven to be distinct then the behaviour of those who visited them would apparently be clearer. Employing the same logic, the defence sought to show the continuity of the street and room with the rest of the city.

Whatever the status of the Little College Street flat in terms of middle-class propriety, what was clear was that Wilde had trespassed in other ways. At the committal proceedings of Wilde and Taylor at Bow Street on 6 April, Gill said that 'it would be shown that the prisoner had the audacity to commit these offences at the Savoy, at a hotel in Piccadilly, and even at his own house in Tite Street when his family was away'.[68] In his summing-up Judge Alfred Wills was aghast that sex between men might have taken place at the Savoy Hotel and had in the first instance gone unreported by the chambermaid. 'It is a state of things one shudders to contemplate in a first class hotel,' he said.[69]

The prosecution painted a picture of gross trespass on public, domestic and pseudo-domestic turf on the one hand, whilst on the other constructing a perverse 'other' space in Little College Street which appeared to nurture dissident desire. This sense in both the Cleveland Street and Wilde scandals recurred in reporting of other cases. The West End actor Arthur Mellors, prosecuted in 1906, and the murdered artist Archibald Wakley, whose inquest received wide coverage in the same year, both lived outside middle-class domestic arenas: in a small flat in Victoria and a studio in Bayswater respectively. Both also used public spaces to find or entertain partners: Mellors in the West End theatres, Wakley in Hyde Park. Earlier in 1895 John Goodchild, the man prosecuted for having sex with a Jewish match boy, made forays from the room he rented above a chemist's shop into the East End streets to find sexual gratification. Judged by middle-class expectations of domesticity each of these men was an outsider. Their private space in the city enabled rather than inhibited their dissident desires; the policing function of the family home was absent. The day after Wilde was found guilty the *Chronicle* berated the lack of wholesome domestic influence: 'The herding of boys in great schools, their too early separation from their homes and association with their mothers... all these things, coupled with the tasteless luxury that rich parents hold out as a poisonous lure to idle young men and women, afford a terrible wide margin for the gradual perversion of heart and intellect.'[70] The *Telegraph* editorial, meanwhile, saw Wilde's 'superfine art', and all it represented, as the 'enemy' of 'the natural affections, the domestic joys, the sanctity and sweetness of the home'.[71] The middle-class home was set in opposition to these spaces and desires, making Wilde's activities in Tite Street particularly abhorrent. When his effects were auctioned to pay his debts, the sale attracted almost universal coverage in the press. The 'dispersal' of his possessions seemed a kind of poetic justice: the familial domestic space could not harbour these activities and survive.[72]

This use of city space by men seeking sex with other men blurred the conceptual boundaries between public and private. Assignations were made at private parties, like those at Little College Street or Fitzroy Square, in the streets, in public toilets, in parks and through friends in West End restaurants and bars. They were consummated *in situ* or in private rooms, in bachelor chambers in St James', in the pseudo-domesticity of West End hotels or even in the family home. The city centre, as opposed to the suburbs, was shown to be permissive of homosexual activity in its public, private and more liminal aspects, and a fluid movement between them was suggested. A transition between the public and private was commonly outlined – indicating the potential dangers to the unsuspecting of both the city street and of heavily curtained rooms. A chat in the park led to improper suggestions in Wakley's studio; an invitation on Piccadilly gave way to the obscenities of the Cleveland Street brothel; a restaurant meal in Soho to gross indecency in a room at the Savoy. The prohibition under the Labouchere Amendment of such activity anywhere was apparently flouted everywhere in central London.

It was in conjunction with this set of spaces that a sexually dissident body was delineated. Importantly, men were not labelled as homosexuals or inverts by the newspapers or courts during the period and the emphasis continued to be on what they had done. Although stereotypes were elaborated, this emphasis on criminal sexual acts meant that men were assumed to have misbehaved as a result of a profound moral debasement and an inability to exercise self-control, rather than for any constitutional reason. The courts and press were largely uninterested in the arguments about inherent sexual identity being propounded by sexologists. Thus even though Justice Wills, who had tried Wilde, noted a 'strain of insanity' in James Smith in 1897, it did not stop him from passing the maximum sentence of two years with hard labour. Smith had only been released from jail in 1895, having served eighteen years of a life sentence for sodomy.[73] Wilde's appeal for early release on similar grounds in the previous year, which cited degeneration theorists Max Nordau and Cesare Lombroso, was also turned down.[74] The offence was too gross to admit excuse. Nonetheless, reports of the bigger cases in particular often included lengthy descriptions of the behaviour of defendants and witnesses, building up images of distinct, though no less culpable, types. Wilde was almost obsessively described and he became, as Sinfield and Cohen both argue, the clearest prototype of the urban homosexual. Cohen shows how, in coverage of the first trial, Wilde's languid and aesthetic stance was contrasted to Lord Queensberry, who became 'a virtual icon of outraged masculinity'.[75] Illustrations in the *Morning Leader*, Cohen goes on to observe, depicted Wilde as a grotesque figure, with bloated face and enlarged nose and lips. His physicality and mass were emphasised and contrasted to the more respectable (and bearded) 'intelligent philistines' of the jury.[76] The Russian émigré poet Marc-André Raffalovich echoed these depictions in his damning account of Wilde after the trials: 'one could not see him speak without noticing his sensual lips, his discoloured teeth, and his tongue which seemed to lick his words'.[77] On his conviction the *Evening News* commented that Wilde 'was the perfect type of his class, a gross sensualist, veneered with the affectation of artistic feeling too delicate for the common clay'.[78]

This image is fed and refined by precedent and subsequent figures appearing in the dock and witness box. *Reynolds* described Jack Saul of the Cleveland Street case as 'a filthy loathsome and detestable beast' and the *Star* remarked on his effeminacy and theatricality. His demeanour was markedly different from the editor Parke, who took the guilty verdict and the pronouncement of sentence 'like a man'.[79] Whilst Saul prowls Piccadilly in the image in the *Illustrated London News*, Parke is shown sitting pensively with his wife (see fig. 8). As Morris B. Kaplan observes, Saul and men like him were seen 'to have fallen outside the dominant structure of class relations in Victorian England'.[80] Instead they seemed to have assumed a distinctive identity associated with their metropolitan lifestyle and profession, rather like the protagonists in *Sins of the Cities of the Plain*. This was of course not the case for other urban 'rent', like the telegraph boys and soldiers, whose class status was intrinsic to their attraction. In the Fitzroy Square case of 1894, the newspapers reported the spectacle of two men, Arthur Marley and John Severs, making their first police court appearance in women's clothes.[81] In 1895 Wilhelm Julius was said in *Reynolds* to be a 'very effeminate-looking individual' and Henri Müller, arrested in Oxford Street in 1906, was described standing in the dock 'with one black glove on and holding a handkerchief. His face had been carefully shaved and slightly rouged and was of a feminine cast... He wept while in the dock.'[82]

In other cases descriptions were less detailed, but still gave an impression of a particular type. William Jones, who had been seen 'frequenting' a urinal just off Oxford Street in 1901, was said to be 'a tall, unwholesome looking individual'.[83] Later in 1908, in an apparent allusion to Wilde, Herbert Blythe was said to be a 'clean-shaven, well-dressed man' and a 'higher critic'.[84] Back in the Wilde trials, the witness Arthur Mavor was described as a 'slim dandified young man, in a painfully high and stiff collar', and Charles Parker was 'a slim clean-shaven lad with a fair girlish face'.[85] *Reynolds* remarked on 'the saddening spectacle' of a 'large number of well, even fashionably dressed men' at Wilde's committal proceedings, who 'for more than an hour... waited, walking up and down, smoking cigarettes, laughing and joking, trying to learn what truth there was in the report that further arrests were intended'.[86] Taylor had, according to the *Star*, a particularly suspect mouth and smile. It was not fleshy and sensual like Wilde's, but instead narrow and effete. The paper described the 'cynical smile' which 'hovered round his thin lips'.[87] Later they reported his 'sickly smile' and Wilde was described being followed into court by 'the simpering Taylor, who smiled all over his weak open mouth'.[88] In the absence of other distinguishing features the fascination with his mouth stressed both effeminacy and corporeality. Gill Davies notes a similar preoccupation amongst the urban explorers and novelists who wrote about the East End. The mouth, she suggests, represented 'the physicality of the body and its threat to rational, middle-class sensibility and ideology'.[89]

The bodies of Wilde, Saul, Muller, Horton, Taylor and others were each interpreted by journalists, and in turn by the reading public. Stereotypes were evoked, clarified and endorsed, rendering the pariah recognisable in a number of forms in the city streets: as fleshy and decadent; weak and effeminate; or more generally as 'unwholesome' and 'beastly'. The cross-dressing connection was also repeated, and other subsidiary markers included a penchant for fashionable dress and a lack of facial hair. The fact that defendants were clean-shaven was invariably reported, and the suspect members of the Hammersmith amateur dramatics group discussed in the last chapter were said to be 'terribly' close shaven.[90] Facial hair functioned as a symbol of masculinity and respectability during what Allan Peterkin calls the late-Victorian 'beard boom'. Those without were associated with fashion, bohemianism and an avant-garde – but also possibly worse.[91] A month after Wilde's conviction Cesare Lombroso noted in the *Contemporary Review* that 'the interchange of sexual characteristics (absence of beard, &c.)' was a functional sign of atavism. The 'degenerate' was defined further here, and aligned closely with the 'homosexual'.[92] It was possible, Lombroso and the newspapers suggested, to read identity and character directly from the body.

Origins were also important: nationality and accent were frequently noted in the papers, and it is certainly possible that police xenophobia made foreigners more vulnerable to arrest. Saul was said by *Reynolds* to 'speak with a foreign accent',[93] Müller's nationality was mentioned in the first sentence of the article in the *People*, and at a time of increasing tension between Britain and Germany the papers stressed the Germanic origins of Julius Walters, who was arrested for approaching men in East India Dock Road whilst dressed as a woman in 1908, and Ernest Sneider, who surrendered himself to the police in 1910 in an attempt to elude a blackmailer.[94] In the Goodchild case of 1895 the fact that the match boy, Jon Abrahams, was Jewish, was mentioned repeatedly, alongside suggestions that he complied willingly with Goodchild's advances.[95] These factors were not primary indicators of dissident desire, but they came in apparent confirmation, shaping and conflating images of the urban sexual deviant and the dangerous foreigner. As part of the intensifying debate about immigration in the 1890s, the Rev. G. S. Reaney complained of the familiarity of East End 'aliens' with the vices 'common to the deeper depths of Continental cities'.[96] As in the 1700s and early 1800s, the foreigner was a convenient scapegoat for the extent of homosexual and other vice in London.

These spaces and bodies gained added importance in the newspapers since, as Cohen demonstrates, they stood in for mention of the sexual acts themselves. The newspaper reader often had to gather clues from details of place and appearance in order to discern the crime, which was often not made clear. Whilst the courts heard descriptions of sexual acts, the newspapers referred to 'gross indecency' or 'unnatural', 'infamous' or 'unnameable' offences. Sometimes references were even more oblique and the reader was left guessing what was at issue. In the 1912 case against John Hill and Robert Freeman it was unclear from press reports what they were saying to the men they approached in Charing Cross Road. Earlier in 1898 Robert Clibburn was convicted of blackmail and sentenced to seven years' imprisonment, but the threats he issued to Charles Deck were only suggested by the fact that Deck was on the Embankment at night with an actor when he was approached, his fur coat stolen and money demanded for its return. Acute readers might also have remembered Clibborn as one of the men who attempted to blackmail Wilde, and deduced from this – together with the implications of a night-time walk along the Embankment and the theatrical company – the possible nature of the threats he used to extort money.

Reports of the inquest into the murder of Archibald Wakley in 1906 were similarly evasive and Wakley's evening visits to Hyde Park to meet soldiers became crucial to the conclusions drawn by the newspaper readership. Having heard about these visits, the foreman of the inquest jury asked an acquaintance of Wakley, a soldier named Walker, what had happened when he had visited the artist's studio: ' "I am sorry to have to put this question but I want a plain answer. You will understand what I mean. Now do I understand that the deceased suggested something to you to which you objected?" "Yes Sir", replied Trooper Walker, who afterwards stared down, and swung, with a military style, head erect out of the court.'[97] The euphemistic question and answer, which are far from 'plain', shed no real light on what had happened, unless the reader had picked up on various indicators and understood what 'something to which you objected' might mean. The reader was left to draw conclusions as to the nature of Wakley's desires from the place where he and the trooper had met, from the sketches he kept in the studio and from an unspecified injury. The foreman meanwhile assumed it would be Wakley who made the objectionable suggestion and did not question why Walker visited Wakley in the first place, having only met him casually in Hyde Park. These assumptions about Wakley's guilt were set in opposition to Walker's military aplomb in the courtroom, during a period of considerable sensitivity about the moral and physical condition of the army.[98] In each of these cases the unmentionable nature of homosexual relations made the circumstances of the crime, where it was supposedly committed and who was present decisive to the reader's understanding. Ed Cohen thus points out that during the Wilde trial banal details of visits to the Savoy and chambers in St James' had to stand in for more graphic descriptions offered in the courtroom.[99]

'LIFTING THE VEIL' ON VICE

Accompanying these descriptions came a rhetoric of exposure. When Wilde was finally prosecuted the *Illustrated Police News* reported that a 'canker' had been brought 'to light'.[100] The imagery was typical. The cases were seen by the press as the means through which urban depravity could be exposed and removed. During the Cleveland Street scandal the *Star* admitted its reticence in 'dragging into the light of day and topics of conversation the foul loathsome slimy things that are hidden out of sight', but announced that the time had come to break the silence, to lift the 'veil' and 'expose' the men involved 'to the view of justice'.[101] This idea of concealed lives and the need to render them visible was crucial to the maintenance of sexual order since it brought with it a regime of watchfulness and vigilance.

Police surveillance was a common aspect of these cases. The Cleveland Street house was monitored and Lord Somerset was followed as part of the investigations into the 1889 scandal. The whole case only started because Charles Swinscow had been observed at the GPO with an unusually large quantity of money for a telegraph boy. Four years later police watched the house in Fitzroy Square, and in the Wilde case it transpired that Taylor's rooms had surreptitiously been searched by police.[102] Wilde was tailed after the libel trial collapsed and Mellors and Horton were kept under observation in 1906 and 1912 respectively.

Park keepers were also on the look out for homosexual activity, although they do seem to have been less vigilant than the police, making the LCC-controlled parks – basically those outside the central area of the city – potentially more permissive spaces for discreet homosexual fraternisation.[103] Arrests nevertheless took place there, and in 1909 twenty-one-year-old Arthur Humphries was fined £5 at Old Street Police Court in 1909 after he was 'observed' entering a public lavatory in Victoria Park with sixteen-year-old Joseph Purt.[104] In the same year a keeper in Battersea Park arrested Frederick Harrison and Thomas Rhodes after seeing them 'commit an act of gross indecency' in a urinal. They were subsequently sentenced to fifteen and twelve months with hard labour respectively.[105] The LCC's Theatre and Music Halls Committee was perhaps more attentive in matters of public morality. Between 1890 and 1892 1,200 inspections of music halls were made, reflecting the council's mounting concern. The LCC refused to grant new music halls alcohol licences after 1894 and although they did not actually close halls down for immorality on stage during the period, their power to do so probably induced self-censorship and made hall managers responsive to protests from the council. In 1897, for example, a Moorish bath scene was dropped from a show at the Palace Theatre following an approach from the Theatre and Music Halls committee.[106]

This policing was supplemented by a wider watchfulness or nosiness on the part of members of the public. In the Lord Euston libel case Ann Morgan offered detailed information about the number of men who had entered and left number 19 Cleveland Street. She claimed to have seen between fifty and sixty men entering the house over time. In the Fitzroy Square affair police had been tipped off by a neighbour and in the blackmailing case of 1895, held in the midst of the Wilde trials, part of the evidence was supplied by Joseph Hawkins, a corn dealer, who had observed George Mooney and George Wilton 'frequenting the lavatory [just off Oxford Street] for months past'.[107] In 1902 Prince Francis Joseph of Braganza and two men were landed in court by the evidence of a Mr Burbage, who claimed to have watched the three men having sex through a hole in the bedroom door at his house in Lambeth.[108] Finally, the inquest into the murder of Archibald Wakley in 1906 heard testimony from George Miles, a salesman from Whiteley's department store. On 23 May he had seen Wakley 'coming along the road in the company of a soldier of the Royal Horse Guards'. Wakley had entered the house followed by the soldier, 'the latter hesitating a moment. The soldier had spurs on, and no light had gone on in the room once they had entered.'[109] These were not casual observations, but the product of careful attention to what must have appeared suspicious behaviour: large numbers of men entering a single house, men visiting public toilets a little too frequently, an aristocrat taking two men into a room in a lodging house, an artist in the company of a guardsman, and so on. These witnesses were attuned to the unconventional and the scandalous.

These signs were also picked up by blackmailers on the lookout for potential victims. Statutes against homosexual activity had legislated these other criminals into existence. In *A History of Penal Methods* Ives suggested that there was an established blackmailing fraternity in London. 'A number of most villainous gangs are always badly wanted by the state,' he noted, adding: 'certain blackmailers are almost as "known" as politicians or actors, only the witnesses and victims will not come forward, and the police cannot get legal evidence enough to put before a jury.'[110] Clibburn, for example, was at large for at least nine years before being prosecuted for attempting to blackmail Charles Deck on the Embankment in 1998. Ives noted that, around the time of the Cleveland Street scandal, Lord Euston had been involved in a 'tussle' with Clibburn, who he described as 'a young renter and blackmailer'. Six years later he figured in the Wilde case.[111] Ives' scrapbooks include around two blackmail cases each year but these represent only unsuccessful blackmailing operations. In a condemnation of both the blackmailer and urban homosexual adventuring Ives observed in his diary after the conviction of four men in 1894 that: 'the law steps on two or three, and squashes them with a heavy tread; and fifty scamper off and prey on the putrefaction of the great cities'.[112] The journalist George Sims pointed the finger at foreigners in 1908, claiming that foreign syndicates of blackmailers and bullies operated from Soho cafés and pubs which were 'the fertile breeding beds of crime and anarchy'.[113] 'There is a numerous army of blackmailers in London,' one paper claimed in the same year, 'and the nefarious crime of blackmail...is on the increase.'[114]

Between men in search of sex, blackmailers, park keepers, the police and watchful bystanders, a circle of vigilance was established. In the 1895 black-mailing case, for example, the blackmailers Mooney and Wilton watched for victims; the man who gave Mooney money at the exit of the toilet had presumably looked out for sex; the corn-dealer Hawkins had observed the blackmailers' activities; and finally the police had watched the comings and goings to clarify and verify details of a complaint made by Westly Francis, from whom Mooney and Wilton had previously attempted to extort money. The regime was effective only because of the anonymity of each observer. It was important that the man entering the toilet did not realise he was being followed by a blackmailer and that neither of them was aware they were being observed by the police or a bystander. Each person, with the exception of Hawkins, was aware of the possibility of being seen, from the police who needed to survey incognito, to the blackmailers and the man in search of sex. The latter two risked hefty prison sentences if they were too obvious, but they still needed to remain visible enough to effect a sexual or monetary transaction. It was a lack of such caution which led to Wilde's downfall, and he pulled out of the libel case only when he realised the extent of surveillance undertaken by the Marquis of Queensberry's private detec-tives. He expected his cosmopolitan milieu to act as a shield and seemed to have been unaware of the number of people who had seen him entering and leaving various establishments, and who deemed, or had been persuaded to deem, such comings and goings suspicious. 'It came as a shock to their preconceived idea . . . that the police in London knew a great many things which they were not supposed to concern themselves with', Wilde's early biographer Frank Harris noted.[115]

The opportunities of the West End were constantly tainted by the pos-sibility of being observed by an astute member of the public, a policeman or a potential blackmailer. Whilst it might have been necessary to betray markers of sexual identity – in dress, demeanour or by visiting particular places – in order to find sexual partners, such behaviour was clearly also dangerous and much rested on careful self-regulation. Ives, for example, saw himself caught between blackmailer and policeman, writing in 1902: 'I know the real dangers in our wretched and hungry streets. No wonder I am wary of common courtesy.'[116]

Despite the rhetoric of exposure emanating from the press there was also a strong sense that homosexual activity was rife, was protected and had not in fact been brought fully 'to light'. This emanated partly from the perpetual euphemism which left judges, jurors, editors and MPs speaking of 'a certain offence', 'the hideous crime' or 'something objectionable'. Labouchere, having himself drafted the hazily worded addition to the Criminal Law Amendment Act, complained in *Truth* after the Cleveland Street affair that the lack of revelation emanated from the unmentionability of the subject: 'ministers have taken advantage of the fact that the subject raised last Friday in the House of Commons was one which, from its nature, renders it impossible to enter into details. Were this not so, I could show that the offence has increased in London to a fearful extent.'[117] This lack of clarity suggested a malevolent presence which haunted the city. Despite an increasingly clear sense of what in fact was being spoken about, the coyness in directly referring to it perpetuated images of a heinous and shadowy criminal fraternity.[118] Comments by judges, MPs and editors confirmed this impression and the idea that the crime was on the increase: Labouchere proclaimed its resurgence at the time of the Cleveland Street scandal; the judge in the 1898 blackmailing case involving Clibborn reported an increase 'in recent years';[119] and during a parliamentary debate about introducing flogging for soliciting offences in 1912 the Liberal Home Secretary, Reginald McKenna, remarked that 'the evil has been steadily growing of late years'.[120] Whilst worrying for the Home Secretary, for men wanting to find male sexual partners in the city such comments were tantalising and spoke not only of the dangers associated with homosexual sex but also of an enduring and apparently expansive subculture.

Cases already discussed demonstrated a confident use of the West End by some men in women's clothes or make-up both before and after the Wilde trials. Evidence brought into court – the incriminating address book found in Mellor's flat, Taylor's notebook from Little College Street, Goodchild's diary from his East End rooms, the slips of paper with addresses on found near Wakley's body – indicated a large social and sexual network, and there was the repeated suggestion of a criminal confederacy between men in the city.[121] The recorder in the Mellors case of 1906, Sir Forrest Fulton, observed that the defendant had belonged to 'another gang' of sexual criminals which he had hoped had been 'rooted out'.[122] Julius Walters, the German caught masquerading as a woman in 1908, was said in court and in the newspapers to be an associate of 'well-known blackmailers and other infamous characters in the West End'.[123] In the same year Robert Gathercole, a cross-dresser spotted by police taking an army officer home, was similarly said to be an associate of men 'of vicious habits'.[124] Earlier, the succession of witnesses at the Wilde trial indicated a circuit of male prostitutes and blackmailers who were not charged or prosecuted.[125]

There was in addition the suspicion that many of these men were protected. Ives suggested that King Edward VII prevented a case involving
Lord Battersea going to court in 1902,[126] and earlier the Cleveland Street
saga was seen as a wide-ranging cover-up orchestrated by the 'old boys'
network. Lord Salisbury, the Conservative Prime Minister, was accused of
warning Somerset of his imminent arrest warrant, the police were accused of
deliberate tardiness and it was suggested that Veck and Newlove's trial had
deliberately been left until last on the list for the day to avoid publicity.[127]
The sentence they received, of nine months and four months with hard
labour respectively, was contrasted in the *North London Press* with that
handed down to a Hackney vicar who was imprisoned for life, presumably
under the statute against sodomy rather than gross indecency.[128] The same
paper reported the anger of 'Hackney workmen' at the permissiveness of
West End high society. One member of the London Fields Radical Club
observed that 'working men are free from the taint' but that 'FOR GOLD
LAID DOWN our boys might be tempted to their fall'.[129] Again, the dangers
of an aristocratic preserve and of 'posing as sharers' in a wealthy, decadent
and degenerate culture were highlighted, resonating with the more general
concern about amorphous class boundaries in the West End streets and
theatres, discussed in the last chapter.

Central London was cast as a sexual playground for the rich, sanctioned
by the clubs and protected by government and police. Indeed, it does appear that whilst aristocrats – Lord Alfred Douglas, Prince Francis Joseph,
the Earl of Euston and Lord Somerset – frequently evaded prosecution,
other men often faced severe penalties.[130] Julius Walters and James Smith,
who were discussed earlier, went to jail repeatedly for their activities, and
in the Braganza case the Prince was acquitted at the request of the counsel
for the prosecution whilst both the men he allegedly had sex with received
two years' imprisonment. The prosecution also assumed these men were
motivated by blackmail, the only reason apart from prostitution it could
conceive for working-class men to have homosexual sex.[131] Wilde was a
stand-in for the louche aristocrat, but he was crucially neither upper class
nor English. Indeed, whilst the *Telegraph* and the *Evening News* issued
vindictive editorials on Wilde's conviction, *Reynolds* argued that the prosecution had been a screen for broader aristocratic homosexual activity in
the city and indicated the prevalence of such activity amongst 'our leisured
and cultured class' and 'Tories'.[132] The paper implied that the emergence
of the Wildean stereotype conveniently obscured other urban 'types' from
view.

Whatever ambivalence surrounded the messages of urban danger and op-portunity, court cases were moments when captured sexual dissidents, emerged to full scrutiny: they could be exposed and expelled from the city as part of a process in which moral codes were adjusted, clarified and rearticulated. For extended periods – six months with the Cleveland Street scandal, two months with the three trials involving Wilde – the cases gripped and apparently appalled the capital. During the debate on the Cleveland Street scandal in the House of Commons, James Rowland, MP for Finsbury, spoke paternally of what the city's inhabitants had been through: 'the people of London have had a great scandal in their midst ... no-one who was in London through the Autumn could have failed to recognise that these scandals have produced a great effect on the public mind'.[133] Lady Blanche Waterford, Lord Arthur Somerset's sister, complained in a letter that 'the whole thing is being hawked in the street, and everyone invents his or her own story to it all'.[134] The tenor was similar during the Wilde trials. Placards and newspaper boys shouted the latest details, and anger greeted those who appeared to have sided with Wilde. Rev. Stewart Headlam, who bailed Wilde out, was threatened with stoning by a mob outside his Bloomsbury home and the publishers of *The Yellow Book* had their windows smashed after it was erroneously suggested that Wilde had a copy of the journal under his arm when he was arrested.[135] Later, and in the absence of the possibility of public pillory, the trials became the focus for urban reaction. In the courtroom the relationship between hegemonic values and sexual dissidence was cast in simplistic binary terms. Labouchere declared in *Truth* during the Wilde trials that the public were appalled by homosexuality, a response which was 'exactly the reverse' of 'a narrow but influential circle in London'.[136] At the conclusion of the case the *Star* noted the cheers 'of the ever virtuous British crowd' which 'had been audible throughout the judge's address'.[137] ' "E'll ave his 'air cut regular now [*sic*]" ' one woman was reported as shouting, relishing the playwright's imminent incarceration and transformation.[138] The inclusion of these details in the newspapers apparently confirmed the popularity of the judgement against Wilde. The city became one, unified in the battle against the sexual pariah. As the early sociologist G. H. Mead argued in 1918, 'the cry of thief or murderer is attuned to the profound complexities lying below the surface of competing individual effort, and citizens ... separated by diversified interests stand together against the common enemy'.[139] Whether or not the cry of pervert actually elicited this collective reaction, the newspapers effectively portrayed it as such in their reporting of the Wilde and Cleveland

Street scandals in particular. Walkowitz describes a similar collective address during the Maiden Tribute case: the press, she argues, treated the public as a 'single moral entity'.[140]

What was so sensational about Wilde's conviction was that a high-profile 'pervert' had been caught and imprisoned, something that had not happened in the Cleveland Street and Maiden Tribute cases, when instead journalists had faced imprisonment. *Truth* thus saw it as 'a storm that will clear the moral atmosphere', whilst the *Daily Chronicle* observed that 'there has been a purge, and we hope London is the better for it'.[141] The *Star* described Wilde's collapse at the verdict: '[he] seemed to have lost control of his limbs. When at last he turned away, between two wardens, he trailed like a man smitten with paralysis.'[142] It was the final step in the gradual expulsion of Wilde from the city. He had been asked to leave the hotel in which he sought refuge after the collapse of the libel action, his name had been taken from the theatre billboards after his arrest and now he was bound for prison, where his ill-health and depression were widely reported. As Cohen convincingly argues, once a convicted sexual deviant, Wilde was described undergoing a transformation: from larger than life, vivacious urban actor to diminutive, ageing wreck, more in line with Taylor, who, already enfeebled, underwent no such mutation.[143] In *Discipline and Punish* Michel Foucault argues that the development of the prison marked a standardisation of punishment, a movement away from a more public model in which the penalty was often symbolic of the crime that had been committed.[144] In this case, however, the press revelled in Wilde's imprisonment as a singularly appropriate punishment for the urban decadent: he was to be removed from the territory that had fed his desires. The *Evening News* commented: 'The brilliant wit was elbowed to the silence of solitary imprisonment, the man of fashion was condemned to shorn locks and the convict's garb; the voluptuary to the hard labour of the treadmill; the poet to the maddening torture of two years hard labour.'[145] The events in the courtroom and his imprisonment provided a figurative pillory through which a set of 'norms' could be forcefully rearticulated and dissident behaviour symbolically expunged.

Of course the case removed only two sexual criminals. It was evident from subsequent trials that the city changed little in terms of the prevalence of homosexual activity. Moreover, however vociferous the newspapers, there were enough indications of sympathy for Wilde to tarnish the image of a city unified in outrage. During the trial itself applause greeted Wilde's defence of same-sex love and in the month following the conviction *Reynolds* published a number of letters expressing dismay at the sentence and sympathy for Wilde. A letter signed 'A woman who believes in Oscar Wilde' took heart from the correspondence: 'I had begun to think, until I read those letters, that there was no gleam of pity or charity for him, for according to a very large section of the press, all seemed merciless.'[146] *Reynolds'* own measured editorial after the conviction sharply contrasted with those of other newspapers. Four years later, *The Adult*, the journal of the Legitimation League, praised *Reynolds* as 'the premier newspaper of enlightenment in England'.[147] Ives detected 'a change in the ethical atmosphere' after the trials and four months later noted that 'the change in public feeling, if one may judge from the gossip in the clubs etc., is truly wonderful; men very hostile a few months ago, now admit this or that, and seem truly on the road to reason'.[148] Whilst club gossip is not a sufficient gauge of public opinion, the trials clearly did not simply reaffirm prevailing attitudes about homosexual activity. They also provoked dialogue and, Ives suggested, some change of heart. In 1909 Ives suspected a jury of acquitting a clergyman they knew to be guilty so as to prevent 'the dreadful consequences';[149] three years later he registered the support of 'a clergyman, a captain and four or five ladies' for a proposal by the Prison Reform League to oppose the extension of legislation against solicitation by men. Just before the outbreak of war Ives wrote of his 'joy' at hearing a magistrate 'denounce the senselessness and cruelty of the sentences passed on inverts' at an meeting of the British Society for the Study of Sex Psychology.[150] The sharp increase in arrests for homosexual activity between 1910 and 1914 was provoking opposition at least in some quarters.

Through the reporting and editing of court cases, the newspaper press produced a version of the 'homosexual' and revealed the places he frequented, his putative domestic arrangements and his concomitant disregard for a middle-class ordering of public and private realms – a disregard tacitly legitimated by the wording of the Labouchere Amendment itself. However, the relationship between homosexuality and the city as described in these accounts was also fraught with contradictions. In the major scandals, which endured in the public memory, and the minor cases, which came as weekly reminders of them, there was the sense of a highly sensitised and vigilant public and police force on the one hand, and on the other of an embedded subculture which was tacitly accepted and even protected. The courts and the newspapers suggested purges and the scope for eradication, yet also revealed an entrenched network. Such a dichotomy indicated the unacceptable nature of these activities whilst also advertising their existence as an integral part of city life. This was vital to the maintenance of the status quo. Some semblance of order in the city was sustained by confronting its inhabitants with the worst urban excesses: the reporting constituted an invocation to moral and social rectitude. Sexual and gender 'norms' took shape and London's imperial image gained clarity and potence partly through the threat supposedly posed by these men. Their dissidence gave a fresh opportunity to espouse English virtues.[151] Moreover, this repeated exposure and outrage meant homosexual activity remained a controllable part of the city's sexual economy. It was impossible for men like Ives and Wilde to function beyond the threat of exposure, prosecution or blackmail. Each of these possibilities became structurally important in their lives and affected the way they used the city: Wilde responding with a flagrant disregard, Ives becoming obsessively secretive and perhaps over-cautious. Those who were caught – Wilde, Taylor, Smith, Newlove, Horton and so many others – suffered the misery of imprisonment, often with hard labour and sometimes for periods far exceeding two years. Others, like Julius Walters, were deported or, like Lord Arthur Somerset and Lord Battersea, forced into exile. Yet although each case and report forcefully communicated the dangers inherent in having sex with other men, the courts and the newspapers also indicated ways in which, and places where, sexual difference could be explored. They suggested that the city was a site of homosexual and homosocial possibility and community. Men necessarily existed within the legal framework and in relation to the powerful newspaper press, but these institutions could not comprehensively control the way men acted on the messages they sent out.

CHAPTER 3

The inverted city

THE CITY AND SEXUAL PATHOLOGY

On 31 October 1898 the Secretary of the Legitimation League, George Bedborough, was fined £100 for selling Henry Havelock Ellis and John Addington Symonds' *Sexual Inversion*. The book argued that 'inversion' was an inborn condition and should not be treated as a crime. 'Its publication', wrote George Bernard Shaw in the league's journal, *The Adult*, 'was more urgently needed in England than any other recent treatise...Until it appeared there was no authoritative scientific book on its subject within the reach of Englishmen and Englishwomen who cannot read French or German.'[1] Bedborough's guilty plea meant that no such defence was offered in court and the book was branded 'a lewd, bawdy, scandalous libel', a verdict which constituted a virtual ban.[2]

The case highlighted an epistemological clash between the law and sexology over the legitimate representation of homosexuality. Ellis' work, and that of the European sexologists who influenced him, drew existing ideas about sexual behaviours and 'types' together into a description and theory of sexual subjectivity. They provided a scientific rationale for desire to be conceptually integrated into an understanding of self and identity, and by postulating that a biological imperative lay behind sexual difference, provided a potent argument for legal change. Even W. T. Stead, whose journalistic work ushered in the 1885 Criminal Law Amendment Act, acknowledged that 'if the conclusions at which [Ellis] arrives are sound, then the principle of the legislation is unsound'.[3] Sexological work was consequently welcomed by many middle- and upper-class 'homosexuals' and 'inverts'. It was Symonds who initially suggested the *Sexual Inversion* project to Ellis,[4] and Ellis and the Austrian sexologist Richard von Krafft-Ebing both received unsolicited case studies from men keen to contribute to their research. The publication of these cases meant at least a degree of self-determination and the results instituted a powerful explanatory narrative. Ives, Carpenter and Symonds were thus much quicker to adopt the new labels and categories than the press and public were to apply them.

Sexology nonetheless reinscribed the division between the sexual mainstream and periphery in essentialist terms, and suggested the pre-eminence of sexual preference as a classifier of identity. It reaffirmed prevailing stereotypes and made men who had sex with other men objects of study and sometimes treatment, rather than active agents in society. The sexological texts published in English during the period also highlighted a trenchant connection between homosexuality and the city, describing urban subcultures across Europe. For some English apologists for homosexual behaviour, including Ellis and Symonds, this urban connection was far from helpful. At a time when sexual continence and responsibility were being touted vociferously by purity campaigners and sections of the newspaper press,[5] a sexual identity rooted in the degenerate and profligate city seemed to stand little chance of acceptance. This chapter takes a step back from London to examine the ways in which the urban association was developed in translations of continental sexology, and also looks at how Ellis, one of the very few English writers on the subject during this period, produced silences which he could not fully sustain around the supposed connection. The theories the sexologists propounded resonated through diverse arguments for the legitimisation of homosexuality and had a long-term impact on understandings of sexual identity. The urban connection as it is imagined in these works is therefore key to the ways in which men engaged more specifically with London.

Gert Hekma charts the development of sexology from an article published in the French journal *Annales Médico-Psychologique* in 1843, in which the mental state of the 'pederast' was analysed rather than the physical sexual act he had been involved in.[6] Debate burgeoned and by the end of the century a series of conflicting and overlapping theories were circulating about possible causes. In the 1860s the German lawyer Karl Ulrichs argued for the existence of an inborn trait characterised by gender misalignment. He developed a highly nuanced series of categorisations based on varying degrees of feminisation in men and corresponding degrees of desire for sex and sexual passivity with other men. He used his claims in his campaign for legitimacy for homosexual relations. Working later, but on similar lines, the German physicians Iwan Bloch and Magnus Hirschfeld, also a vociferous campaigner for homosexual equality, suggested a third sex, existing between men and women. Richard von Krafft-Ebing in Vienna refuted this theory, but agreed that desire for the same sex, together with a series of physical markers of this desire, were largely inherited. Whilst Ulrichs, Hirschfeld and Bloch saw a benign condition, however, Krafft-Ebing initially considered homosexuality to be 'a functional sign of degeneracy', 'a dangerous by-path' from the evolutionary progression. It was a conclusion he retracted in 1901 in a piece for Hirschfeld's campaigning *Jarhbuch für Sexuelle Zwischenstufen* (*Yearbook for Sexually Intermediate Types*), but the English edition of *Psychopathia Sexualis* published in the same year maintained the connection.[7] The degeneracy connection was accepted by Charles Féré and Jean-Martin Charcot, who were working in Paris around the same time, and by August Forel, a professor of psychiatry at the University of Zurich.

Each of these writers also considered the possibility that in some cases homosexual impulses might be acquired rather than inherited. The environment and external factors became significant in awakening a latent predisposition or inciting an entirely new configuration of desire. Most suggested the importance of schools, universities, prisons and military institutions in this process, but also indicated how life in the city might prompt sexual experimentation and excess, as will be shown later. Whilst Ulrichs and Hirschfeld – and, in Britain, Carpenter, Ives and Ellis – were somewhat reticent about these ideas, Bloch, Forel, Féré and Krafft-Ebing gave them more credence. Bloch talked of the 'pseudo-homosexuality' and Forel of the 'compensatory homosexuality' of men in single-sex environments. Féré suggested that it was possible to over-emphasise the hereditary factor at the expense of mere 'licentiousness and depravity' which might follow from particular ways of life. He also considered the potentially damaging influence of homosexuals on nervous individuals who had 'less power of resisting exterior influences'.[8] Forel echoed the sentiment. Krafft-Ebing, meanwhile, theorised an acquired condition born of masturbation or seduction which became irreversible and inheritable after the initial stages. This theory, which owed more to the French naturalist Jean Baptiste Lamarck's idea of 'intelligent' adaptation than to the blind process described by Darwin, heightened the significance of external influences. These were dangerous not only because of the effect they had on the individual but also because of the indirect risk they posed to his progeny.

Whilst the debate about sexual 'abnormality' gathered pace in continental Europe, in Britain the discussion was muted, relatively late in coming and reliant largely on translations of continental writers. The Edinburgh doctor James Burnet complained in 1906 that little work had been done in Britain on homosexuality. 'It is', he remarked, 'a great pity that medical men in this country, with almost unanimous consent, have agreed to ignore the study of sexual science in its bearing on practice.'[9] Later, in 1914, the British Society for the Study of Sex Psychology noted in its statement of *Policy and Principles* that it 'was rather appalling that at a great international medical congress on sex-questions... there is only one official representative from this country, whilst others are sending doctors by the score'.[10] Forster acknowledged the problem in *Maurice* (1914): Dr Barry 'had read no scientific works on Maurice's subject. None had existed when he walked the hospitals, and any published since were German and therefore suspect.'[11] Sexology existed on the periphery of the medico-scientific establishment in Britain partly because of its continental genesis and partly because it connoted not just the search for scientific 'truth' but also a wider social and political reformist agenda. Ellis and Carpenter, who disseminated sexological theory in his writing, were the most vociferous proponents of sexological theory. They were also closely associated with Fabian socialism and the Utopian Fellowship of the New Life, which advocated co-operative living and stressed the importance of a simple – and implicitly rural – life and 'true' relations between individuals.[12] Their radical reputation was underscored by the association both men had with the Legitimation League, which championed the rights of illegitimate children, challenged sexual hypocrisy and was suspected by the police of having anarchist leanings.[13] The Bedborough case bankrupted the league and further marginalised sexual science in Britain. It acted as a major disincentive to publish and sell sexology, and indeed Ellis published subsequent volumes of his *Studies in the Psychology of Sex* in the United States.

There were nevertheless signs that continental theory was being read and applied in England as early as the 1870s. The police surgeon in the Boulton and Park case of 1870, for example, was drawing on continental concepts of the distinctive soma of the sodomite, and especially his 'elongated private parts', when he examined the genitalia and anuses of the accused men.[14] Work published in Britain took longer to emerge, however, and although continental theory was noted in the *Journal of Mental Science*, *The Lancet* and *British Medical Journal* during the early 1880s, it was not until 1884 that the first English 'Case Study of Sexual Perversion in a Man' appeared.[15] The translation of Krafft-Ebing's *Psychopathia Sexualis* (1886) was published eight years later in 1892 and included a lengthy consideration of 'contrary sexual instincts'.[16] It received a cool reception from the medical press and its saving grace was apparently the use of '*terminis technicis*' and the fact that 'particularly revolting portions' were in Latin. Even so the *British Medical Journal* would have preferred that the whole text had been 'veiled in the decent obscurity of a dead language. The more extreme response to Havelock Ellis' *Sexual Inversion* five years later has already been noted. Other texts followed, but none with the singular focus of Ellis' work. Charles Féré's *The Evolution and Dissolution of the Sexual Instinct*, which included a chapter on homosexuality, was published in English in 1904, and August Forel's *The Sexual Question*, which also had some consideration of the subject, in 1905. *Sex and Character*, the work of the young German philosopher Otto Weininger, appeared in translation the following year and was particularly insistent on the congenital nature of homosexuality. The Professor of Sociology at the University of London, Edward Westermarck, included a more sociological chapter on 'homosexual love' in his *Origin and Development of Moral Ideas* (1908) and in the same year Iwan Bloch's *The Sexual Life of Our Times in Relation to Modern Civilisation* finally appeared. It included a consideration of homosexuality from sexological and anthropological perspectives and had initially been aimed at a general readership. In 1907, however, the book was condemned and destroyed by Bow Street Police Court. After an appeal to the House of Lords it was reissued on condition that it was sold only to legal and medical professionals. Whilst complimenting Bloch's erudition, the *Review of Reviews* suggested that it would have been better if 'half the book had never been published for general circulation'.[18]

Freud's *Three Essays on the Theory of Sexuality* was published in English in 1910, and were amongst the first of his works to be translated from the German, bringing with them a rather different understanding of the development of homosexual desire. Freud's theories remained beyond the main current of debate within this period, however, and Chris Waters has argued that in Britain sexological understandings of sexuality largely prevailed over psychoanalytic conceptualisations at least until the 1940s.[19] Other key figures in the European sexological debate, most notably Magnus Hirschfeld, Albert Moll and Veniamin Tarnowsky, were not translated into English before 1914, although they were frequently cited. Hirschfeld was a particularly significant omission given his campaign for homosexual law reform in Germany and his close association with Carpenter and Ives, who saw him as a valuable ally.[20]

The work that was published in English during this time was largely restricted to an elite audience. Ellis and Bloch's texts were both curtailed, Krafft-Ebing made extensive use of Latin and Forel's work had a sub-title spelling out its constituency: it was 'a Scientific, Psychological, Hygienic and Sociological Study for the Cultured Classes'. Even for this elite, sexological texts and related literature could be difficult to get hold of. Hirschfeld complained to Ives in 1906 that his *Jahrbuch für Sexuelle Zwischenstufen* had been 'secreted in some particular room' of the British library, and Carpenter battled with the library authorities over the omission of Ulrichs' works from the catalogue.[21] The library was deliberately restricting access to sexological material and especially to those texts which attempted to legitimise homosexuality.

The significance of sexology in England should not be underestimated, however – particularly for men like Symonds, Carpenter and Ives, who had access to it and discussed it in their own work.[22] Symonds saw sexology providing an acceptable public language for homosexuality and his collaboration with Havelock Ellis on *Sexual Inversion* as a means of gaining legitimacy for inverts; Carpenter propagated the theory of the intermediate or third sex in his writing; and Ives' diary indicates a wholehearted embrace of sexological theory, which he considered a liberatory medical breakthrough. He corresponded with many of the key sexologists, including Magnus Hirschfeld, Edward Westermarck, Havelock Ellis and Iwan Bloch, built up a library of largely German texts on the subject and helped set up the British Society for the Study of Sex Psychology, which held its inaugural meeting at the Hotel Cecil in the Strand in 1913.[23] The society predicated much of its discussion of homosexuality on sexological theory. Earlier, *The Adult* was vigorous in its support of the scientific investigation of sexuality, and other publications such as *The Freewoman*, the *New Age* and the *Humanitarian* gave space to the discussion of sexology, as did the medical press in their review pages. Though it certainly had a much smaller readership than the newspaper press, sexology was at the cutting edge of thinking on sexual behaviour during the period and was embraced by London's radical intelligentsia.

The connection between homosexuality and the city in sexological writing begins at a theoretical and rhetorical level. It resulted firstly from the supposition that sexual pathology in general was linked closely to urban life. At the very start of *Psychopathia Sexualis* Krafft-Ebing noted: 'It is shown by the history of Babylon, Nineveh, Rome and also by the "mysteries" of life in modern capitals, that large cities are the breeding places of nervousness and degenerate sensuality.'[24] The city appeared to be a vital element in the genesis of sexual abnormality and Krafft-Ebing went on to cite the case of a Parisian woman having sex with a trained bulldog as 'a monstrous example of the moral depravity in large cities'.[25]

Degeneracy and nervous disease or neurasthenia were seen to be key determinants in the development of this depravity and both conditions were closely aligned with the metropolis. Sections of the urban population were perceived by many commentators to be transmogrifying into a separate degenerate race apart, as a result of a lack of contact with nature and a deleterious heritage. 'The true-born Londoner', wrote journalist Sidney Low in the *Contemporary Review* in 1891, 'dies out in the third generation, and lives a weakly and stunted Helot.'[26] The East End 'residuum', the poorest of the poor, were especially associated with what Arnold White called 'hereditary unfitness in the arts of progress' and also with ideas of sexual and gender disarray.[27] In the bars of Tiger Bay – also known as Bluegate Fields, where the eponymous hero of Wilde's *The Picture of Dorian Gray* visits an opium den – the *Telegraph* journalist James Greenwood found 'an unbroken scene of vice and depravity of the most hideous sort'.[28] Prostitutes appeared as 'petticoated bipeds' and had 'the air of a Whitechapel fighting man in female disguise'.[29]

Degeneration was not only seen to be a problem of the poor. The journalist, novelist and physician Max Nordau famously elaborated the regression of a decadent monied elite and the literary avant-garde in *Degeneration*, which appeared in German in 1892 and in English just before the Wilde trials three years later. The book was dedicated to the Italian criminal anthropologist and degeneration theorist Cesare Lombroso, and proved immensely popular. Over ten years later, George Bernard Shaw still felt the need to defend the artistic community against Nordau's attacks.[30] Nordau's pathologisation of the aesthete, decadent, mystic and even the realist, involved a catalogue of symptoms which coincided with virtually any transgression of what he terms 'traditional discipline' in the areas of art, morality, fashion and home decoration.[31] These transgressions apparently proliferated in the city and Nordau saw them as an inciting cause of degenerative illness, leading to an abandonment of moral rectitude. The offspring of these men and women lost any sense of moral structure and suffered from physical malformation: 'The growth of long bones is extremely slow, or ceases entirely, the legs remain short, the pelvis retains a feminine form, certain other organs cease to develop, and the entire being presents a strange and repulsive mixture of incompleteness and decay.'[32] Nordau's prognosis for the race if it did not seek to 'adapt itself' was bleak. Looking to the future he saw the majority of men 'cloth[ing] themselves in a costume which recalls, by colour and cut, feminine apparel', whilst 'women who wish to please men of this kind wear men's dress'. In this dystopia 'modesty and restraint are dead superstitions of the past' and same-sex marriage is legalised as 'a majority of deputies have the same tendency'.[33] Homosexuality was described as symptomatic of the wider degenerate malaise: it was, for Nordau, the form of sexual dissidence which could most readily be imagined shaping an alternative, degenerate and decadent urban culture.

Though Nordau's diatribe against a plethora of late nineteenth-century artists and writers appears paranoid and extreme, many of his ideas about the potential effects of city life were echoed elsewhere. Fears about sexual disarray and compromised masculinity and femininity in London prolif-erated in the fiction, journalism and social commentary of the period, and extended well beyond the pages of *Degeneration*. The effeminate aesthete and masculine new woman were the subject of parodies but also of seri-ous concern in the 1890s, and came as an apparent realisation of Nordau's worst fears.[34] Shortly after the publication of the English translation of *Degeneration* in 1895, and just after the Wilde trials, Lombroso reiterated ideas about the interchange of sexual characteristics in, and the perversity of, the degenerate in his piece for the *Contemporary Review*.[35] The eugenic campaigns for national efficiency in the early years of the twentieth century testified to some of these concerns. Ives reported a conversation with radical MP Arthur Priestley in 1912 in which Priestley suggested that the increase in effeminate men and masculine women in London constituted 'the great danger of the times'.[36]

Nordau's association of homosexuality with degeneracy was echoed by Krafft-Ebing, Féré and Forel, whilst Ellis and Bloch – and subsequently also Krafft-Ebing – felt the need to reject it overtly. The connection was difficult to discredit, however, partly because those who refuted it did not offer any substantive evidence as to why homosexuality was *not* degener-ate. The theories of Ellis and Bloch did not differ substantially from those of the sexologists favouring a degenerate rationale and their stance thus seemed rather more political than empirical. All wrote in a post-Darwinian context in which heredity was a key determinant, and 'the criminal', 'the genius', 'the homosexual' and 'the degenerate' were all accounted for through broadly similar theoretical models. The British Society for the Study of Sex Psychology, which saw itself as an arbiter of reason on sexual matters, echoed the language of degeneracy in its discussion of homosexual-ity. The first policy and principles statement suggested that homosexuality was 'breeding apace' in the most 'deplorable underground conditions'.[37] The idea here of uncontrollable proliferation and debased sexual expression resonated with images of the degenerate urban residuum.

Neurasthenia or some other form of nervous illness was a further and less contentious component of the invert's supposed background. Ellis and Krafft-Ebing, who also wrote specifically on neurasthenia,[38] noted a familial history of nervous disorder in many of their case studies and Féré observed that 'sexual inversion is often associated with a nueropathic temperament'.[39] The term 'neurasthenia' was coined by George Beard in the *Boston Medical and Surgical Journal* in 1869 and was later known as shell-shock. During this period, though, it was commonly associated with what the medic John Clarke termed 'the emotional excitement and often unhealthy conditions of life in the great city'.[40] The condition was ill-defined but – or perhaps as a consequence – informed wider commentary on the effects of modern urban living. In his turn-of-the-century work on jingoism, for example, J. A. Hobson argued that cities and towns 'generated' 'a neurotic temperament' which 'sought natural relief in stormy sensational appeals, and the crowded life of the street'.[41] Georg Simmel's *The Metropolis and Mental Life* (1903) theorised a similarly distinctive metropolitan persona arising from the 'intensification of nervous stimulation which results from the swift and uninterrupted change of outer and inner stimuli'. The city dweller, he went on, had to fight to be different, and is 'tempted to adopt the most tendentious peculiarities, that is the specifically metropolitan extravagances of mannerism, caprice, and preciousness... of standing out in a striking manner and thereby attracting attention'.[42] These were all features which recalled images of the invert and homosexual outlined by some of the sexologists. The suggestion throughout was that sexual anomalies might be on the increase as a result of modernity and the confusion of city living: 'the excitement and innumerable pleasures' of the modern metropolis, Forel suggested, was leading to 'a restless and unnatural existence'. 'Sexual excesses in the country' were, he claimed, 'more comfortable to nature.'[43]

By being associated with degeneracy and neurasthenia, homosexuality represented on the one hand a regression to a primitive state and on the other nervous collapse in the face of 'the feverish activity of modern life'.[44] It was both atavistic and a specifically modern disorder, symptomatic of contemporary urban dis-ease and decay. This sense was emphasised through the use of contagion imagery by some sexologists which resonated with longer-standing concerns about the dangers of the congested city. Forel suggested that 'inverts' had to be prevented from 'becoming the centre of infection for their surroundings',[45] whilst Féré regarded 'the invert who obeys his impulses' as 'a corruptive agent'.[46] In *Crime: Its Cause and Cure* (1899) Cesare Lombroso argued that congenital homosexuals were 'a source of contagion and cause[d] a great number of occasional criminals'.[47] This potential led Lombroso, Forel and the anonymous author of a *British Medical Journal* piece written in the immediate aftermath of the Wilde trials, to suggest that homosexuals should be permanently separated from others if they refused to suppress their desires. The *BMJ* writer argued that 'pity cannot obscure the compulsory necessity there is to free society from their presence'.[48]

Aside from the degenerative, neurasthenic and contagious associations which tied sexual pathology to the city, there were wider conceptual links. Urban developments in the last thirty years of the century brought with them heightened concerns about excessive consumption and fears that the chaotic centre of the imperial city was symbolising anything but thrift, productivity and order. The work of the sexologists, meanwhile, looked at sexual *dis*order, not just at homosexuality, and brought to the fore ideas of sexual plurality and sometimes excessive sexual consumption. Harry Oosterhuis has noted that sexology made 'sexual variance imaginable and enlarge[d] the sphere allotted to idiosyncratic desires'.[49] Such variety and idiosyncrasy echoed the increasing, and increasingly visible, heterogeneity of the urban scene. Indeed, Oosterhuis makes the larger claim that sexology marked 'the transition in the urban bourgeois milieu from the ethos of Christianity and productivity, which dictated self-discipline and control of passions, to a consumerist culture of abundance, which valued the satisfaction of individual desire'.[50] It is a contentious argument, not least in postulating such a clear and wholesale shift, but what is nevertheless compelling is Oosterhuis' observation of parallels between images of heterogeneous sexuality emerging from sexological textbooks on the one hand and urban plurality and consumerism on the other.

Finally, the hereditary and congenital understandings of homosexuality in sexology aligned it, and other forms of sexual deviancy, with space and the physical environment. This is because the homosexual was placed in opposition to the heterosexual in terms of the evolutionary process and the civilising march into the future. Krafft-Ebing, Forel and Féré all suggested that homosexuals should not reproduce. Forel even argued that they should be allowed to embark on same-sex marriage as a means of staving off the possibility of a heterosexual union.[51] Ellis' ideas on the issue were unclear, though he and his wife Edith, who provided a case study on her lesbianism for *Sexual Inversion*,[52] chose not to have children and Ellis was a committed eugenicist, advocating elsewhere the voluntary sterilisation of the 'unfit'.[53] Bloch did not propose any such prohibition or self-denial but assumed instead that homosexuals had no instinct for reproduction and that they were 'intrinsically anti-evolutionistic'. He wrote: 'The greatest spiritual values we owe to heterosexuals not to homosexuals. Moreover, reproduction renders possible the preservation and permanence of new spiritual values...The monosexual and homosexual instincts are permanently limited to their own ego [and are] therefore, in their innermost nature, dysteleogical and anti-evolutionisitic.'[54] Bloch explained the homosexual through evolutionary theory but imagined him existing outside the actual process and the grand meta-narrative of development. He was in the here and now and this position was partially reflected in his status in these texts as a subject of study – distinct and separate from the scientist who, however sympathetic, framed and rationalised his experience.

The theories the sexologists put forward, and to some extent the methodology they used, thus emphasised the distance of the homosexual from the heterosexual progressive 'norm'. This separation was aligned with the putative distance between the concepts of space and time: the male heterosexual existed on the temporal developmental path, whilst the homosexual, by being thrown off that path and rendered a passive subject of study, was associated with (and limited by) his immediate physical environment.[55] Whilst the masculinity and middle-class status of the men in the case studies made them sharers in the heterosexual progressive culture, their newly consolidated inverted identity aligned them with space and a cyclical temporality which Julia Kristeva famously describes as 'women's time'.[56] Disenfranchised and 'degenerate' groups like the East End poor were in a similar position and tended to be seen as creatures of their environment rather than part of the progression into the future. For the homosexual, as for the degenerate and the neurasthenic, the city was the typical habitat.

METROPOLITAN CASE STUDIES

The diagnostic, rhetorical and theoretical connections between the city and sexual pathology were apparently confirmed in the commentary and case studies sexological texts included. Those 'suffering' from other sexual abnormalities tended to be described in the various works as isolated individuals, but the homosexual was generally shown to be part of a social milieu and in willing and consensual relationships. He was repeatedly linked to a social scene based around the theatres, parks, streets, bars and restaurants of major European cities, and was shown to have a particular personal investment in urban life.

The shaping of the invert or homosexual as a type owed much to popular stereotype, as has been observed, and effeminacy was a frequently noted characteristic. Krafft-Ebing carefully categorised different degrees of effeminisation and Bloch distinguished between the effeminate and the 'virile' homosexual, noting a clear complexion and a lack of facial hair in the former and the tendency of both to have skin that 'almost always feels warmer than their environment'.[57] Féré suggested that homosexuals 'are exceedingly vain and given to lying' and commented on their inability to whistle and their liking for 'the dress of the opposite sex'.[58] Forel noted that homosexuals 'generally . . . have a banal sentimentalism . . . are fond of religious forms and ceremonies [and that] they admire fine clothes and luxurious apartments'.[59] These characteristics were closely associated with the sophistry and luxury of a particular fashionable urban set, and more specifically to prevailing stereotypes of the decadent or dandy.[60] The context of these observations – amidst the recapitulation of congenital and hereditary theories of homosexuality – suggested that these features were biologically rather than culturally or socially determined. The lies, banal sentimentalism, fine clothes and so on appeared to be intrinsic to the homosexual condition and added an essentialist twist to the depictions in the newspapers. Amongst the sexologists published in English during the period it was only Ellis who emphasised the indistinct invert. 'The average invert', he wrote, 'moving in ordinary society, so far as my evidence extends, is most usually a person of average general health, though very frequently with hereditary relations that are markedly neurotic.'[61] Despite stressing elsewhere the exceptional artistic contributions inverts often made – a classic justificatory line – Ellis here used the trope of normality as a means of making them more acceptable. He thus referred to the 'average' invert, moving in 'ordinary' society, being of 'average' health, albeit with a neurotic heredity.

The idea of a distinct soma and demeanour in men involved in homosexual activity was certainly not new, but sexology consolidated the idea and gave it scientific authority. Weeks persuasively argues that the sexologists 'produced the definitions in order to understand a social phenomenon which was appearing before their eyes: before them as patients, before the courts, in front of them as public scandals, on the streets in a still small but growing network of meeting places'.[62] Such scandals and networks were chiefly associated with cities and this was where the sexologists worked: Krafft-Ebing in Vienna, Ellis in London, Féré in Paris, Forel in Zurich and Bloch in Berlin. Their work in consequence tended to extrapolate general conclusions from the experience of an urban middle class; from men who, Oosterhuis notes, 'could pursue their idiosyncratic desires not as short-term random diversions from fixed social roles and family responsibilities, but on a more regular basis as part of their lifestyle'.[63] On the basis of evidence from men with these freedoms it was much easier for the sexologists to envisage an exclusive and distinctive homosexual identity and hardly surprising that it was closely associated with the city.

Kraft-Ebing expressed sympathy for the homosexual in *Psychopathia Sexualis* – a sympathy which developed, Oosterhuis argues, as he moved from work in asylums to private practice and academia in Vienna.[64] By the time he wrote *Psychopathia Sexualis* he was hearing from and dealing with men of a different class, one more akin to his own. He nevertheless outlined a pathological condition and an abnormal configuration of desire, which he saw being exacerbated by the modern metropolis. There is sometimes a tension in the work, however, between Krafft-Ebing's commentary and the voices of the subjects he examined. They frequently testify to an urban subculture which provided support, sex and social contacts, detracting somewhat from Krafft-Ebing's take on homosexuality.

In one of the case studies an 'effeminate' doctor noted that it was at the opera house in 'the capital' (presumably Vienna) that he learned from an old man 'the secrets of male love for males, and felt [his] sexuality was excited by it'. The old man told the doctor that 'male-loving men were accustomed to meet on the "E" promenade', and he began to visit the area. Subsequently he moved to the country, where he had 'to live like a nun' and only 'began to live again' when he returned to the city.[65] Another case followed a similar pattern. The patient went to university in 'the city' at nineteen and 'began to be dandified, wore striking cravats, and shirts that were low cut; he forced his feet into narrow shoes, and curled his hair in a remarkable way'. 'This peculiarity', Krafft-Ebing commented, 'disappeared' when he left university and returned home. The subject added, though, that on moving to Vienna 'by means of some recommendations, I gained entrance to various circles of people like myself'.[66] He abstained from sex for some time by using cocaine and living in the country before being arrested for having sex with a man just outside the city walls.

These case studies indicated a particularly close relationship between the city and homosexuality. In the first there is a sense of an urban confederacy, as the old man shares knowledge which allows the doctor access to a sexual subculture and his own latent desires. Similarly in the second, the man gained 'recommendations' into a milieu of people 'like himself' in Vienna. The shift from third to first person in this part of the case study is suggestive of a new-found independence. Earlier, at university, the city appeared to have had a peculiar power over him: the impulse to transformation and his dandification apparently came from the material context. For both men it is only by escaping the city, and in the second case also by resorting to cocaine use, that homosexual desires and an associated lifestyle could be evaded. The metropolis nevertheless continued to exert a powerful draw. It was where the first was able to 'live again', whilst the second came to the city limits to reconnect with what he had given up.

In his section on 'non-pathological pederasty' Krafft-Ebing abandoned case studies and used his own voice to detail the seduction of adolescents by 'old *roués*' in organised groups in cities, 'one of the saddest pages in the history of human delinquency'.[67] He cited Veniamin Tarnowsky's research in St Petersburg, where pederasty was apparently cultivated in 'institutes', and A.Coffignon's *Paris vivant: la corruption à Paris* (1889), which unfolded a complex hierarchy of seduction in the French capital. Krafft-Ebing turned finally to 'the demi-monde' of Berlin, and to a 'women haters' ball' of February 1884.[68] The journalist he cites describes seeing acquaintances transformed at the ball: his shoe-maker to a troubadour and his haberdasher to Bacchus, for example. The faces were familiar, but they had reinvented themselves – or had been reinvented – in their movement to this separate, extravagant urban arena. Krafft-Ebing's account in this section confirmed what had emerged in the preceding case studies: an essentially urban phenomenon which was not confined to one isolated city, but was a feature of them all, from Paris to St Petersburg. This urban circuit of homosexuality was further indicated by the subject of another case study who mentioned the subcultures of Berlin, Vienna, Leipzig, Hamburg and Paris.[69] Each of these places apparently had a decadent *demi-monde* with coherent and organised groupings of initiates. These went largely undetected by the casual passer-by but were uncovered by the prying journalist, rigorous sexologist or confessing case study. A mobile, wealthy and self-confident homosexual was outlined, a figure able to move around and between various European cities.

Within these cities specific places were particularly closely associated with homosexual activity. They became not just the settings for erotic transactions, but, like the city more broadly, seemed to incite them. Museums were avoided by one man because of the frisson he gained from the statues, whilst another could not resist: 'I revelled in the sight of pictures and statues of male form', he wrote, 'and could not keep from kissing [them].'[70] Yet another was aroused by 'lower houses' in the city: 'the dark entrance, the yellow light of the lamps, and all the surroundings have a particular charm for me' he noted.[71] The buildings themselves seduced him, on account, he conjectured, of the soldiers who 'frequent such places' in search of female prostitutes. Similarly, in one of the few illustrative case studies in Féré's work, a predilection for crowded city spaces was seen to be symptomatic of the subject's homosexuality. The man had felt 'impelled to enter public establishments, cafés, halls, assembly rooms' or anywhere where he might be pushed against other men.[72] In another case, noted in the introduction, the subject's formative experience was in a crowded commuter train where he became fascinated by an officer.[73] These places and experiences, and not just somatic signs or familial history, became important in Féré's diagnosis and reflected concern about what the modern metropolis made possible. This concern is also evident in *Psychopathia Sexualis*: Krafft-Ebing included one case who described moving 'to the capital' to 'force [him]self to cohabit with a woman' only to discover his voracious sexual appetite for men; he claimed to have had six hundred sexual partners there.[74]

The city was a 'salvation' for just one of Krafft-Ebing's cases, in which a man being blackmailed was inspired to give up having sex with men by an earlier edition of *Psychopathia Sexualis*. He sought help and hyp-notism from the doctor in Vienna and was transformed.[75] It seems that Krafft-Ebing's Vienna was potentially redemptive, quite different from the counter-culture of the homosexual, which confirmed and induced flawed desires and effeminacy. What nonetheless emerges through several of the case studies is the sense of community and belonging that might come with city-living.

Iwan Bloch acknowledged this more fully than Krafft-Ebing in *The Sexual Life of Our Time*: 'Whilst in the smallest provincial towns and in the country homosexuals are for the most part thrust back into themselves, compelled to conceal their nature or at most to communicate with isolated individuals of like nature with themselves, in the larger towns from early days the homosexuals have been able to get in touch with one another.'[76] Bloch described homosexuals disempowered in the provinces but imagined the city as a place of potential self-determination. Thus whereas Krafft-Ebing imagined the city seducing the individual, in Bloch's account it granted permission and made things possible. He indicated a distinctive urban homosexual subculture and style. In every large town, he claimed, there were certain streets and squares, clubs and health resorts, which were frequented by homosexuals. Bloch described, for example, the dark lateral alleys of the Champs Elysées in Paris and the thickets between Place de la Concorde and the Allée des Vieves as places which 'served, from the com-mencement of twilight, for the rendezvous of homosexuals'. 'They would not tolerate here the presence of any heterosexuals; they closed the entrance with cords, and placed guards at the openings of the alleys, who demanded a password from every comer. Even the police did not venture into this dark region.'[77] The tables were turned as the heterosexual was displaced through a homosexual colonisation of parts of central Paris. In the process grand boulevards gave way to an enclosed 'dark region' with closely guarded 'entrances', 'openings' and 'alleys'. This sequestered space was figured with at least the suggestion of anality, as topography and sexuality intersected. In this way the space became, in Bloch's depiction, especially appropriate to the men who used it and the city particularly accommodating. He acknowledged that such possibilities were 'now' restricted to Turkish baths, including one in Place de la République, and various brothels, of which he detailed two. But even this reduced 'scene' offered exclusive arenas in the very centre of the city.

These descriptions of actual places and streets in Paris gave solidity to Bloch's vision of a homosexual fraternity. In Berlin he was similarly particular, claiming that it 'doubtless' had many more 'social unions of homosexuals' than any other city. He cited Hirschfeld's reports of dinners, summer festivals, cafes, pubs, restaurants and annual picnics, and described a soldiers' promenade popular with homosexual men. Bloch maintained the association of effeminacy with homosexuality evident in Krafft-Ebing's descriptions and similarly recounted a visit to an 'Urning's Ball' in Berlin and other cross-dressing parties in Paris.[78] He also referred to 'effeminate street Arabs' with soft skin and breasts who were 'children of the great towns',[79] suggesting a kind of causal relationship between the city and the effeminate homosexual. Bloch largely avoided Krafft-Ebing's negativity and celebrated the opportunities such a semi-permanent and cohesive subculture afforded and the cosmopolitan diversity it indicated. Bloch saw the city as empowering: if the fact of being observed and categorised through 'the medical gaze' in some ways robbed the homosexual of agency, it was in his relationship with the city – at least as Bloch envisaged it – that he regained it.

What is especially striking about Ellis' *Sexual Inversion* in the light of these continental texts is its tendency to contain and excuse mention of the urban context. He was careful not to guide men to particular places in London through his writing and feared that the city might denigrate the invert by implicating degeneracy on the one hand and effeminacy or public indecency on the other. Ellis' friend Edward Carpenter complained that 'since the field of [the sexologist's] research is usually a great modern city, there is little wonder if disease colours his conclusions'. He went on: 'In the case of [Albert] Moll who carried out his researches largely under the guidance of the Berlin police... the only marvel is that his verdict is so markedly favourable as it is.'[80] Havelock Ellis apparently shared Carpenter's concerns, but despite this, and the wider appeal by many English sexual and social reformers to a fantasy of a redemptive rural idyll, the city was difficult to avoid. This was partly because of England's urbanised culture, partly because of the strong existing associations between homosexuality and the city, and partly because of the European sexological writing in which the connection was being made so explicitly.

Ellis conceded that cities were gathering grounds for homosexual men: 'it is true that in the solitude of the great modern cities it is possible for small homosexual coteries to form, in a certain sense, an environment of their own favourable to their abnormality'.[81] He was grudging in the concession, however, admitting only the possibility of isolated groups in the anonymous and lonely modern city. No embedded subculture was outlined and the city was largely sidelined in the rest of the text. Details of male prostitution in Hyde Park and around Albert Gate in London, for example, appeared as a footnote not to a discussion of the dynamic of homosexual life in the city, but to Ellis' contention that there was 'a considerable lack of repugnance to homosexual practices...among the lower classes', who, he went on, displayed 'a primitive indifference' in sexual matters.[82] The case studies themselves largely lack geographical context, though there are some notable exceptions which suggested the significance of the urban scene and exposed Ellis' own reticence in his commentary. In the 1897 edition, for example, the subject of one case study outlined a personal homoerotic geography of London, communicated in the third person:

When he was about thirty years of age his reserve and his fear of treachery and extortion were at last overcome by an incident which occurred late at night at the Royal Exchange Theatre, and again in the dark recesses of the Olympic Theatre when Gustavus Brooke was performing. From that time the Adelphi Theatre, the Italian Opera, and the open parks at night became his fields of adventure. He remarks that among people crowding to witness a fire he found many opportunities.[83]

Given the lack of detail in most of Ellis' other cases, the specificity here is intriguing. London was cast as an arena for sexual adventure, with liaisons emerging from the chaos of the city, and also from particular places, notably the theatre and the urban crowd. The city was central to the development and expression of this man's sexuality. Significantly, though, this was one of the case studies dropped from the 1915 edition of *Sexual Inversion* for being 'less instructive' than the others.[84] In this later edition there was, however, a detailed description of an ostensibly heterosexual man's adventures in New York. It described a visit to a male brothel where effeminacy ruled: the 'boy-prostitutes' 'bore fanciful names, some of well-known actresses, others heroes in fiction, his own [the prostitute the man talks to] being Dorian Gray'.[85] Subsequently, he met an 'invert' in Broadway, and wrote: 'with him in his room whence I had seen him emerge, I passed an apocalyptic night.

Thereafter commerce with boys only in spirit ceased to be an end; the images were carnalised, stepped from that framework into the streets.'[86] The case vividly illustrated the genesis of homosexual expression in and through the New York streets and brothels, where a set of fantasies met reality. Ellis, however, argued that the case was atypical: '[It] presents what is commonly thought to be a very common type of inversion, Oscar Wilde being the supreme exemplar, in which a heterosexual person apparently becomes homosexual by the exercise of intellectual curiosity and esthetic [*sic*] interest. In reality the type is far from common.'[87] The effeminate 'boy-prostitutes' and the men who had become inverted through their 'intellectual curiosity' were exceptional according to Ellis, and the significance of context and environment were again downplayed. The case study of John Addington Symonds was similarly shorn of geographic detail, even though Symonds was specific in his *Memoirs* about the places which fired his fantasies and desires. As Wayne Koestenbaum points out, we lose the sense in *Sexual Inversion* of 'how closely [Symonds'] ineffable desire abutted actual places and actual men'.[88]

This reluctance to validate the significance of the urban context in *Sexual Inversion* becomes more obvious when we look at some of Ellis' other work. In *The Criminal* (1890) the environment was described as a significant factor in the development of the criminal psychosis and in a later piece, *The Nineteenth Century: A Dialogue in Utopia* (1898), Ellis noted the stifling and denaturing effect of Victorian urban architecture. Finally, in *Sex in Relation to Society* (1910), Ellis ascribed the cause of prostitution not to atavism, as Lombroso had done, but to 'the fascination of the city . . . the brilliant fever of civilisation [that] pulses around them in the streets'.[89] Each of these accounts indicated the deleterious effects of the urban environment and this explains Ellis' reticence about the city in *Sexual Inversion*. He was firmly committed to the reform of attitudes towards homosexuality and may well have felt that a detailed consideration of inversion in the metropolis would have debased it. Thus whilst the city cropped up a number of times in the various editions of *Sexual Inversion*, Ellis drew back from it and his typical invert was cut loose from his geographical context. Indeed, those cases which mention the city in *Sexual Inversion* implied an urban perversion of the inverted passion. The man who recounted his experiences in London was one of only three out of twenty-seven in the 1897 edition who was directly described as effeminate – a characterisation Ellis was keen to challenge[90] – whilst the aesthetic American in the 1915 edition was, as we have seen, marked out as exceptional. The original appendix piece by 'Dr K', which discussed the significance of environment and culture in shaping the inborn inverted instinct, appeared only in the two 1897 editions and was dropped from subsequent editions.

In his conclusion to *Sexual Inversion* Ellis suggested that society 'cannot be expected to tolerate the invert who flaunts his perversions in its face'.[91] Once 'flaunt[ed]', observed in anything other than his sexological panopticon, inversion became 'perversion', a term he avoided in the rest of the text. The limits of Ellis' tolerance were exposed. However, the case studies of other sexologists, the newspaper reports considered in the last chapter and those urban cases he did include in *Sexual Inversion* all spoke of such visibility, detracting from the more discreet and 'normalised' figure Ellis was attempting to outline. He sidelined the city from his discussion as a distraction, but the vividness of the cases that did mention it confirmed the widely credited association nonetheless, particularly as Ellis made no explicit disavowal. The city and what it made possible haunted the text and proved difficult for Ellis to eliminate.

EROTIC ANTHROPOLOGY

Sexology's metropolitanism meant that homosexuality was cast as a determinedly urban phenomenon. A network of cities extending across Europe was indicated, one which seemed to eclipse national or regional identifications for the men involved. This arose partly because the case studies focused chiefly on mobile, monied and often well-travelled middle-class men, and partly because sexology developed as a pan-national discourse. Cases detailing life in Vienna thus sometimes appeared alongside others centring on Paris, Berlin, London or New York. This was especially true in those works – like *The Sexual Life of Our Time* and Xavier Mayne's *The Intersexes* (1908)[92] – which drew wholly or partly on the research of earlier sexologists.

Erotic anthropology supplemented and elaborated this impression. European sexology and science, Rudi Bleys suggests, informed the anthropological gaze at other cultures, and various anthropological accounts resonated with developing images of the urban homosexual in sexology.[93] Lisa Sigel, moreover, indicates links between these fields of writing and an elite group of collectors and pornographers in London in the 1880s. The Cannibal Club – a sexually libertarian but reactionary sub-group of the Anthropological Society of London – wrote, collected and translated a range of erotic literature. Members categorised sex and collated sexual experience rather as the sexologists did.[94] They showed little reticence in describing extremes of sexual behaviour, and whilst Ellis felt a political imperative to normalise, deviance was their stock-in-trade. The association of homosexuality with effeminacy, degeneracy and decadence was thus readily affirmed.

Sir Richard Burton was a prominent member of the Cannibal Club, and in the terminal essay to his translation of *The Arabian Nights* he supplemented the sexologists' theories of homosexuality with a thesis which suggested that geography and climate were determining factors in the emergence of homosexual desire. *The Arabian Nights* was privately printed and distributed in ten volumes to hostile reviews. The *Edinburgh Review* compared it unfavourably to other versions such as Edward William Lane's 1839 edition, which had been reprinted in 1883, and John Payne's translation, which appeared for private circulation between 1882 and 1884. The reviewer observed that whilst Lane's edition might be suitable for the library, and Payne's, which he saw as vulgar in places, for a gentleman's study, Burton's was suitable only for the 'sewer': 'When [Burton] might have really added to our information on the general life of the Mohammedans, he has preferred to constitute himself the chronicler of the most degraded vices.'[95] The reviewer seemed to accept the private titillation for gentleman that might have been offered by Payne's version, but the content of Burton's rendered it beyond the pale. Burton had chosen to include the tale of 'Abu Nawas and the Three Boys' – a story omitted from Lane's collection – which tells of how three youths were seduced by Abu Nawas through verse. More significant though was his 'Sotadic' theory of homosexuality. Burton described the existence of a 'Sotadic Zone' which covered the area between the northern latitudes of 30 and 43 degrees and included the Iberian peninsula, Italy, Greece, Northern Africa, the Punjab, Kashmir, China, Japan and Turkistan. Within this zone homosexual behaviour was, Burton argued, especially common. The theory is confusing, not least because he also talked, without explanation, of 'born pederasts' and of 'pederasty' being 'carried' from one country or area to another through trade routes and colonisation.[96] Despite this, his conclusions lent a certain credence to presumptions about excessive homosexual indulgence in these areas. He further suggested that homosexuality 'of course prevails more in the cities and towns of Asiatic Turkey than in the villages' and was also common in Tunis, Tripoli and Algiers, as well as 'the cities of the south Mediterranean seaboard'.[97] The Chinese, meanwhile, were 'so far as we know them in the great cities . . . the chosen people of debauchery'; 'their systematic bestiality with ducks, goats and other animals is equalled only by their pederasty'.[98]

Many of Burton's observations were echoed in *Untrodden Fields of Anthropology: Observations on the Esoteric Manners and Customs of Semi-Civilised*

Peoples by Dr Jacobus X, the alias of Louis Jarolliot. It was published in French in 1895 and then in English in 1898 by Charles Carrington, who had worked for pornographers in and around Soho in the 1880s and early 1890s before moving to Paris in 1895 to set up his own bookshop and publishing concern, using mail order to distribute his books in England.[99] His publications included two of Jacobus X's works, Féré's *The Evolution and Dissolution of the Sexual Instinct* and various pornographic novels, indicating further the cross-over and possible cross-fertilisation of ideas between sexology, erotic anthropology and pornography.

Carrington acknowledged Dr Jacobus X's debt to Burton in a lengthy preface, which attempted to justify the work. 'Our aim', he wrote, 'has been precisely the same as had in view by Sir Richard Burton, who was not afraid to illustrate his books on travels and voyages with facts of real anthropological interest.'[100] He defended *Untrodden Fields of Anthropology* against accusations that it had an 'improper character' by noting that Jacobus X 'writes with the frankness of a medical student... laying open as with a scalpel, and exposing the vices of people who have brought depravity to the level of a fine art'.[101] Carrington utilised surgical metaphor to suggest his disinterested objectivity, though the image also suggests something more sinister and violent. The text certainly served sexual voyeurism as much as the expansion of anthropological knowledge and provided wide-ranging and detailed accounts of various sexual proclivities. It observed that 'the East enjoys the wretched privilege of being the chief nucleus of pederastic vice' and like Burton suggested that such vice was particularly rife in China.[102] In North Africa, meanwhile, the Arabs were said to be 'inveterate pederasts' who could be met in 'public squares and the Moorish cafes'.[103]

Throughout these accounts there is a tacit connection between sexual 'vices' and high art and culture, and in this way they incorporate a subtextual commentary on the European decadent movement, signalled at the outset of *Untrodden Fields of Anthopology* by Carrington's comments about raising 'depravity to... a fine art'. Jacobus X claimed that the Chinese were analogous to the ancient Romans in their levels of 'abandonment' and detailed the elaborate appliances – such as the 'anal violin' – pederasts used.[104] Both texts showed art and sex being brought together in the quest for sensual novelty in distant places, though their descriptions probably tell us more about fantasies of sexual possibility and activity amongst men in Europe than the cultures the texts ostensibly discuss. Indeed, the works referred frequently to European sexual mores, conflating them with ideas of Oriental degradation. They showed the supposed sexual plentitude of distant, exoticised cultures and simultaneously indicated the proximity of such pleasures to European readers – especially those in Paris, London, Berlin and Amsterdam. Jacobus X, for example, cited Krafft-Ebing's account of 'the women haters' ball' in Berlin and noted that 'the vices, practised with such revolting cynicism in Asia, were carried out with unseemly audacity in the great cities of Europe'.[105] Burton noted that: 'Outside the Sotadic Zone... the vice is sporadic, not endemic: yet the physical and moral effects of the great cities, where puberty, they say, is induced earlier than in country sites, has been the same in most lands, causing modesty to decay and pederasty to flourish.'[106] Burton went on to mention scandals in London and Dublin and suggested that Berlin 'is not a whit better than her neighbours'.[107] Burton and Jacobus X both also highlighted homosexual activity in Paris and devoted several pages to the Allée de Vieves episode described in *The Sexual Life of Our Time* and also in Pisanus Fraxi's bibliography of erotica, *Centuria Librorum Absconditorum*.[108] The details of this and other scandals allowed Paris to emerge as the European centre of homosexual activity in texts ostensibly concerned with other places entirely. The textual co-existence of Paris and the sexualised East intensified the city's homoerotic associations. These were further underscored by Henri d'Argis' *Sodomé* (1888) and Coffignon's *Paris Vivant* (1889). Sections of the latter appeared in English in Jacobus X's subsequent work *Crossways of Sex: A Study in Eroto-Pathology* (1904), along with further extensive details of homosexual antics in the Parisian streets, cafés and parks.[109]

These texts reiterated the internationalism and metropolitanism suggested by the sexologists, and for English readers also underscored the long-standing association of homosexuality with foreigners and foreignness. That the bulk of these works emanated from continental Europe, and from Paris, Vienna and Berlin in particular, further suggested that homosexuality was their peculiar interest and problem. In England, attempts to stifle *Sexual Inversion* and *The Sexual life of Our Time*, and the reticence surrounding *Psychopathia Sexualis*, spoke of concerns about the influence they might have, and so implicitly of a lack of faith in the hereditary theories they foregrounded. There was a fear of the continental vices which might insinuate their way further into London life; vices which by the 1890s appeared to be securing a stronger foothold in a decadent and aesthetic avant-garde.

CHAPTER 4

The decadent city

'AGAINST NATURE'

'The degenerate', Max Nordau reported, could be seen 'in the vanishing day at the Paris Champs de Mars Salon or the opening of the Exhibition of the Royal Academy in London';[1] he was also to be found in 'a suburban circus; the loft of a back tenement... or a fantastic artist's restaurant, where the performances... bring together the greasy *habitué* and the dainty aristocratic fledgling'.[2] In his home he sought to replicate the over-stimulation of the city streets: 'everything in [their] houses aims at exciting the nerves and dazzling the senses'.[3] For Nordau these different places framed the degenerate and provided a stage on which his symptoms – amongst them an amoral sensuality and perversity – were played out. Within months of the appearance of the English edition of *Degeneration*, Oscar Wilde went to prison after his own mapping of London – which included a top-class hotel, private dining rooms, heavily curtained chambers and his Tite Street home – had been evoked for the judge, jury and newspaper-reading public. Nordau and the prosecuting counsel in the Wilde case used a series of urban spaces to confirm degeneracy on the one hand and gross sexual misconduct on the other. They connected degeneration and homosexuality with aestheticism, decadence and the flouting of middle-class convention in the city.

Aestheticism, Regenia Gagnier notes, 'resisted the Victorian values of utility, rationality, scientific factuality, and technological progress'.[4] These values were dismissed in favour of the isolated beautiful moment, the only utility of which was the pleasure it could give. Art, aestheticism proclaimed, existed simply for its own sake. The Oxford don Walter Pater famously concluded his book *The Renaissance* (1873) with what amounted to an aesthetic manifesto. 'Art', he wrote, 'comes to you proposing frankly to give nothing but the highest quality to your moments as they pass, and simply for those moments' sake.'[5] Artists and writers no longer needed to defer to a pre-ordained natural or moral order in their work and the imperative was instead to seek beauty, the ultimate arbiter in the valuation of art and literature. The corollary of this aesthetic conception of art was that life too should be cut free from 'natural' archetypes. 'What we have to do', wrote Pater, 'is to be forever curiously testing new opinions and courting new impressions, never acquiescing in a facile orthodoxy.'[6] Orthodoxy in general and the prescriptiveness of nature in particular were held in tension with aestheticism and were the factors against which aesthetic artists and critics like Wilde and Pater reacted. Aestheticism provided a model for a complex identity based on beauty and the senses, rather than on social and cultural conformity or biological determinism.

This understanding had significant implications for the individual's relationship with time and space. In his conclusion to *The Renaissance*, Pater indicated the power of personal reflection to 'dissipate' and reconfigure the 'cohesive face' of external objects, a process which modulated the individual's sense of self and subjectivity in 'a strange perpetual weaving and unweaving of ourselves'.[7] This shifting subjectivity could, Pater suggested, shape experience of the material world and allow for some dramatic transformations. In Wilde's dialogue piece 'The Decay of Lying' (1889), for example, the aesthetic domestic fashion for all things Japanese cast Piccadilly in a new light. Vivian comments:

If you desire to see a Japanese effect, you will not behave like a tourist and go to Tokyo. On the contrary, you will stay at home and steep yourself in the work of certain Japanese artists, and then when you have absorbed the spirit of their work and caught their imaginative manner of vision, you will go the same afternoon and sit in the park or stroll down Piccadilly, and if you can not see a Japanese effect there you will not see it anywhere.[8]

Wilde's flippancy here carried with it a profound, and profoundly aesthetic, comment on the effect shifts in perception had on the way the self and the environment might be experienced. Subjectivity, physical context and perception become interdependent, with a change or conscious manipulation of one prompting the others to shift and re-form. In this case, domestic study and rearrangement aided the perceptual recreation of the public realm. At a lecture in London in 1883 Wilde claimed that with this kind of aesthetic vision 'even Gower Street' could be beautiful.[9] The public spaces of the city in this sense became private, colonised to the interior artistic vision of the subject. Whereas later nineteenth-century realist and naturalist writers like Emile Zola and George Gissing represented individuals as creatures of their environment, woven into the social fabric – a metaphor George Eliot famously elaborated in *Silas Marner, The Weaver of Raveloe* (1861) – this aesthetic ethos suggested a mode of self-determination and mastery over the environment, at least for an elite. Both Gissing and Wilde offered detailed domestic descriptions but whereas for Gissing they underscored the material plight of the inhabitants, trapped within particular spaces and their associated orthodoxies, in Wilde's work the accumulation of detail indicated a quest for new sensation and experience, a retreat from social reality into what Jean Pierrot calls 'an inner paradise furnished with the utmost luxury and refinement'.[10]

When Oscar and Constance Wilde moved to 16 Tite Street in 1885 their interior decoration not surprisingly marked a rejection of prevailing domestic convention. It was, Charles Hirsch noted, an 'artistic interior' with 'bizarre furnishings, tapestries and ornamentation'.[11] The library was redone in North African style and for the dining room the Wildes employed E. W. Godwin, the influential designer of Anglo-Japanese furniture. Each chair, wrote Wilde, was 'a sonnet in ivory ... the table a masterpiece in pearl'.[12] Wilde valued Oriental art and furnishings in particular because of their 'frank rejection of imitation' and 'dislike of the actual representation of any object in Nature, of our own imitative spirit'.[13] *Punch* famously poked fun at these aesthetic fashions in the late 1870s and early 1880s, and Max Beerbohm described the craze in *The Yellow Book* just prior to Wilde's prosecution: 'Peacock feathers and sunflowers glittered in every room, the curio shops were ransacked for the furniture of Annish [*sic*] days, men and women fired by the fervid words of Oscar Wilde, threw their mahogany into the streets.'[14] Symbols of Victorian propriety were rejected with the introduction of furniture and ornamentation which invoked other times and spaces and signalled a break with tradition.

The aesthetic validation of the individual perspective and the quest for beauty in art and life became closely associated with decadence. Decadence focussed not just on the pleasure and intensity of looking but also on novel experience and experimentation for all the senses. Thus the value of Oriental and North African art lay for decadence not only in its rejection of mimesis but also in the kind of sensual and erotic associations elaborated by Richard Burton and Jacobus X. It drew on the idea of the decaying luxury of 'advanced' civilisations, depicted most famously by Edward Gibbons in *The Decline and Fall of the Roman Empire* (1776–8), a book whose message reverberated across the nineteenth century. For the symbolist poet Arthur Symons decadence had 'all the qualities that mark the end of great periods...an intense self-consciousness, a restless curiosity in research, an over-subtilising refinement upon refinement, a spiritual and moral perversity'.[15] Whilst aestheticism sought personal epiphany and uplift through beauty, the decadent movement explored sensual novelty however debilitating.

The links between aestheticism and decadence were well-established. This was partly because of the shared emphasis on sensory intensity, partly because they had common roots. Both movements were associated with a French literary tradition, extending from Theophile Gautier through Baudelaire, Rimbaud and J-K. Huysmans. R. V. Johnson indicates the importance of aspects of English Romanticism and Renaissance theatre, as well as work in German by Goethe and Winkelman. Pater also signalled the impact of the ancient Greeks, especially in their valuation of beauty. In late nineteenth-century England they were connected with the poets Arthur Symons, Ernest Dowson and Lionel Johnson, and with the illustrator Aubrey Beardsley. Pater's luxuriant prose echoed some of the writers of the French tradition, and as we have seen his conclusion to *The Renaissance* seemed to endorse more than the aesthetic quest for beauty, particularly in its exhortation to 'discriminate in every moment some passionate attitude in those about us'.[16] Pater withdrew his conclusion from the 1877 edition, explaining in a footnote when it was virtually reinstated in 1893 that it had been 'omitted...as [he] conceived it might possibly mislead some of those young men into whose hands it might fall'.[17] Pater clearly saw decadence potentially licensing not only enhanced aesthetic perception and artistic fervour but also other dissident activities and pleasures.

Aesthetic and decadent perspectives also developed partly through the artefacts of Empire, which could be seen in the huge warehouses of London's docks, in the new department stores of the West End, at the British Museum, the Colonial Conference of 1888 and the Colonial and Imperial Exhibition of 1894. Foreign and 'exotic' art forms and cultures were proudly showcased in the city, paradoxically sparking domestic and artistic trends which contravened prevailing norms and represented 'alien' and 'foreign' values and passions. Various writings – *Don Leon*, *Sins of the Cities of the Plain*, Burton's *Arabian Nights* and Jacobus X's *Untrodden Fields of Anthropology* – elaborated these associations and detailed a supposedly rapacious indulgence in homosexual sex in these 'other' places. When Edward Carpenter edited his homoerotic anthology of friendship, *Iölaus* (1902), he included extracts from Stanley Lane-Poole's *Turkey* (1888), James Silk Buckingham's *Travels in Assyria, Media and Persia* (1829) and a number of thirteen and fourteenth-century Persian poets.[18] These writings and cultures provided important reference points for middle- and upper-class men exploring aestheticism and decadence and male–male friendships and relationships.

As the last chapter observed, Paris was the place where Oriental eroticism, aestheticism and the decadent impulse for sensual exploration were seen to intersect. This urban conjunction was captured especially strikingly by Joris-Karl Huysmans in *A Rebours*. The novel exerted a huge influence on English aesthetic and decadent writers, especially in its representation of the relationship between the city, gender and sexuality. It is the mysterious work which so influences Dorian Gray, and its lavish interiors are replicated in parts of Wilde's novel and also in the pornographic work *Teleny* (1893).

A Rebours, which has been translated as both *Against Nature* and *Against the Grain*, was published in 1884 and presented, according to Arthur Symons, 'the history of a typical decadent' and 'the main tendencies, the chief results, of the decadent movement in literature'.[19] Huysmans had initially been associated with Zola's *Médan* group of Realists, producing *Marthe* (1876), a story about a prostitute in a licensed brothel, and *Les Soeurs Vatard* (1879), which was dedicated to Zola and dealt with working-class life. *A Rebours*, however, was written in a different vein: it drew on Baudelaire and Mallarmé, as well as the lives of a number of the Parisian decadents with whom Huysmans had had contact. It centres exclusively on the quest of the aristocrat Des Esseintes for new sensation and experience and is set largely in his secluded home. It offers lengthy descriptions of his acquisitiveness and also includes sections on his former exploits in Paris. The novel has little narrative impulse, and as David Mickelsen suggests, it is made up of 'a succession' of scenes which have no necessary interrelation.[20] This succession amounts to a structure which privileges space over time; the various settings and Des Esseintes' activity within them impede the narrative progression of the novel and draw the reader in rather than on-wards. The same structure can be seen in a less excessive form in both *The Picture of Dorian Gray* and *Teleny*, and shows, Edward Soja argues, a deep understanding of 'the instrumentality of space amongst the aesthetic and decadent avant-garde'.[21]

In his introduction to the abridged 1922 translation of the novel, Havelock Ellis described the hold 'the feverish activities of Paris' had over Huysmans: '[They] fixed his attention... with the concentrated gaze of a stranger in a strange land, held by a fascination which is more than half repulsion.' The idea of the personal quest evoked by 'the tincture of Parisian modernity' was, Ellis suggested, explored and echoed in the novel.[22] Des Esseintes searches ceaselessly for new sensation: he collects artificial flowers, then grotesque real flowers that appear unnatural; he buys a tortoise and has it gilded and encrusted with jewels; he investigates perfumery, revelling in its artificiality; and casts seafaring paraphernalia around part of the house so that 'he was able to enjoy quickly, almost simultaneously, all the sensations of a long sea-voyage, without ever leaving home'.[23] He manipulates and controls his environment to invoke distant experience, sensation and beauty. This decadent sensibility becomes more sexualised in the Parisian sections of the novel, and in chapter nine three encounters are recounted in quick succession. Each one derives its eroticism from the setting and helps to build a vivid sense of what the city – and especially its streets and places of entertainment – could offer in an exploration of desire. The first is with an American female acrobat called Miss Urania, whom Des Esseintes observes performing at the circus. As he watches her, admiring her suppleness and agility, he imagines a shift in gender: 'after being a woman to begin with, then hesitating in a condition verging on the androgynous, she seemed to have made up her mind and become an integral unmistakable man'. Des Esseintes 'got to the point of imagining that he for his part was turning female... This exchange of sex between Miss Urania and himself had excited him tremendously.'[24] Miss Urania's performance of 'suppleness and strength', her name signifying ambiguous sexuality, the carnivalesque context of the circus and Des Esseintes' passive role in the circus audience, allow for a gender-shift in his fantasies.[25] 'He was seized with a definite desire to possess this woman, yearning for her just as a chlorotic girl will hanker after a clumsy brute whose embrace could squeeze the life out of her.'[26] Des Esseintes wants sex with her as if she were a man, but in such a way as to maintain his own hold on power: this is *his* fantasy, created out of the performance *he* watches. He wants to possess this 'woman' – her 'true' gender definitively reasserted for a moment – and force her to play a particular role in his imaginary fragile girlhood. Out of place and performance he constructs and controls a fantasy of gender mutability which yet preserves him as the locus of power, dictating the erotic events. When they come together, however, she subverts the illusion by 'being positively puritanical in bed' and forcing him to 'resume the man's part'.[27] The woman's muscular body is not enough to sustain Des Esseintes' interest: what excited him was the fantastical exchange of conventional gender roles which the circus made possible but which revert in the mundane bedroom.

He is somewhat more successful in his second encounter in a café with a ventriloquist 'with greasy hair parted on one side near the temple like a boy's'.[28] His sexual relations with this boyish girl rest on her ability to throw a masculine voice behind the bedroom door, which denigrates her and frightens him:

'Open up, damn you! I know you've got a cully in there with you! But just you wait a minute, you slut, and you'll get what's coming to you!' Straight away, like those lechers on the river bank, in the Tuileries Gardens, in a public lavatory or on a park bench, he would temporarily recover his powers and hurl himself onto the ventriloquist, whose voice went blustering on outside the room.[29]

The erotic charge arises from the evocation of other places beyond the bedroom. First it comes from the space behind the door and the man who hammers on it, but this in turn is related to the frisson of cruising in the city's public spaces. He manages to have sex with the girl, who loses her gender to become simply 'the ventriloquist', only because she maintains for him the fantasy of an encounter with a man through a chain of spatial associations which lead to cottages and cruising grounds.

The final relationship of the chapter provides a consummation of these thinly veiled homoerotised affairs with a mannish woman and a boyish girl with a man's voice. It springs from a real juncture of roads and avenues:

As he was walking by himself along the Avenue de Latour-Mausbourg, he was accosted near the Invalides by a youth who asked him which was the quickest way to get to the Rue de Babylone. Des Esseintes showed him which road to take, and as he was crossing the esplanade too, they set off together . . . They gazed at each other for a moment; then the young man dropped his eyes and came closer, brushing his companion's arm with his own. Des Esseintes slackened his pace, taking thoughtful note of the youth's mincing walk.[30]

This encounter is specifically mapped out, with their meeting place and destination mirroring the social status of their encounter and future relationship: they meet at 'Invalides' and head off together for 'Babylone'. The city streets are foregrounded in the depiction of the meeting and also narrate and foreshadow events. Their walk through these streets allows Des Esseintes to 'read' the boy's body along sexological lines and begin to act upon the possibilities it suggests. Whilst the meeting is given a precise mapping and extended description, the relationship itself is abstracted into what appears to be the decadent zenith: 'never had he submitted to more delightful or stringent exploitation, never had he run such risks, yet never had he known such satisfaction mingled with distress'.[31] The episode is omitted from the 1922 translation introduced by Ellis, along with the reference to 'lechers' in the Tuileries Gardens evoked in the liaison with the ventriloquist.[32] The culmination of this triad of relationships is thus censored and their homoerotic undercurrent curtailed, though these parts had of course long been available to readers of French like Wilde.

City spaces created the erotic charge in each of these encounters, allowing for the elaboration of fantasy and for sexual experimentation. More specifically, the city permitted an exploration of homosexual desires; they may have been '*invalide*' and 'Babylonian' but they were apparently accommodated and incited by the decadent French capital. The explicit artifice of the built environment reflected, sanctioned and facilitated these performances of mutable gender and sexuality, just as Des Esseintes' isolated home allowed him to explore other roles and sensations, destroying his health in the process.[33]

The decadent impulse charted in the novel impels Des Esseintes into overtly constructed realms, the domestic sphere and the city; places where nature does not obviously constrain and compel him. In this respect, the city was the ideal setting for decadence and aestheticism.[34] Writing in 1913, Holbrook Jackson noted hyperbolically that in the 1890s: 'Art threw a glamour over the town, and all the artificial things conjured by that word ... Poets ... found romance in streets and theatres, in taverns and restaurants, in bricks and mortar and the creations of artificers.'[35] The variety of different spaces in the city moreover suggested the possibility of wide-ranging experimentation with perception and sensation. The city was, like 'Art' in the preface to *The Picture of Dorian Gray*, 'at once both surface and symbol',[36] it was a material locale which signified the scope to act 'against nature'. As such it was as integral to the aesthetic and decadent pose and experience as the private space of the home.

Paris was clearly the archetypal decadent city, but in England London was the nearest counterpart. It was 'a pale shadow' by comparison,[37] but those interested in aesthetic and decadent ideas of art and life continued to live and work there, despite remaining, according to Jackson, 'spiritual foreigners in our midst'.[38] London was where the periodicals associated with aestheticism and decadence were published, principally *The Yellow Book* (1894–5), *The Savoy* (1896), *The Pageant* (1895–6), and *The Dome* (1897–1900). The city provided a convenient arena for privileged men to experiment with dress and desire and to publish work and illustration which explored aesthetic and decadent ideas.[39]

It was also a prominent theme within decadent writing of the 1890s. In '*Impression du Nuit*: London' (1899), Lord Alfred Douglas meshed material, mental and sexual geographies as he imagined the city at night as a woman through which men 'creep like thought'.[40] Symons similarly figured

London as both seductive and malevolent in 'City Nights' (1891).[41] In both poems the city functioned as a screen for the projection of erotic fantasy.[42] Wilde returned repeatedly to London in his work, transforming it through his aesthetic gaze in 'Symphony in Yellow' (1889) and '*Impression du Matin*' (1881).[43] In his short story 'The Sphinx Without a Secret' (1891), Lord Murchison tells the unnamed narrator of his infatuation for the mysterious Lady Alroy. In a gentle parody of the decadent drive for new sensation, and perhaps also of London's capacity to provide it, the woman's dark secret turns out to be tea-drinking in a room in Soho, which she had rented precisely to heighten her enigma. Murchison tells his story in Paris, and the reference is typical: the French capital was drawn repeatedly into aesthetic and decadent depictions of London to effect an imaginative transformation. It was significant both to Wilde's *The Picture of Dorian Gray* and the anonymous *Teleny*, texts which outlined, with varying degrees of explicitness and to different audiences, the fantasy of a city rich in homosexual possibilities.

DORIAN GRAY AND TELENY'S DECADENT OUTINGS

The Picture of Dorian Gray is, of course, the better known of the two works. It is the tale of a man whose portrait takes on the signs of his transgressive behaviour and age, leaving him unaltered in appearance. It was first published in 1891 by Ward Lock to a generally resistant press. Gagnier argues persuasively that the reception was not to do with the subject matter. Some of Wilde's short stories had dealt with related themes and *The Picture of Dorian Gray* in any case fulfilled the perceived need for moral censure by killing off the protagonist at the end. The problem, she suggests, was the milieu and setting Wilde chose to depict, the focus on louche aristocracy and the debt the text owed to the aesthetic and decadent movements. Partly as a result, the novel unnerved some reviewers, especially given its veiled homoeroticism. A former friend of Wilde's, W. E. Henley, observed in the *Scots Observer*:

The story – which deals with matters only fitted for the Criminal Investigation Department or a hearing in camera – is discreditable alike to author and editor. Mr Wilde has brains and art and style; but if he can write for none but outlawed noblemen and perverted telegraph boys, the sooner he takes up tailoring (or some other decent trade) the better for his own reputation and the public morals.[44]

Henley, like the counsel for the prosecution in the Wilde trials five years later, was able to identify the hints at homosexual desire in the novel and connect them to the Cleveland Street Scandal which had erupted a year earlier. The novel is not explicit, but the obsession Basil Hallward and Lord Henry have with Dorian, the gaps and silences around many of Dorian's exploits, the trail of ruined young men, the circuit of places and even the choice of an ancient Greek name for the protagonist, make Henley's extrapolations perfectly plausible. The luxuriant furnishings signify at least a generalised Eastern sensuality, whilst the descriptive passages, the poised, mannered opening pages and the debt to *A Rebours* clearly link the work to the decadent tradition. In a move worthy of Des Esseintes, Dorian has nine large-paper copies of the first edition of the book imported from Paris and bound in different colours to suit his changing moods.[45]

Teleny was published two years later in 1893. Charles Hirsch claimed that the manuscript was the work of a number of authors, including Wilde. He described how the developing manuscript was dropped off and picked up from his Coventry Street bookshop around 1890, just as Wilde was writing *The Picture of Dorian Gray*. It was subsequently passed on to Leonard Smithers, who published 200 copies in 1893, having clumsily, according to Hirsch, 'transferred the drama to the other side of the channel' for fear of shocking 'the national pride of his British subscribers'.[46] Further editions appeared in 1899, 1903 (in which Wilde is named as the author) and in 1906. A French edition of 1934 restored the supposed London setting of the original manuscript, though the specific geography remains vague.

Although there is no direct corroboration of Hirsch's story, the novel's uneven style is suggestive of shared authorship,[47] and so of a circle of men, possibly centred around Wilde, working together to construct a decadent fantasy of homosexual life and sex in London. The transposed setting might have fooled some, but, as Hirsch points out, the Embankment, Soho Square and parts of the East End would have been discernable in the narrative, at least to those who knew London. In a preface to the French edition, omitted from the earlier English versions, Teleny is said to be buried 'au Cimetière de Brompton' in Earls Court,[48] and one or two other specific places in London – the Queen's Hall and Belgravia, for example – are mentioned elsewhere in this putative original. In the English edition circulating during the period and discussed here, the setting is equivocal, suggesting both London and Paris, and so hinting at the mutability of the urban scene. The novel is structured as a dialogue between Des Grieux, a wealthy trader, and an unnamed male friend. Des Grieux relates the story of his sexual development, which centres on his intense emotional and sexual relationship with Teleny, a Hungarian musician. Des Grieux and Teleny identify themselves as constitutionally interested in the same sex but they also desire and have sex with women. A preference is suggested but the possibilities for these men are not curtailed.

The depictions of homosexual and heterosexual love and sex are not interchangeable, however. Sex between men, whilst always tacitly associated with death, also carries with it multiple sensual possibilities and new levels of ecstasy and intensity. Heterosexual love, meanwhile, is associated by Des Grieux with 'a quiet chatty drawing room flirtation'[49] and heterosexual sex with disease, abuse and enclosure. The bodies of the female prostitutes he visits early in the novel are 'cadaverous and bloated' and contained in a building which mirrors and prefigures them: the brothel looks as if it had 'some loathsome, scabby, skin disease'.[50] The maid he attempts to seduce is locked in her room before being assaulted by Des Grieux and raped by the coachman. These disturbingly violent and misogynist depictions of sexual relations with women take place in the circumscribed spaces of brothel and bedroom, to which the men have access, but from which the women can only escape through death: one of the prostitutes dies of consumption and the maid commits suicide from her bedroom window. Des Grieux's mother is the only woman to emerge unscathed from heterosexual relations, although her lover, Teleny, commits suicide once he realises they have been discovered by Des Grieux himself. By contrast sex between men occurs in public, semi-public and private space which are part of a fluid urban circuit.

Teleny was written for a different audience and with a more obviously sexual purpose than Wilde's novel, and comparisons between them need to be made with caution. Examining them together, however, begins to reveal similar conceptualisations and fantasies of the city and homosexual experimentation. Moreover, *Teleny*'s conclusion suggests an amoral reworking of the ending of *The Picture of Dorian Gray* and gestures to the potential elaboration of a decadent sexual agenda, which is more conclusively closed down in Wilde's novel.

The two novels are both set in the present, in an age of electric doorbells and telegrams, and the possibilities or dangers they are concerned with are thus explicitly contemporary. Despite this, in *The Picture of Dorian Gray* in particular the imperatives of time are evaded. Whilst time's passing, and Dorian's atavism, are dramatically registered through the ageing and degenerating portrait – one of the few temporal indicators – there is a sense of timelessness as the ever-youthful Dorian explores the city. Although the narrative structure draws the reader through the novel in a fairly conventional progression – as Dorian moves from innocence to corruption and then to punishment – in other ways it pulls us into the protagonist's world where the developmental path and the conventional process of ageing are sidestepped in favour of a decadent accumulation of sensual experience. Pleasure in the novel is experienced for itself and in the moment. It is essentially unproductive and unrelated to any hopes for the future. So, whilst the novel has a stronger narrative impulse than *A Rebours*, the spaces Dorian moves between in his search for new sensation are key.

This alignment of dissident desire with space comes as a muffled echo of the sexological accounts of the homosexual or invert discussed in the last chapter. Whilst Bloch, Ellis and the others saw a biological imperative at work, however, Wilde portrays a more complex genesis and experience of desire. Dorian is the offspring of Lady Margaret Devereux and 'a subaltern in a foot regiment' – a pairing suggestive of the liaisons between aristocrats and soldiers in Hyde Park and nearby brothels – but both are dead.[51] He is also Lord Henry's protégé and Basil Hallward's artistic subject, but he leaves both behind him: displacing Henry as the focus of the narrative voice and murdering Basil once he is in on his secret. Dorian reflects on the effect of 'a strange poisonous germ' passed on to him by his forebears through the generations, but his fascination is with their dreams and fantasies rather than a pathological bequest: 'Were his actions merely the dreams that the dead man had not dared to realize?'[52] Wilde suggested but did not insist upon the factors which shape Dorian's subjectivity, unlike Gissing, who delineated the co-ordinates of identity much more precisely. Dorian is described 'trying to gather up the scarlet threads of his life, and to weave them into a pattern; to find his way through the sanguine labyrinth of passion through which he was wondering'.[53] There is no purposeful journey here but rather an echo of Pater's weave and W. T. Stead's sexual labyrinth, evoked in his 'Maiden Tribute of Modern Babylon' articles of 1885. Wilde sidesteps the city's new thoroughfares, stations, hotels, theatres and shops and instead utilises other representations and understandings of the city which might mirror and represent a complex internal map of desire.

The early part of *The Picture of Dorian Gray* focuses on Lord Henry Wootton, his aesthetic tastes and his West End circuit. Details of the latter – communicated through a description of an afternoon stroll – would almost seem superfluous except that the places mentioned were not merely fashionable but also had other associations for those familiar with London's homoerotic history. He begins in St James', which had long-standing associations with homosexual activity and was known in the 1880s and 1890s for its homosocial club-life, bachelor chambers and the London and Provincial Turkish Baths in Jermyn Street, as chapter 1 observed. From there, Lord

Henry crosses Piccadilly, where Jack Saul had touted for custom for the Cleveland Street brothel, and visits an uncle in the bachelor chambers of the Albany. He then goes through the Burlington Arcade, which had featured prominently in the sensational Boulton and Park case of 1871 and from where dyed green carnations, supposed symbol of transgressive desire in Paris, could apparently be purchased.[54] Lord Henry continues to Hyde Park, notorious for its guardsman 'rent', and then on to Soho and a draper's in Wardour Street, where he goes 'to look after a piece of old brocade and had to bargain for hours for it'.[55] It was from a draper's in Soho that the fictional Jack Saul was first solicited in *Sins of the Cities of the Plain*, a novel Wilde reputedly purchased in 1890, and it is tempting to put a similar gloss on Lord Henry's hours of bargaining for fabric. Whether W. E. Henley was also aware of these associations when he suggested Wilde should enter tailoring is not clear, though Christopher Breward has noted a contemporary suspicion of draper's and clothing retailers.[56] Soho and Piccadilly also had a reputation for an indeterminacy in terms of place and identity, as we have seen. In outlining this walk Wilde touched on a secretive map of the city without revealing its precise associations: it would have been available to some but not all of the novel's readers.

Dorian absorbs this mapping of the West End but he soon moves beyond it. Watching the 'fascinating' and 'terrifying' people in the park and Piccadilly fills him with a 'mad curiosity' and awakens 'a passion for sensation'.[57] He strikes out and 'wanders eastward' into 'the labyrinth of grimy streets', not as part of the philanthropic project he is engaged in with Lady Agatha, but in search of beauty, 'the real secret of life'.[58] The visit is described in direct speech, largely without narratorial intervention, and the East End becomes Dorian's creation. Echoing contemporary depictions of the area by some of the urban explorers,[59] it is a mapless space which both repels and seduces Dorian. Here he enters the theatre, a place which allows him to create a fantasy around the actress Sybil Vane. She transforms herself before Dorian's eyes from Juliet to a 'pretty boy in hose and doublet and a dainty cap' and back again,[60] in a performance which echoes those of Fanny and Stella, the fictional Miss Urania in *A Rebours* and the more circumscribed transformations on the music hall stage. Dorian is fascinated by her and his own spectatorial role and he returns repeatedly as if to confirm his new-found desires. Lord Henry aptly diagnoses what has happened to him in terms of space and movement: 'out of its secret hiding place had crept his Soul, and Desire had come to meet it on the way'.[61]

It is when the space ceases to be secret, described by the narrator rather than Dorian, and when Lord Henry and Basil visit the theatre as well, that the fantasy and the desires evaporate. Sybil ceases to fulfil the requirement of the space – just as Miss Urania does in *A Rebours* – and she stops performing. As Rachel Bowlby observes, she 'abandons the sexual, historical and imagistic mobility of her artistic persona for the third-rateness of finding a true, consistent self'.[62] The fantasy and transformatory potential of city spaces remain only as long as Dorian himself shapes and controls it; as with Des Esseintes these fantasies are cursed when they intersect with the social realm beyond.[63] Dorian, uninterested in this orthodoxy, ceases to desire Sybil and retreats through the city to his luxurious bedchamber in Mayfair. The theatre loses its mystery and is soon specifically located. The *St James' Gazette* reports that the Royal Theatre, Holborn was the site of Sybil's 'death by misadventure'.[64] The theatre is no longer the locus of desire in the midst of the labyrinth, but is instead mundanely mapped in Holborn, near Covent Garden, and much further west than we expected. The location was not incidental: the Royal Holborn Empire in High Holborn (see Figure 4) was a popular music hall venue, and like other halls featured both male and female crossing acts. The nearby Royal Holborn Amphitheatre and Circus, also in High Holborn, was the scene of a notorious act in 1870 in which a boy pertaining to be 'a great female gymnast', 'M'lle lulu', sang a song with the refrain 'wait till I'm a man'.[65]

The theatre and the whole romantic episode are subsequently erased by being rendered unspeakable. Dorian tells Basil 'if one doesn't talk about a thing, it has never happened. It is simply expression, as Harry says, that gives reality to things.'[66] The homoerotic implications of Lord Henry's walk and 'bargaining for fabric' remain unspoken and maintain their potency precisely because they are oblique. Following this example and his own tryst with Sybil, Dorian does not detail his exploits and they become mysterious and insubstantial as a result. The reader cannot piece together the full extent of his personal map of the capital, a map which would perhaps reveal the nature of his desires. We can only guess the implications of the places that are mentioned and what it is about him that 'was so fatal to the lives of young men'.[67]

Dorian's use of the city reveals its expansiveness: each place leads somewhere else and has somewhere beyond it where it might be possible to find new pleasures. We do not experience Dorian's townhouse as entirely separate but are made aware of the garden, the square outside and the balcony on to which Dorian steps after murdering Basil. The schoolroom which houses the painting is significantly private and not open to the public gaze, but it is also bathed in light during the day, not shut away in the dark. Beyond the house and the square is Piccadilly and 'the little Italian restaurant in Rupert Street',[68] which the same night gives way to the 'dingy box' in the theatre. From here Dorian moves into the fantasy spaces evoked by Sybil – 'the forest of Arden' and 'an orchard in Verona' – and backstage, the scene of his equally fantastic relationship with her.[69] Then there are the 'distant parts of Whitechapel' and 'the dreadful places near Bluegate Fields', where the journalist James Greenwood had found mannish female prostitutes.[70] At home he evokes other sensual and exotic locales by burning 'odorous gums from the East' and giving 'curious concerts' in which 'yellow-shawled Tunisians plucked at the strained strings of monstrous lutes [and] slim, turbaned Indians blew through long pipes'.[71] There is a fluid movement between public and private spaces, between self-created interiors and the labyrinthine, secret and hidden aspects of the metropolis, and Wilde uses this interplay to indicate a complex exploration of desire and identity.

Dorian's decadent engagement with the city is facilitated by his ability to keep these spaces separate from each other whilst maintaining his mobility between them. His independent movement through the city, by foot and cab, maintains his secret and disguises his locale and destination. Whilst we are given a detailed mapping of Gissing's 'nether world',[72] in *The Picture of Dorian Gray* we get fragments of the city cobbled together as Dorian passes through them.

This rendition of London is of course based on assumptions of possibility consistent with Dorian's masculinity and class, and the depiction of the city in the novel replays familiar urban dynamics. Most obviously his journeys east replicated those of philanthropists, urban explorers and 'slummers'. The allusions to his exploits there reproduced conceptions of the East End poor as sexually pliant and ideas of the 'sensual', 'bestial' and 'revolting' Limehouse Chinese providing a passport to fantastical other worlds through opium.[73] Dorian's sensual acquisitiveness tapped into the expanding consumerist possibilities of the West End, and the transformation and transgressive use of the city by night were familiar from renditions of both heterosexual and homosexual sexual activity. There are, for example, echoes in the novel of a contemporary depiction of the night-time scene at the Haymarket: 'They come out in strange and fantastic garments, and in glaringly gas-lit rooms screech and gabble in wild revelry. The street corners are beset by night prowlers. Phantoms arrayed in satin and lace flit upon the sight. The devil puts a diamond ring on his taloned finger, sticks a pin in his shirt and takes his walks abroad.'[74] The revelry and the dashing, deceptive appearances both figure in *The Picture of Dorian Gray*, and in both this extract and the novel the demonic and dangerous underbelly of the city is personified – as the devil and Dorian respectively. These ideas were recapitulated in the coverage of the Ripper murders of 1888 and earlier in Robert Louis Stevenson's *The Strange Case of Dr Jekyll and Mr Hyde* (1886). Wilde, Bartlett notes, was in some ways merely repeating 'the clichés of a descent into London's underworld'.[75]

The novel nevertheless indicates the possibilities of the city, and there is a marked contrast between Dorian and other figures who do not or cannot act upon its potential. Dorian's imitators are 'frozen in Mayfair balls' and 'sit like shop dummies in Pall Mall club windows'.[76] Those ruined by Dorian find themselves shut out: Lord Henry's sister, Lady Gwendolen, is excluded from society and when Dorian asks Adrian Singleton why he is in the opium den he replies 'where else would I be?'[77] Of the working-class characters, the carters only know Covent Garden and London at dawn, and Sybil and James Vane feel and look out of place in the park. They return from their walk on the set route of a public bus, which 'left them close to their shabby home in the Euston Road'. Euston Road had, according to contemporary journalist Robert Machray, 'as malodorous a reputation as any in London'.[78] Their excursion is predictable, traceable and public, and confirms their economic and social standing. Dorian, meanwhile, sustains his fantasies and evades detection partly because of his perpetual youth, but partly because he is mobile and the precise co-ordinates of his personal map of the city remain unclear, even if its general patterns are 'clichéd'. Wilde presents a version of the city which remains private; which destroys and debilitates, perhaps, but which also permits an elaborate negotiation of subjectivity. This opacity is the means through which Wilde suggests a departure from convention and what Steve Pile calls 'administrative rationality'.[79] Whilst the bedroom and the family home might define and specify marital sexual relations, here it is the multiplicity of spaces and untracked movements between them which indicates Dorian's transgressive sexual appetite.

In this sense the novel resonates with the ethos of individualism Wilde outlines in his utopian polemic, 'The Soul of a Man Under Socialism', also published in 1891. In the novel, however, Wilde explores the complexities of such a vision in an unreformed and class-bound culture, and, in consequence, the possibilities of the city are also tainted by a fear of scandal. Dorian is ultimately afraid to leave London in case the mutating portrait is discovered: the city which enables his exploration of his 'myriad lives' and 'myriad sensations' also traps him. In the East End, scene of drug-induced reveries, he is threatened by James Vane; the theatre is both squalid and fantastic; his home is the scene of his extreme acquisitiveness and wild concerts, but also has the schoolroom with the decaying portrait. The schoolroom itself holds both the picture and a mirror, which disgust and delight him in turn. Each of these spaces reflect Dorian's own duality and become a projection of his decadent pose, a pose which holds both the promise of sensual intensity but also presages his debilitation. Wilde thus depicts an intricate relationship between the city and the self. It is mediated by broader representations of the city and characterised by possibility and constraint; London is conceived as a place where individualism both flourishes and founders. When Dorian plunges the knife into the painting in the final passage of the novel a personal transgressive odyssey is brought to an end: the formal divisions between inside and out, the public and the private are re-established and the policeman makes his entrance.

Given this orderly ending it is telling that *The Picture of Dorian Gray* was still perceived by Lord Queensberry's defence to be 'calculated to subvert morality and encourage unnatural vice'.[80] Wilde explored and represented the complexity of the city, which, as we have seen, was understood in multiple, shifting and unstable ways. This constituted part of the novel's threat since it implicated unruly and ineffable identities and desires. In the month of Wilde's prosecution the anarchist, communist, 'aesthetic sensualist' and decadent were compared and conflated in *Blackwood's Magazine*. 'The aesthetic sensualist and the communist', it noted, 'are nearly related . . . The unbridled licentiousness of your literary decadent has its counterpart in the violence of the political anarchist.'[81] In the West End streets and Soho cafés these suspect figures constituted a profound threat. They represented a destabilisation of existing ideologies and, whilst they had a different ultimate objective, brought with them overlapping ideas about the importance of the individual. They were seen to reside at the heart of the city and presented a challenge to home, city, nation and empire. The sexual anarchy that Elaine Showalter identifies in London's literary culture at the *fin de siècle* was thus perhaps reason enough for the prominence of *The Picture of Dorian Gray* in the trial of its author: the eponymous hero takes his cue from a book after all, and conflates psyche and city in an evasive and individualistic exploration of desire and identity.[82]

Teleny elaborated this potential for decadent experimentation in the city, and with a more restricted audience the writers were able to be much more explicit. As in *Sins of the Cities of the Plain*, the city itself is an erotic component. Steven Marcus suggests that urban location is incidental to the eroticism of Victorian pornographic texts, but in *Teleny* the diverse spaces of the metropolis are pivotal, even though they are sufficiently oblique to implicate both London and Paris.[83]

Des Grieux's relationship with Teleny takes some time to consummate and involves a protracted topographical foreplay which draws him through various real and fantasy spaces. It begins in a concert hall, unspecified in the English edition, but located as the Queen's Hall, Langham Place in the later French version. Teleny's performance that evening transports Des Grieux to Egypt, ancient Greece, the 'luxuriant loveliness' of the Alhambra – the Moorish palace in Grenada but also the famous music hall in Leicester Square – and 'the gorgeous towns of Sodom and Gomorrah, weird, beautiful and grand'.[84] The space of the concert hall is transformed by Teleny's performance into a sequence of homoeroticised places, culminating in a vision of the pianist standing naked in 'a rain of rubies... that was consuming the Cities of the Plain'.[85] The end of the concert leaves Des Grieux sexually exhausted: 'I was powerless to applaud, I sat there dumb, motionless, nerveless.'[86]

Des Grieux is drawn back repeatedly to Teleny's recitals, and, as with Dorian Gray, it is art and performance which transform his understanding of his desires. In their wake Des Grieux is reluctant to return home and instead takes to the streets. One evening he finds himself drawn towards Teleny's house – in a quiet street in Belgravia in the French edition[87] –, and on another he follows him to the 'Quai de ____', a cruising area which maps readily on to the Embankment and Embankment Gardens in London. Here Des Grieux finds an effeminate dandy, an 'old wiry simpering man' and a 'strong, sturdy' workman cruising.[88] It is an abject area in which desire and disgust are mingled. Men 'spring up' and 'disappear' suddenly, and Des Grieux loses himself and his purpose among them:

I had been so taken up with all these midnight wanderers that I had lost sight both of [Teleny] and Braincourt, but all at once I saw them reappear. With them was a young Zouave sub-lieutenant, a dapper and dashing fellow, and a slim and swarthy youth, apparently an Arab. The meeting did not seem to have been a carnal one... the soldier was entertaining his friends with his lively talk.[89]

The Quai is transformed by darkness and Teleny and Braincourt become like the other erotic spectres, magically materialising in front of Des Grieux. There are possibilities for sex with a range of men, who accord with archetypal figures of homosexual fantasy: the working-class youth, whom Ives delighted in; the soldier, who attracted Symonds and Ashbee; and the Arab, whom Burton and Jacobus X suggest had a predilection for sex with men. Aside from these objects of desire, there are the sexual consumers: the bohemian artist, the aristocrat and the dissipated old man. These men were not having sex, however, and the 'Quai de___' seems also to be a social space, somewhat like the roped-off area between Place de la Concorde and the Allée des Vieves in Paris discussed in the last chapter. Uninitiated into this milieu, and, as a middle-class merchant, failing to accord with any of these archetypes, Des Grieux wanders off directionless and finds himself 'standing in the middle of the bridge, staring vacantly at the open space in front of [him]'.[90] The riverside and the concert hall – both places for respectable recreation – have become overtly sexualised, challenging Des Grieux's conceptualisation of both the city and his own desires. He questions his own sanity and contemplates suicide but in the midst of this crisis Teleny appears and the pair begin to have sex on the bridge 'amidst the thickening fog', once again taking homosexual experimentation into darkness and obscurity.[91] Des Grieux and Teleny continue to have sex in the cab as they travel through the city and as they 'grope [their] way upstairs in the dark' at Teleny's house. Their union culminates in a secret chamber, 'a room', Teleny tells him, 'prepared to receive you, and where no man has ever set foot'.[92] Here they have anal sex, an act clearly prefigured by their passage through the house and the lengthy description of their ultimate destination, which has 'warm, soft, quilted' walls and floor.[93] The sequence of spaces and the movement between them are explicitly sexualised, appearing to both mirror and produce Des Grieux and Teleny's acts and desires.

This meshing of place and sex continues in the exclusive subculture Des Grieux now finds himself in. From a secret balcony at Braincourt's house, for example, Des Grieux watches Braincourt's fantastical experiences at the concert enacted in front of his eyes. He sees a great room decorated with 'lewd art worthy of Sodom or Babylon' in which bodies are, as Neil Bartlett suggests, 'converted into objects, luxuries, additions to a fabulous collection':[94]

On faded old damask couches, on huge pillows made out of priests' stoles . . . on soft Persian and Syrian divans, on lion and panther rugs, on mattresses covered with a variety of cats' skins, men, young and good-looking, almost all naked, were lounging by twos and threes, grouped in attitudes of consummate lewdness . . . such as are only seen in the brothels of men in lecherous Spain, or in those of the wanton East.[95]

The men are syntactically held over until the second half of the description and are offered up by the luxurious divans and rugs; they become part of an elaborate tableau of Mediterranean and Oriental debauchery. It is another magical fantasy space like the cruising ground, but this is for a wealthy elite who can afford its creation and control the participants. Alan Sinfield rightly points out that these 'gatherings' are initially unavailable to Des Grieux and it is only when he is invited in by the aristocratic Braincourt as a result of his affair with the bohemian Teleny that he gains entry.[96] Des Grieux is comforted by his observation that 'men of the highest intelligence, of the kindest heart, and of the purest aesthetic feelings, were – like [him]self – sodomists'.[97] The search for new sensation – which previously presented Des Grieux with effeminate old men, 'sturdy' workmen and female prostitutes – was accompanied by the fear not of moral retribution but social degradation: hell, he imagines, would be made unbearable by 'the low society we might meet there'.[98] Now these 'low' figures, fixed in their class and the spaces appropriate to them, are left behind. The society of wealth, bohemianism and decadence he moves on to generates a homoerotic circuit in which he can be a free agent and explore a variety of roles. Preparing for the masquerade, for example, Des Grieux is told of the potential personas he might take on – he could dress as a woman, soldier, sailor or tightrope dancer. At Teleny's request he finally dons 'a tight-fitting cycling suit', perhaps like the one Ives sometimes wore.[99] The city opens out for Des Grieux and becomes his own decadent playground.

In *The Picture of Dorian Gray* sexual activity and identity are figured through a series of urban spaces and are sustained for as long as the full extent of the circuit can be kept secret. Once the revelation occurs the spaces available contract and the decadent gloss dissipates. A similar outcome attends Des Grieux's exposure. When the scandal of Des Grieux and Teleny's affair 'had appeared in every newspaper' and Teleny's suicide note has become public property, Des Grieux becomes the subject of a 'famous clergyman's... edifying sermon' which prophesied that 'he shall have no name on the street' and 'shall be driven from light into darkness, and chased out of the world'.[100] As in *The Picture of Dorian Gray*, a conventional spatial dynamic is reimposed. The twist here is that Des Grieux, unlike Teleny and Dorian Gray, lives to tell the tale. His banishment is into the darkness and the anonymity of the streets – both of which were associated with dissident sexual activity. Des Grieux promises to detail further amorous adventures, involving his mother and Braincourt, and, more intriguingly, his *Doppelgänger*. As Des Grieux runs frantically through the streets after finding his mother having sex with Teleny, he collides with his 'own image'. It is this man who subsequently rescues Des Grieux from the river after a second suicide attempt. Des Grieux's anonymous interlocutor asks him if he ever saw his double again and Des Grieux replies 'that is another strange incident in my too-eventful life. Perhaps', he adds teasingly, 'I'll tell you some other time.'[101] The suggestion of further adventures beyond the text inverts the conclusion to Wilde's novel. There it is Dorian's relationship with his double, the painting, that both facilitated his decadent lifestyle but also ultimately kills him. In *Teleny* there is at least the suggestion of an amorous engagement between the two. The novel thus reworks the conclusion of *The Picture of Dorian Gray* and suggests further adventuring. Des Grieux's personal geography is curtailed after he is branded a sexual outlaw, but there is still potential for experimentation: existing in contravention of the prevailing moral order – and in a pornographic novel – yielded its own sexual possibilities.

Desire, identity and the city became mutable when viewed through an aesthetic and decadent prism, and the interaction of these three factors suggested apparently boundless scope for new sensation. However, whilst these two texts existed, in different ways and to varying degrees, on the margins of acceptability, and foregrounded the pursuit of pleasure and sensation, they also bolstered the status quo and drew on existing social structures and spatial dynamics to explore homosexuality and decadence. As Lisa Sigel comments in her work on Victorian pornography 'the desire to escape a conventional morality did not provide an instantaneous escape from the straightjacket of conventional social dynamics'.[102] Men trying to conceptualise an alternative sexual system had difficulty reaching outside the trenchant cultural and indeed subcultural norms which structured their lives and relationships.

In 'Paris, Capital of the Nineteenth Century' Walter Benjamin rounded on the aesthetic slogan 'l'art pour l'art', noting that: 'the solemnity with which it is celebrated is the corollary to the frivolity that glorifies the commodity. Both abstract from the social existence of men.'[103] The comparison is instructive since in these texts aestheticism and decadence are philosophically and practically dependent on the ability to consume. Money and position not only enable the domestic transformations enacted by Lord Henry, Dorian, Teleny and Braincourt, but also allow these men to participate in homoerotic and homosocial circuits and to pay the cabmen to transport them between the clubs, restaurants and theatres. These aesthetic and decadent fantasies of city space were dependent on privilege and rested on the maintenance of existing social structures. Securing new pleasures and sensations required an underclass to facilitate them; the mechanised servants envisaged by Wilde in 'The Soul of a Man Under Socialism' are nowhere to be seen in these novels. This kind of urban sexual experimentation was apparently the preserve of an elite group, with walk-on parts for soldiers, servants, workmen and exotic foreigners. The aristocratic and bohemian figures transgress boundaries, between public and private and east and west, for example, but they also reaffirm them, since it is the act of transgression itself which is rendered erotic.[104] The boundary and the space on the other side are essential, as are the restricted figures who serve as foils to the mobile protagonists. In *Teleny* the desires of the foreigners and lower-class men and women are obscured or invented as receptive and ubiquitous, just as they often were in sexology, the anthropological texts of Burton and Jacobus X, the newspapers and the earlier pornographic work, *Sins of the Cities of the Plain*.

The power dynamics and economic realities that structured city life nonetheless impinge on the decadent urban pleasures depicted in the texts. Decadence and aestheticism placed the onus on the individual and suggested his autonomy, but in *The Picture of Dorian Gray* and *Teleny* this is something the protagonists ultimately lose or never really possess. The fact that their experiences are individualised and not shared also means that social interaction almost inevitably disappoints. The cities over which Des Esseintes, Dorian Gray and Des Grieux imagine some sort of mastery ultimately defeat them because these cities have an existence in the novels beyond the imaginations of these figures. The disappointments or disasters each of them experiences emanate from the intrusion into their fantasies of wider social and economic structures on which their philosophies of experience are paradoxically reliant; London thus seems both to invite and thwart fantastical recreation and sensual indulgence.

THE DECADENT MENACE

This implicit constraint and an associated predictability was ridiculed in numerous parodies of the aesthetic and decadent movements, and of Oscar Wilde and his circle in particular. Chief among them were W. S. Gilbert's comic opera *Patience* (1881), George Du Maurier's cartoons in *Punch*, particularly between 1879 and 1885, and two novels, Robert Hichens' *The Green Carnation* and G. S. Street's *Autobiography of a Boy*, both published in 1894. Each of these works centred on London and defined the aesthete and decadent precisely, producing a constrictive stereotype from a stance supposedly predicated on individualised and unique sensual experimentation. *The Autobiography of a Boy* is the fictional memoir of Tubby, a young effeminate aesthete who lives in Jermyn Street. It is prefaced by an apology from the 'editor': 'I perceived that if I published it in all its length nobody would read it: his life in England was not various, his orbit was circumscribed, the people he met and the situations he faced had a certain sameness, the comments he made on them dealt in repetitions.'[105] *The Green Carnation* similarly trades on the restrictiveness of the aesthetic pose in a parody of Wilde, his circle and *The Picture of Dorian Gray*, which makes an appearance in the novel as *The Soul of Bertie Brown*. The two central characters, Araminth, 'who smacked essentially of cities',[106] and Lord Reggie, his young sidekick, are involved in some predictable transgressions: 'There are moments when I desire squalor, sinister mean surroundings, dreariness and misery. The great unwashed mood is upon me. Then I go out from luxury. The mind has its West End and its Whitechapel. The thoughts sit in the park sometimes, but sometimes they go slumming.'[107] Dorian's abject wanderings, complex psyche and driven search for new sensation become facile and his sins banal: 'we are to sin on the housetop and in the street, instead of in the privacy of a room with a door locked', reports Lady Locke, adding: 'what will the London County Council say?'[108] Lord Reggie is described mincing through the opera house in a rendition of Wilde and his friends' theatrical late entry to the premiere of *Lady Windermere's Fan*.[109] Lady Locke observes that he is 'not a man at all'.[110] *The Autobiography of a Boy* similarly mocks the compromised masculinity of the aesthete: Tubby despairs of the 'mania for outdoor sports that afflicts the country' and is more concerned about whether his smoking jacket matches his new rug.[111]

Concerns for English masculinity were voiced more seriously in a cluster of articles around the same time. The *National Observer* noted shortly before the Wilde trials: 'The time has surely come when there should be an end of this, and when every man who cares for the manhood of literature should lift his pen against so disgraceful a crew.'[112] The writer Grant Allen, though keen to challenge late Victorian sexual hypocrisy, expressed anxiety about the contravention of gender norms: 'we see that each man and each woman holds his virility and her femininity in trust for humanity and that to play fast and loose with either . . . is fraught with danger for the state and for future generations'.[113]

The danger became more pressing with the trials of 1895 when Wilde, decadent art and gross indecency were conflated in court and in condemnatory newspaper editorials. His writing was used as evidence against him and was discussed in conjunction with details of his apparently excessive sexual and culinary consumption and the luxurious surroundings in which this consumption had often taken place. If the domestic interior could prompt an aestheticised or decadent vision of the world outside, it could also incriminate: speaking not only of the occupant's artistic philosophy but of behaviour at odds with prevailing sexual and social norms. The *Evening News* labelled Wilde 'one of the high priests of a school which attacks all the wholesome, manly, simple ideals of English life, and sets up false gods of decadent culture and intellectual debauchery'.[114] The *Star*, at the opening of the trials, was more circumspect. It claimed that 'the literature of the decadence contains much which is admirable and something that will live' but also noted that beside the 'saner element' 'there has existed a parasite, an excrescence, an aberration which diligent advertisement has made more or less familiar to the public against its will'. The piece concluded: 'the ultimate effect of recent disclosures should be to strengthen health and right and reason – that kind of art which Plato had in mind when he spoke of the refreshing winds that blow from healthy regions'.[115] The *Telegraph*, finally, reiterated the French connection: 'Everybody can see and read for himself, and every honest and wholesome-minded Englishman must grieve to notice, how largely this French and Pagan plague has filtered into the healthy fields of English life [undermining] the natural affections, the domestic joys, the sanctity and sweetness of the home.'[116] At a time of particular tension between France and England following the French alliance with Russia in 1894, such influences were especially threatening, and these commentators tended towards the promotion of a cleansing and tacitly pastoral Englishness. Decadence was the inverse: it was French, urban, excessive, contagious and parasitic, vampirically draining the nation's life blood. It anarchically threatened a vaunted if illusory English domestic and social orderliness.

That Bram Stoker began *Dracula* in 1895 is thus hardly surprising, and Stoker's ambivalence towards Wilde and the decadent menace is evident in the text. Talia Schaffer shows how a careful reading of the dates and detail in the novel indicates a close association with Wilde's experience and aspects of Stoker's own biography, particularly his intense friendships with men.[117] An analogy between the novel and contemporary critiques of decadence and degeneracy is certainly compelling: the novel imagines a foreign invader with ambivalent desires, prowling the city for victims, existing apart from the domestic arena and potentially sapping the health of the new generation. This figure is also alluring, however, and Stoker seems sometimes to be in the thrall of the sexually transgressive undercurrent of the work. The novel uncovers the potential for sexual transgression and disorder in the city, and to an extent revels in it. However, whilst in *The Picture of Dorian Gray* the pleasures and consequences are focussed on an individual, in *Dracula* there are wider implications and there is a more pressing need for action. The defeat of the vampire marks not only the end of a lone sexual pervert but also the salvation of the family, future generations and the nation. The individual intensity of *The Picture of Dorian Gray* opens out into an analysis of potential national crisis and eleventh-hour redemption in Stoker's novel, reflecting wider fears of imperial and racial decline.

Alan Sinfield and Ed Cohen both show Wilde's conviction to be a key moment of definition; it was the point at which diffuse indicators of homosexuality cohered into a fixed stereotype and the long-parodied aesthetic and decadent pose became a more serious threat. The emergence of Wilde as an archetypical homosexual headed off, Sinfield suggests, 'the Victorian exploration of diverse models of same-sex relations'.[118] The publicity attending Wilde's strident pose and his ultimate downfall, and the potential suggested by his writing, provided an obvious – though not the only – template and frame of reference for those seeking to explore and to condemn homosexuality in the capital and beyond. The male prostitute in the New York case study in Ellis' *Sexual Inversion* went by the name of Dorian Gray, for example, drawing on the potential suggested by Wilde's fiction. Conversely, E. M. Forster's fictional Maurice uses Dorian's creator to describe his desires and identity to Dr Barry: he is 'an unspeakable of the Oscar Wilde sort'.[119] It is important to observe, though, that if the trial manufactured an infamous image of the modern homosexual, it did not comprehensively stall the circulation of other ideas and explanatory narratives, as the other chapters show. Neither did it usher in a period of increased constraint and puritanism, as Holbrook Jackson seductively claimed in 1913: 'The chance romances of the streets were abandoned for the reputedly more certain realities of home life. Bohemians cut their locks, shed their soft collars and fell back upon suburbia... even dandyism of thought and word disappeared; for once you live in the suburb, there is nothing left but to become ordinary.'[120] Despite the mythology surrounding the *fin de siècle* and the decadence of the 1880s and the early 1890s, there was a limit to the libertinism and abandon of the pre-trial period, just as there was to the supposed restrictiveness of the years that followed. In Wilde's prison 'letter', *De Profundis*, London in the early 1890s emerged as a place where free will might be surrendered as well as exercised. Wilde described London and the affairs he had there as suffocating and ruinous. The text detailed containment within a circuit of restaurants, clubs and hotels, intrusions into his home and chambers, and an attempted escape to Paris from London and his lover. In this account the city that created him, gave him his celebrity and permitted his pose, initially distracted him from his art, and finally led to his literal incarceration. The tension between urban liberation and debilitation which runs through *The Picture of Dorian Gray* is rendered even more vividly in *De Profundis*, and in the final pages Wilde imagined abandoning the city and embracing nature: 'She will cleanse me in great waters, and with bitter herbs wash me whole', he wrote.[121] Wilde envisaged a fragmentary urban self in *The Picture of Dorian Gray* but in *De Profundis* this is set against the potential for a unified, complete, 'natural' being, a figure who preoccupied the writers examined in the next chapter.

After the trials there was no purge of homosexual activity and nor was there a sudden drop in convictions. Arrests and prosecutions continued, rising intermittently, but showing no dramatic change until 1911, almost fifteen years after Wilde's imprisonment. Men clearly did not 'retreat to suburbia' as Jackson claimed or abandon the city for the continent as Frank Harris suggested.[122] These accounts of events obscure the fact that a subculture endured in the city. It was perhaps more discreet but it was nevertheless determinedly present. Men cruised for sex in the city's streets and parks, and also continued to be involved in exclusive subcultural activity. Roger Casement found plentiful sexual opportunities for casual sex in London in the years immediately preceding the Great War, and Ives' Order of the Chaerona continued to grow in the post-Wilde era. In 1912, Madame Strindberg opened the Cave of the Golden Calf club in Heddon Street, just off Regent Street, which developed a reputation for sexual freedom and tolerance of same-sex relations.[123] The Marquis of Anglesey, Iwan Bloch reported, could be seen in the first years of the new century walking confidently through Mayfair in perfume and rings and with a 'pink-ribboned poodle'.[124] Robert Ross, Wilde's loyal friend and literary executor, maintained both his aesthetic demeanour and his place in society, including his friendship with the Asquiths.[125] Periodicals associated with decadence were launched after Wilde's conviction; *The Savoy*, which appeared in 1896, was provocatively named after the hotel with had featured prominently in the trials. Wilde's plays continued to be performed and his collected works were published in 1908, in an acknowledgement of his cultural importance.[126] The influence of Wilde and the movements he symbolised were not easily curtailed. 'The cult of Wilde', as Philip Hoare terms it, endured, and the playwright's work continued to have an impact – with additional homoerotic resonances – post-1895. Even though *The Picture of Dorian Gray* and *Teleny* did not envisage a radical disturbance of the social order, they were significant in suggesting the scope for an individualised engagement with the city and homosexual desire. They drew on the flux of urban life and the associations of other places to depict the city as an arena which sustained, for a time at least, a dissident sexual lifestyle.

CHAPTER 5

The Hellenic city

The decadent meeting of the self and the city imagined by Huysmans, Wilde and the anonymous authors of *Teleny* was problematic for men like John Addington Symonds, Edward Carpenter and George Ives. The explicit rejection of nature and the emphasis on lush interiors, artifice and performativity went against the grain of the sexological biological imperative and the neo-Hellenic conceptualization of relations between men to which these men subscribed. The metropolitan context seemed to degrade homosexuality and made it appear part of a wider urban malaise. Symonds, for example, noted the 'disease' of effeminacy in modern cities and that 'in modern society the inverted passion has to be indulged furtively, spasmodically, hysterically'.[1] In *Homogenic Love* Carpenter wrote that in 'the great cities there are to be found associated with this form of attachment prostitution and other evils comparable with the evils associated with the ordinary sex attachment'.[2] Ives was more specific, wishing Wilde's set would be 'less extravagant and more real' and finding the 'style of the men' in a Parisian bar 'contemptible'. He was also dismissive of the 'silly inverts' dancing in the streets on Bastille day.[3] This urban frivolity seemed to him to be a betrayal of the emancipatory 'cause', apparently confirming the imagery filtering through the newspaper press of a hedonistic and degraded lifestyle and, perhaps more importantly, compromising the version of masculinity Ives and these other men were each keen to affirm in their renditions of the homosexual or invert. The city was nevertheless difficult to avoid and their appeal to Hellenism was itself in part based on an idealised version of Athenian democratic citizenship.[4] The ancient Greeks, together with fantasies of a rural idyll, nevertheless provided an escape within the modern city and also framed a new politics of homosexuality there.

Wilde's evocation of ancient Greece at his trial and his appeal to nature in *De Profundis* resonated powerfully with contemporary ideas of Englishness. The transformation of central London in building projects of the second half of the nineteenth century was part of an attempt to secure a triumphal imperial image for the city and nation.[5] Yet national identity was often more closely aligned with images and fantasies of rural England, especially as the nation became more urbanised and culturally and economically centralised.[6] 'London', wrote the early sociologist Georg Simmel in 1903, 'has never acted as England's heart, though often as England's intellect and always as her money bag.'[7] The harsh and disquieting realities of rural life were sidelined in images propagated by a middle- and upper-class elite who had been nurtured through the orderly worlds of the public schools, often in semi-rural settings.[8] This vision combined images of tamed nature and settled communities, apparently directly at odds with the chaos and social instability of London in particular. Indeed, nature was repeatedly enlisted in the attempted salvation of the city and the city dweller. Ruskin extolled the virtues of architecture which reconnected with nature in *The Stones of Venice* (1851–3)[9] and Charles Kingsley wrote of the potential reimposition of social order though new ruralised suburbs encircling London. He saw urban discontent being soothed with the balm of pseudo-country living. William Morris' *News from Nowhere* (1891) famously reimagined London as a socialist and ruralised utopia and Havelock Ellis' *The Nineteenth Century: A Dialogue in Utopia* (1899) similarly emphasised the radical and restorative power of rural life. In the 1880s and 1890s the Arts and Crafts movement, Guild of Handicrafts and Utopian Fellowship of the New Life associated themselves strongly with an ideal of rural working and living practices.[10] These groups were nevertheless each based in London, at least initially, indicating again the peculiar tension between the imperative for radical groups to engage with the city[11] and the potent redemptive utopian fantasies which clung to the countryside.

Alongside the pastoral many Victorian commentators appealed to ancient Greek culture, society and philosophy. Figures as diverse as John Stuart Mill, Matthew Arnold, Charles Kingsley and Benjamin Jowett, the Oxford scholar, saw in Hellenism the potential to reinvigorate national life.[12] If Kingsley valued the rural for its ability to temper discontent, he valued the ancient Greeks for their emphasis on the development of body and mind in tandem. In 'Nausicaa in London' (1873), for example, he compared the supposed perfection of ancient Greek bodily form to the modern urban degenerate. In the British Museum he found:

Fair and grand forms; the forms of men and women whose every limb and attitude betokened perfect health and grace and power, and self-possession and self-restraint so habitual and complete that it had become unconscious...I had been up and down the corridors of those Greek sculptures, which remain as a perpetual sermon to rich and poor amid our artificial, unwholesome, and, it may be, decaying, pseudo-civilisation.[13]

Kingsley noted the Hellenic onus on physical development and argued that exercise and outdoor activity were the means through which the effects of urban degeneration might be avoided and English 'virtues' recovered. He suggested that through exercise and mental rigour the 'mothers of our future rulers' might measure up to the idealised figure of Nausicaa, the daughter of Alcinous, King of Phaeacians in Homer's *Odyssey*.[14]

Matthew Arnold and J. S. Mill found in Socratic and Platonic thought a philosophy which stressed independence of opinion and self-development. 'The Greeks', wrote Arnold, 'pursued freedom and pursued gymnastics not mechanically, but with a constant reference to some ideal of complete human perfection and happiness.'[15] Jowett meanwhile made Plato central to the reformed Greats curriculum at Oxford as part of his drive to develop a 'civic elite' serving nation and empire.[16]

In art, architecture, education, politics, philosophy and social reform, the ancient Greeks were evoked and compared to Victorian society, either as a mirror to English virtues or as an endorsement to do better. More specifically, ancient Athens seemed to indicate how, with a comprehensive social philosophy and sense of direction, urban life could serve as a force for social unity and order rather than fragmentation. Evelyn Abbot's *Pericles and the Golden Age of Athens*, which emphasised the putatively unifying social structure of the city, was published in 1891, whilst Plutarch's *Lives of the Noble Grecians and Romans*, containing an account of the foundation of Athens in the 'Life of Theseus', went through at least fifteen complete editions between 1850 and 1914.[17]

Both Hellenism and pastoralism promised stability, a counter to degeneracy and a clearer idea of national identity. They heralded other spaces, including Athens, Arcadia and the English greenwood, and used the muscular body as a symbol of health, vitality, personal endeavour and self-restraint.[18] At a time when fears about the city were focussed on the degenerate, criminal, prostituted and effeminate body, these versions of corporeal perfection provided an important counter. An athletic physique could signify not only personal vitality, but also national strength and prowess.

The appeals to Hellenism and pastoralism in the name of urban and national revival were echoed in writing by many middle- and upper-class men who sought justification for their homosexual desires. Their appeal to the ancient Greeks tied a particular conceptualisation of homosexuality closely to national- and class-bound culture, as well as to movements for social reform. Whilst pastoralism allowed for claims about the naturalness of desire, Hellenism conjured a social system in which homosexuality had supposedly been an accepted and integrated part. It provided two particular justificatory strands. The first centred on the Theban bands, who were described in 'The Life of Pelopidas' in Plutarch's *Lives of the Noble Grecians and Romans*.[19] The bands were composed of men fighting alongside their male lovers and were revered for their bravery. They stood undefeated until the Battle of the Chaerona in 338BC, when Greece was colonised by the Romans. Ives named the support and pressure group he formed in the early 1890s after the battle and repeatedly imagined his own fight for legitimacy in terms of martial force, persistence and bravery. In 'A Problem in Greek Ethics' (1883) John Addington Symonds described their defeat presaging the decay not only of a unique form of comradeship but also of a supreme military spirit.[20]

The second line of justification blended ideas of martial prowess and stoical comradeship with the Hellenic pedagogical philosophy of self-development. The crucial texts were Plato's *Republic* and *Symposium*. The love of an older man for a beautiful youth could lead to a love of beauty and wisdom itself, it was argued, and so aid the emotional and spiritual growth of the citizen. The youth, meanwhile, benefited from the older man's wisdom and gained an induction into Athenian life. Less directly, the ancient Greek invocation to self-realisation, so valued by John Stuart Mill, fed into Symonds' argument for the acceptance of individual impulses, implicitly including homosexual desires. 'We must acknowledge', he wrote in *Studies of the Greek Poets*, 'the value of each human impulse, and aim after virtues that depend on self-regulation rather than on total abstinence and mortification.'[21]

Both justificatory strands found a cogent symbol in Greek statuary and the image of the perfect male body – and so also in the British Museum galleries, as chapter 1 observed. As for Kingsley and the proponents of physical culture, such statuesque perfection signified an ordered understanding of identity and desire. Walter Pater noted in his deeply homoerotic piece on Johann Winckelmann that the Hellenic male nude showed 'man at unity with himself, with his physical nature, with the outward world'.[22] With their unbroken surfaces and fixed relationship to their surroundings, statues seemed to provide a model of certainty in the face of complex desires and amidst the confusion of the modern city.[23]

Late Victorian homophile writers were selective in their seizure of the ancient Greeks. They stressed pedagogy and comradeship and sidelined the repressive and hierarchical nature of Athenian culture. Athenian life was neither so stable nor so democratic as many in the later nineteenth century chose to believe. Men often used sex with youths, women and slaves to affirm their position as citizens rather than as part of a pedagogical process or a meeting of minds.[24] Neither did the Athenians provide a model of exclusivity in sexual taste being touted by the sexologists and the writers considered here. Ancient Greece nonetheless represented something of a panacea for many men; it provided a private logic for dissident desires as well as a wider model for legitimacy. Symonds, Carpenter and Ives each described adolescent epiphanies prompted by Greek statuary,[25] and Wilde eloquently used Platonic logic at his trial to justify his friendships with younger men. Linda Dowling comments: 'Against [the] older discourse of the English common law . . . Wilde deployed a new and powerful vocabulary of personal identity, a language of mind, sensibility and emotion, of inward and intellectual relations.' The self-conscious assumption of these values, Dowling goes on to argue, fed into modern understandings of homosexual identity, as men began to see that their homoerotic desires might 'belong to human experience in its fullest historicity and cultural density'.[26]

These men used a particular version of Hellenic history to situate their experiences and understandings of homosexuality. It provided an argument for reform, a place for homosexuality within society, a physical ideal, an arena in which to take imaginative resort and a language in which to discuss male love and beauty – a language which sidestepped the prevailing legal and journalistic vocabulary. Finally, Symonds, Carpenter, Ives and Pater were elaborating an existing and accepted discourse. As such it was harder to contest than the decadent and aesthetic movements, which, despite being rooted in part in the same Hellenic valorisation of beauty, did not have the same cultural kudos. This is true even though there were increasingly clear lines connecting 'Greek love' to the acts of gross indecency reported in the papers.[27] Most obviously, Wilde's invocation of Greek love in court failed to win him an acquittal, bringing the Hellenic ideal into close proximity with his sexual behaviour. Homoerotic work drawing on Hellenism nevertheless continued to be published throughout the period and, the critic Timothy d'Arch Smith shows, until at least the 1930s.[28] It had become a barely obscured code which yet enabled continuing communication about an outlawed set of practices.

A key conduit of this literature in the late 1880s and early 1890s was *The Artist and Journal of Home Culture* under the editorship of Charles Kains Jackson. The journal, Laurel Brake demonstrates, skilfully managed to carry 'homosexual material and keep the homosocial reader on board without offending his male and female heterosexual readers'.[29] It did this partly through the evocation of ancient Greece, which could serve both homophile and national culture. The homoerotic vein was nevertheless pronounced. Virtually every edition during Jackson's tenure included poetry which evoked the fantasy of youths with the idealised bodies of Greek statues bathing naked, and often there were also articles and reviews which reinforced such Hellenic and pastoral themes and images. This material suggested ordered identifications and stable power relations between a voyeuristic narrator and the bathing boys. The effect was achieved partly through the specific exclusion of urban referents which might complicate the picture. The final issue of *The Artist* with Jackson as editor – April 1894 – contained multiple images of male homosexuality. These included Lord Alfred Douglas' love poem for a sixteen-year-old boy, 'Prince Charming', a bathing ballad by John Gambril Nicholson, a review of the decadent artist Aubrey Beardley by Theodore Wratislaw – whose poem 'To a Sicilian Boy' had been published in *The Artist* the previous year –[30] and Jackson's own 'The New Chivalry', written under his pseudonym PC, the initials of his middle names. 'The New Chivalry' suggested that whereas the Old Chivalry found its ideal in the 'youthful feminine ideal', 'the flower of the adult and perfect civilisation will be found in the ... exaltation of the youthful masculine ideal'. The piece went on to argue that this new civilisation would especially value 'Nature's most intimate and instructive bond of sympathy', Jackson's euphemism for homosexual relations. This he legitimised through nature and by evoking the Hellenic 'tenderness of elder for younger'.[31] In a letter to Jackson, written from Wilde's chambers in St James', Douglas called the piece 'brilliant and daring'.[32] Whether it also presaged his departure from the journal is unclear; Brake suggests there may also have been a financial and commercial imperative.[33] Whatever the reasons, *The Artist* changed considerably under its new editor, Lord Mountmorres, an Oxford contemporary of Douglas. Douglas complained of the appointment in a further letter to Jackson: 'I never heard that he was at all sympathetic. I know he was recently married.'[34] With Mountmorres as editor the format and style were altered, and the 'Journal of Home Culture' suffix was dropped. In September 1894 an obituary to the 'old' magazine was published, which acknowledged both the escapist and idyllic fantasy in which the journal had indulged to that point and the 'bitter' practicality of its business thereafter.

> A change is to come over the nature of our dream. After fifteen years wandering through the peaceful land of perpetual afternoon *The Artist* is to set forth a commercial warrior to conquer the regions of money and trade, and henceforth it will lead its followers, not through the valleys... and veil-like, slow-dropping waterfalls, but in the busy haunts of men amid the strife and turmoil of the city.

The piece went on to herald 'the deadly, bitter, unwelcome return to life and reality' as the reader 'rise[s] and set[s] out to haggle in the crowded mart'.[35] The writer explicitly noted a return to the city, from which the journal had apparently turned its back, but s/he also suggested that this departure had in any case only been a flight of fancy, and that the 'business' of art, artists and the magazine itself were grounded in 'reality', in the 'crowded mart' of the metropolis.

Jackson's demise as editor did not mark an end to published versions of the Hellenic and pastoral fantasy. *The Studio: An Illustrated Magazine of Fine and Applied Arts* – a competitor, suggests Brake, for the 'pink market niche' between 1893 and 1894[36] – published Wilhelm von Gloeden and Frederick Rolfe's photographs of naked male youths in ancient Greek and North African settings and costumes in its second issue of June 1893, alongside an article called 'The Nude in Photography'.[37] The imagery once again suggested the homoerotic freedom and possibilities of an idealised 'elsewhere'. In Von Gloeden's case this 'elsewhere' was the Sicilian fishing village of Taormina, which he made famous from the 1890s through his photography and which, Lisa Sigel suggests, was repackaged as a 'latter-day Greek polis', attracting wealthy men keen to share in the fantasy.[38] George Ives collected images printed in other magazines, including one of two naked youths embracing, with the by-line, 'The spirit of ancient Greece recreated for the camera',[39] and there were also novels and collections of poetry published throughout the period which explored homosexual attachments via similar themes and images.[40] Mention of the city in this work was infrequent and disparaging but it also becomes clear that the Hellenic idiom and the references to contemporary Greece and Italy were a means of legitimising and sustaining a set of desires in more immediate, though less ideal, times and places. In *The Artist*, for example, mention of the city was minimal in the years 1888 to 1894, as the editorial after Jackson's departure suggested. Yet the journal's advertisements and commentaries on plays and exhibitions were focussed on London and the West End.

The Artist also noted the appearance of the 'exquisitely pure' green carnation in town, along with instructions on its manufacture and a revealing denial that they were unmanly or effeminate.[41] *The Artist* was published in London – by Wells, Gardner, Darton and Co – and Jackson and many of the contributors also lived in the city. It functioned as a rallying point for a group of well-educated upper-middle class and upper-class readers and contributors whose social and sexual lives seem to have centred on London.[42] Ives and Douglas' letters to Jackson indicate a sense of common cause and register some of the harsh realities associated with homosexual life in the city. In 1893, for example, Douglas asked for help from Jackson 'in the name of the cause' for 'a poor man Burnand [of Buckingham Palace Road] who is now awaiting trial'.[43] Later he wrote again, demanding from Jackson an explanation as to why he had given up the editorship: 'I look in vain for any sympathetic matter [in the latest edition]. Surely you have not deserted the cause and deprived us of our only organ of expression.'[44] The vision of open unconstrained pastoral and Hellenic spaces in the journal carried the reader out of the urban mêlée and provided sustenance for life within it. Indeed, given the strong existing links between homosexuality and the city, these fantasies themselves evoked, and were predicated upon, the urban antithesis.

The ambivalence towards the city implicit in these escapist fantasies also ran through the *Memoirs* of John Addington Symonds, which he was writing in the immediate aftermath of the Cleveland Street scandal and during Kains Jackson's tenure at *The Artist*. Symonds drew consistently on the ancient Greeks in his personal relationships with men and in his arguments for the reform of attitudes towards homosexuality. The former were described in detail in his *Memoirs*; the latter were outlined most vigorously in 'A Problem in Greek Ethics' (1883) and 'A Problem in Modern Ethics'(1891). Symonds found the aspects of the city which drew Dorian Gray east too unpredictable and overpowering to accommodate his more ascetic vision of desire in which self-realisation was coupled with self-control and social responsibility. He nevertheless returned repeatedly to the metropolis in his writing to track the genesis of his desires and the sexual crises he experienced, from his boyhood fantasies of 'sailors, such as [he] had seen about he streets of Bristol' to his fleeting encounter with a 'young grenadier' in 1865 in an alley between Trafalgar and Leicester Squares – an area described by Sala as a 'choked up labyrinth of noisome courts and alleys' before the construction of Charing Cross Road in 1887.[45] Symonds refused the grenadier's proposition and 'broke away from him with a passionate mixture of fascination and revulsion'.[46] He experienced a similar sensation later when he saw a 'rude *graffito*' – 'an emblematic diagram of phallic meeting, glued together gushing', accompanied by the words 'prick to prick so sweet' – scrawled on a wall 'in the sordid streets' just to the west of Regent's Park. Symonds wrote:

> Wandering [one] day for exercise through the sordid streets between my home [near Paddington Station] and Regents Park I felt the burden of a ponderous malaise...While returning from this fateful constitutional, at a certain corner, which I well remember, my eyes were caught by a rude *graffito* scrawled with pencil upon slate. It was so concentrated, so stimulative, so penetrative a character – so thoroughly the voice of vice and passion in the proletariat – that it pierced the very marrow of my soul...now the wolf leapt out: my malaise of the moment was converted into a clairvoyant and tyrannical appetite for the thing which I had rejected five months earlier in the alley by the barracks. The vague and morbid craving of the previous years defined itself as a precise hunger after sensual pleasure, whereof I had not dreamed before save in repulsive visions of the night.[47]

Symonds found himself profoundly affected by the urban fabric. Not only did the 'sordid streets' seem responsible for his 'malaise', but the *graffito* incited and focussed his desires. The labyrinthine aspect of London produced appetites which were, for him, vicious and predatory. What disturbed him particularly was the precision the urban context gave them: 'vague cravings' become 'concentrated' and 'precise', apparently precluding human and admitting only genital contact. In these 'sordid streets' Symonds was transported into his tortured dream world and the city became nightmarish. Morris Kaplan convincingly argues that this encounter, together with others described by Symonds in the *Memoirs*, indicate contradictory impulses: 'animal desire', a quest for comradeship and an attempt to 'domesticate' same-sex desire in line with prevailing notions of middle-class respectability.[48]

Symonds' response to 'the voice of vice and passion in the proletariat' shifted in his move to the Graubünden in the Swiss Alps. There he enthused about the purity and simplicity of the people and their unity with their surroundings. 'When I came to live among peasants and republicans in Switzerland', he wrote, 'I am certain that I took up passionate relations with men in a more natural and intelligible manner – more rightly and democratically – than I should otherwise have done.'[49] Symonds reported that he 'kept aloof' in the Graubünden 'from those who had been sophisticated by residence in foreign cities'.[50] He shielded himself from what he saw as his own potentially depraved longings by shunning the city and those who lived there. The metropolis introduced something more disturbing than

Symonds could countenance and instead he sought to frame his desires with a philosophy of rural comradeship. Switzerland softened the implications of abuse that often accompanied reports of cross-class relations in the city and which were of course powerfully suggested in the Cleveland Street scandal.

The city nevertheless provided solace for Symonds and he was also able to locate his Hellenic and pastoral ideal of homosexual relations within the urban context. In his *Memoirs* he recounted a visit to London from Switzerland in 1877 during which he visited a male brothel near the Regent's Park Barracks on Albany Street. With a 'strapping young soldier' Symonds 'enjoyed the close vicinity of that splendid naked piece of manhood'. After sex he 'made him clothe himself, sat and smoked and talked with him, and felt, at the end of the whole transaction, that some at least of the deepest moral problems might be solved by fraternity'. He added: 'I met him several times again, in public places, without any thought of vice.'[51] The brothel provided a specifically urban but also insulated space where Symonds could conjure comradeship out of sex in a way that the chance encounter with the grenadier and the *graffito* in the 'sordid' streets seemed to preclude.[52] The possibility of ambush was removed and Symonds maintained control: he visited the brothel voluntarily, not through importuning, and directed the relationship with the soldier – 'making' him dress and talk after sex, for example. It was this that rendered the whole event acceptable for Symonds, ironically allowing him to derive a sense of reciprocity – 'we parted the best of friends, exchanging addresses' – from the indulgence of what he called his 'sophisticated passion'.[53] This passion, he seemed to assume, was not – or could not be – shared in the same way by his working-class companion. The sex and post-coital conversation in the brothel nevertheless did their work for Symonds and the relationship did not implicate urban vice for him but a more laudable and 'respectable' fraternity. With this man by his side, the public spaces they met in subsequently were less threatening, less likely to evoke his 'wolf of desire'. We do not know what the soldier made of the meeting, or of the construction Symonds put on it, but for Symonds himself it was part of what was most promising about 'masculine love'. 'Where it appears', he wrote to Edward Carpenter in 1893, 'it abolishes class distinctions, and opens by a single operation the cataract-blinded eye to their futilities.'[54] He does not seem to conceive that it might have been precisely the cross-class nature of their liaison which so excited him.[55]

The metaphor of blindness in his letter to Carpenter is significant because gazing is a key erotic modus operandi of Symonds' work, from his

Studies in the Greek Poets (1879) to his elegiac *In the Key of Blue* (1893), in which he observes his Venetian lover Augustus Fusato in a series of tableaux around Venice.[56] The gaze seems almost to stand in for sex, as it does for the narrators watching the bathing youths in the poetry in *The Artist*. Fleeting exchanged glances, like those Ives reported and enjoyed as he walked and cycled around London, are, Henning Bech suggests, key to ideas of modern homosexual identity. As we saw in chapter 2, the play of visibility and invisibility, and recognition and misrecognition, were important to the homosexual dynamic in London during the period. This complex urban experience contrasts with the supposedly more stable and certain gaze and to what Bech describes as the 'all-embracing visibility' associated with the countryside.[57] Symonds hankered after this apparent simplicity and paradoxically he sometimes found it in London. As he watched the men bathing at the Serpentine in Hyde Park and at the Embankment ponds he was able to indulge in fantasies of cross-class connection whilst again avoiding the disturbing untempered passions he experienced elsewhere. In his poem 'The Song of the Swimmer' (1867), a poem pasted into the manuscript of his 'Memoirs', he described the scene at the Embankment in epic terms: 'a young rough' is transformed into 'a Greek hero' as he strips and enters the lake. 'His firm and vital flesh, white, rounded, radiant, shone upon the sward ... I followed him with swift eyes, as a slave his master.' The narrator's soul – personified as feminine in line with the conceptualisation of the 'Uranian' as a man's body with a woman's soul – pursues her hero for an erotic embrace: 'My soul was not less ardent than his joy. She thrust her arms about his breast; she felt his arms throb, the dew drops dried beneath her clasp.' Finally, 'the rough' kneels upon the grass and 'quickly resumed his clothes'. 'The beautiful bright god was hidden; the hero disappeared.'[58] A similar scene at the Embankment ponds is described in the published *Memoirs*.[59] As was observed in chapter 1, many men – Walter Pater, E. M. Forster and the poet A. E. Housman among them – found a similar potential for stillness, contemplation and fantasy in the British Museum statue galleries. These places were particularly valuable precisely because they were in the midst of the frenetic city.

Symonds was searching for stable sexual identifications framed by Hellenic self-control, Whitmanesque comradery and rural muscularity. Yet in his *Memoirs* and poetry particular parts of London were used to mark out his desires and the development of his sexual and political philosophy. He defined his brand of inversion in specific opposition to the random 'vice' of the labyrinthine city streets and the lack of self-control they invited and represented, but he also found comfort and the scope to indulge in some neo-Hellenic hero worship at the Serpentine and Embankment ponds, and in the brothel, where he brought to his relationship with the guardsmen a sense of the camaraderie he had found in Switzerland and Venice. The meanings Symonds found in these spaces were partly determined by broader discourses touting urban depravity on the one hand and pastoral simplicity and Hellenic self-possession on the other. As with Wilde, a radical disassociation from domineering languages of the city and society was impossible, and they braced Symonds' work. His language resonated with Kingsley's description of the degenerate city, the wholesome countryside and the inimitable Greeks in 'Nausicaa in London', for example. However, the very ideas of variety, dislocation and chaos which characterised the city during this period and before, and the confusion of histories and possibilities London presented, also allowed for what was particular in these explorations and experiences of desire. The conjunction of diverse spaces and meanings meant there was somewhere even in the metropolis which could affirm rather than disrupt his fantasies and sexual ethos.

REFORM AND THE URBAN SCENE

Symonds' dedication to comradeship and fraternity was partly derived from his passion for the work of American poet Walt Whitman. He claimed that Whitman's poetry carried him 'back to ancient Greece – to Plato's *Symposium*, to Philip gazing on the sacred bands of Thebans after their fight at Chaerona'.[60] Whereas Symonds' relationship with the city was uneasy, tinged with sadness and a longing for elsewhere, what is striking about Whitman's verse – and especially the 'Calamus' sequence in *Leaves of Grass* (1855) – is the centrality of the city to his exploration of the relationship between homosocial bonds, selfhood and democracy. He deftly closes in on the American metropolis and uses it simultaneously as a material setting for the 'swift flash of eyes offering me love' and as a broader metaphor for fraternity and connection. Whitman's narrator partakes in the city's sexual pulse: he 'penetrate[s] its light and warmth' and feels the scope for an exhilarating comradeship and strident self-expression.[61] London was rarely described in terms of 'light' and 'warmth', however, and Symonds backed away from a similar level of enthusiastic engagement. Carpenter and Ives shared some of this ambivalence but they also found the city to be symbolically and practically important in the embryonic movement for the reform of attitudes towards homosexuality.

Carpenter has been closely associated with a return to the land, and indeed he lived for much of his life on a smallholding at Millthorpe near

Sheffield with his working-class lover, George Merrill. In his epic poem *Towards Democracy*, however, he turned repeatedly to the metropolis and found it to be a potent metaphor for the fraternity which he saw driving change. The four parts of *Towards Democracy* were published separately between 1883 and 1902. Initially they sold slowly and received little critical attention, but after the publication of the first collected edition by Swann Sonnenschein in 1905 Carpenter became something of a celebrity, and he received 'pilgrims' from all over the country, and beyond. By 1916 16,000 copies of the book had been sold. The text itself is composed of a single lengthy prose poem (part one) and three additional sections which contained shorter pieces. The work outlined Carpenter's political and social vision and demonstrated a clear philosophical and stylistic debt to Whitman.[62]

The figure of 'democracy' is the lynchpin of the series and is repeatedly imagined in iconic, homoerotic terms. In the poem 'As a Woman of a Man', for example, the male narrator describes Democracy's 'huge limbs naked' and his 'stalwart erected member', and promises, 'I will drain thy lips and the secret things of thy body, / I will conceive by thee, Democracy.'[63] Carpenter imagined an explicitly sexual and fecund engagement with this complete, unified and perfect figure. Democracy is like one of the free-standing Greek statues, and the encounter yields spiritual, philosophical and political progeny. He appears in various forms throughout the text, at times assuming the narrative voice, at others, as here, the subject of it. In the first part 'disrespectable Democracy' is a 'black and horned Ethiopian' whose 'powerful brows and huge limbs please me well' and shortly after he discloses himself as Pan: 'goat footed and sitting on a rock – as to the Athenian runner of old'.[64] This mutable, omniscient and invariably male deity forms a unifying thread through the diverse spaces evoked in the text, moving between them and emphasising their simultaneity:

I am a seeing unseen atom travelling with others through space or remaining centuries in one place; again I resume a body and disclose myself...I enter the young prostitute's chamber, where he is arranging the photographs of fashionable beauties...and stay with him; we are at ease and understand each other...I dance at the village feast...I go down to the sea with fisher folk...The budder of roses bends among the low bushes...the bathers in the late twilight, almost dark, advance naked under the trees by the waterside, five or six together, superb, unashamed, scarcely touching the ground.[65]

Carpenter undermined ideas of spatial hierarchy at this and similar moments in the poem, foregrounding a range of spaces and including those redolent of homosexual desire like the male prostitute's bedroom and the pond-side, a favourite setting for the poets whose work appeared in *The Artist*. The poem repeatedly opens the reader's awareness to these other places, with each one envisaged as part of a vast web connecting diverse peoples and cultures. It is this spatial dynamic, rather than a strong linear narrative, which structures the text and in this sense there is overlap with some of the work discussed in the last chapter. The focus is not on one character and his sensual adventuring, however, but rather on a series of parallel spaces, stories and figures. The literary critic Scott McCracken describes it as an atemporality through which a new subjectivity might be imagined.[66]

This use of space in the poem relates in part to a radical tradition which saw change in environment as crucial to wider shifts in social and political consciousness. This included the projects of Charles Fourier in France and Robert Owen in Scotland in the 1820s and 1830s, as well as later movements such as the Guild of Handicrafts and the Utopian Fellowship of the New Life. Morris and Ellis' utopias also foregrounded environmental transformation.[67] The reinvention of space, and, most notably in Morris, the integration of nature into the city, were seen as central – practically and symbolically – to the liberation of the subject and the reformation of society. In *Towards Democracy* Carpenter similarly drew heavily on pastoral imagery and focussed on space and its effects. He did not outline a reformed space, however, and instead encouraged a different perspective on existing spaces and their potential to yield a sense of comradeship. His vision combined the idealised rural muscularity of 'democracy' with the seductive fabric and figures of the metropolis. The enervated urban expressions of homosexuality which Carpenter, Ives, Symonds and Ellis criticised elsewhere were reinvigorated, and the social and political possibilities of the city were recaptured partly through the erotics of urban life.

Democracy is drawn especially to outdoor spaces and to places of confluence rather than separation, in marked contrast to the aesthetic interiors detailed in parts of *The Picture of Dorian Gray*, *Teleny* and in coverage of Wilde's trials. In St James' Park desire and democracy intertwine: the mysterious stranger 'easy with open shirt and brown neck and face' attracts everyone around him and embodies 'one of the slowly unfolding meanings of democracy'. 'The delicate lady secretly loathes her bejewelled lord and desires piteously the touch of this man's muscular lithe, sun-embrowned body.'[68] This seizure of the democratic potential of the city parks resonated with the aspirations of the new London County Council, which sought to endorse a new sense of citizenship and belonging through the development of municipal recreation facilities, and by turning the attention of the city dwellers from indoors to out.[69]

More intriguing than Carpenter's frequent recourse to urban parks in the poem, though, is his deliberate engagement with aspects of city life which Symonds found troubling and which were the subject of broader comment and concern. In the city crowd and also in images of urban criminality and degeneracy Carpenter found a democratic promise:

At night I creep down and lie close in the great city – there I am at home – hours and hours I lie stretched there; the feet go to and fro, to and fro, beside and over me . . .
     You, soaring yearning face of youth threading the noisy crowd, though you soar to the stars you cannot escape me.
     I remain where I am. I make no effort. Wherever you go it is the same to me: I am there already.[70]

The passage in some ways echoes the imagery associated with the urban predator: Democracy creeps through the streets, lies in wait, is inescapable. He also picks out – it is tempting to say cruises – the 'soaring face of youth' in the urban crowd. However, this 'predator' is transformed into a redemptive force and is envisaged representing a positive rather than degenerate set of desires. The destructive and perverted forces of the city are transfigured by the incorruptible force of democracy; the dangerous streets harbour not a sexual monster but an omnipresent guardian angel. The 'noisy crowd', meanwhile, potentially yields connection and sustains rather than dissolves identity. It is a vision that recurs forcibly elsewhere in the poem:

Through the city crowd pushing wrestling shouldering, against the tide, face after face, breath of liquor, money-grubbing eye, infidel skin, shouts, threats, greetings, smiles, eyes and breasts of love, breathless, clutches of lust, limbs, bodies, torrents, bursts, savage onslaughts, tears, entreaties, tremblings, stranglings, suicidal, the sky, the houses, surges and crest of waves, white faces from afar bearing down nearer nearer, almost touching, and glances unforgotten and meant to be unforgotten.[71]

A collection of diverse impressions, from the ecstatic to the desperate, are equalised here in an outpouring of jumbled adjectives and nouns. The passage represents the multiplicity of the urban crowd but there is also a rhythmic movement which unifies the elements into an eroticised totality: from an alienating entry to 'breath of liquor, money-grubbing eye, infidel skin', to an orgasmic surge in the middle of the passage ('eyes and breasts of love, breathless, clutches of lust, limbs, bodies, torrents, bursts'), a post-orgasmic despair (of 'tears, entreaties, tremblings'), and finally, from the passionate embrace of the crowd, enduring memories, reiterated in the first line of the stanza that follows: 'I do not forget you: I see you quite plainly.' The crowd is imagined as a sexual experience and whilst chaotic it does not assail 'conscious personality', as Carpenter's contemporary Gustav le Bon suggested it might.[72] Whilst le Bon and other commentators variously imagined crowds breaking down identity, propriety, class and ideas of Englishness,[73] Carpenter cast them as settings for intimate encounters and for desires which could drive social, cultural and political change.

The power of comradeship to pull people together into a new social formation suggested a political productiveness in a set of desires elsewhere conceived as sterile, degenerate or nostalgic. The Hellenic ideal of masculine love, which was seen to embody and produce social stability and progress, was conjured anew within the contemporary urban scene. Moreover, a temporal generative dimension to homosexual desire, denied by the sexologists, was recovered. In a paper given to the British Society for the Study of Sex Psychology Carpenter noted that 'the loves of men for each other and similarly the loves of women for each other may become factors of future human evolution just as necessary and well-recognised as the ordinary loves which lead to the births of children and the propagation of the race'.[74] Carpenter envisaged a productive social, pedagogical, philanthropic and artistic role for the invert, extending his sphere of influence beyond the immediate physical environment which, in the fields of writing considered in previous chapters, tended to enclose and define him. Instead, in *Towards Democracy* Carpenter used the city to stress the place of the invert within – and as a productive member of – the social body. The alternative and removed spaces outlined in the poetry discussed earlier would not have served his purpose so well and he attempted to buck the impulse to secrecy, removal and enclosure in the representation of homosexuality. His conceptualisation of the city helped him in this and although Carpenter moved between many different places in *Towards Democracy*, he returned repeatedly to the metropolis and to a series of urban 'types'. He picked out, for example, 'the carefully brushed and buttoned young man walk[ing] down Piccadilly', reminiscent of the men described attending the Wilde trials;[75] the 'young prostitute' in 'his chamber' 'arranging photographs of fashionable beauties'; the 'young man who organises his boys from the slums';[76] and the 'poor lad born in the slums' who finds his long-lost friend, 'a man twice his own age ... a large free man, well acquainted with the world, capable and kindly', 'in a little street off the Mile End Rd'.[77] Women and their relationships with each other are also described in the poem,[78] though significantly they are less frequently imagined in a specifically urban context, highlighting both the closeness of the association for men and the somewhat different construction of ideas of lesbianism during this period.[79]

These vignettes often have the ring of anecdotes about them, of tales told about experiences in the city, of lovers and comrades found there. Unusually, the stories sometimes recreate the perspectives of working-class men and they become subjects rather than simply objects of desire. Of the 'poor lad born in the slums', for example, we are told that 'many spoke to him, asked him to come and have a drink, and so forth; but still it was no satisfaction to him; for they did not give him what he needed'.[80] In another case a sick man working twelve-hour shifts in a 'wretched tailor's den' in the city meets a man 'of athletic strength and beauty' at the 'casual little club he was in the habit of attending'. This man 'came and championed and nursed him, and stayed whole nights and days with him and loved him'.[81] Whilst Symonds focussed on his own 'sophisticated' passion for working-class men, these episodes represent them actively seeking similar comradely bonds through London pubs, working men's clubs and university settlements. It is a representation of the East End and London more broadly which is markedly different from those discussed earlier. Like Whitman, Carpenter saw the city as a place which might facilitate and sustain homosocial bonds. He reinflected visions of the urban labyrinth in *The Picture of Dorian Gray* and Symonds' *Memoirs*, and eschewed both Dorian's trenchant individualism and Symonds' revulsion. Instead, Carpenter found a potent force of human connection in the diverse spaces and distinctive experiences of the metropolis.

Carpenter looked at homosexuality as part of a wider vision of social renewal and reform, and positioned it clearly on his broad socialist and democratic agenda. The 'stories' of homosexuality embedded in *Towards Democracy* are narrated alongside others of heterosexual comradeship, showing the general power of desire and interpersonal relations to effect change. George Ives held Carpenter and his values in high esteem, trumpeting him as one of the 'four leaders of Hellas' – alongside Whitman, Symonds and Wilde.[82] Whilst Carpenter's conceptualisation of an 'intermediate sex' was essentially conciliatory, however, Ives developed a more combative stance in his evolving politics and in the language he used. He envisaged a dichotomy between 'them' and 'Us' – the latter always capitalised – and referred to 'the battle', the 'fight', to 'traitors' and to 'the cause'. Ives communicated a keen sense of personal injustice and of his own exclusion which related both to his homosexuality and his illegitimacy, and he was more specifically focussed on the legitimisation of homosexuality than Carpenter, who turned down an invitation to join the exclusive and 'issue specific' Order. It is tempting to conjecture that Ives' narrower focus arose out of his proximity to an urban subculture, to the blackmailers, police and the courts which made the need for self-protection acute and the battle for legitimacy especially urgent. He was keenly aware of the pressures on men who had sex and relationships with other men in London and the ways in which they were depicted in the newspaper press. Ives' Order, his writing and his sense of self were shaped in specific relation to a felt marginalisation within the city. Carpenter experienced this marginalisation too, and apart from the ideals he communicated through his writing, he took an active part in protests against specific injustices, especially when they involved censorship.[83] Carpenter was, however, one step removed from the urban scene in Millthorpe, and this distance is perhaps reflected in the way homosexuality is figured as part of a broader landscape in his writing and politics.

Ives perceived his Order – and 'workers for the cause' more generally – as 'an elect' for whom comradeship, selflessness, mutual support and commitment to the movement for reform were uppermost. Despite the evident elitism of the organisation, Ives' rhetoric, especially in his conceptualisation of the cause as a 'faith', echoed that of Carpenter, Whitman, Symonds and, more broadly, the emergent socialist movement.[84] The self-consciousness of members of the Order, the conceptual links with contemporary socialism and the martial prowess associated with the Theban Bands, allowed Ives to imagine a strident political fight for legitimacy, a fight which was moreover connected explicitly with London. It was there that Ives felt the greatest sense of common cause and the closest comradeship. The Service of Initiation for the Order appropriately included Whitman's eulogy to democracy and fraternity in 'a city invincible', 'a new city of friends'.[85]

Whilst the achievements of the grouping as a whole and the seriousness with which it was treated more generally remain obscure, Ives' dogged commitment to it is beyond doubt. He saw it practically as a campaigning and pedagogical body, a means through which prejudice might be challenged, networks of contacts established and pressure brought to bear on figures of influence. He cultivated friendships with several prominent sexologists including Havelock Ellis and Magnus Hirschfeld, and broached the topic of law reform with George Bernard Shaw, the MP John Burns and others.[86] He attended – and translated at – a meeting of reformers, including Magnus Hirschfeld, Carpenter, Kains Jackson and about twenty others, in August 1913 at the Hotel Cecil in the Strand,[87] was active in the

British Society for the Study of Sex Psychology and eagerly recorded and passed on developing theories and ideas. In 1901, for example, he sent 'Ellis' great work' to Australia: 'It cost me £2 but I look upon it as a duty. Let us spread the truth, the blessed seed of knowledge.'[88] Earlier, in 1894, he published a justification of same-sex love in the *Humanitarian*, predicated on the ethos of self-development and an Hellenic pride in the body and the 'sex instinct'.[89] In 1896 he gave Frank Harris 'some bits of evidence from official papers to show the home secretary' in the hope it might 'rescue or alleviate the sufferings of poor Oscar'.[90]

Ives' diary includes extensive notes on various texts dealing with homo-sexuality – including those by Ellis, Carpenter and other sexologists – and for the benefit of the future 'students' he confidently anticipated he provided verso notes, decoded some initials and encouraged them to 'dig further on'.[91] His scrapbook similarly testifies to his commitment to re-form, and he included reviews of works on homosexuality as well as extracts from them. He also paid close attention to homosexual activity in other cities, especially Berlin, Paris and Vienna, and his attempts to develop new contacts and launch new branches of the Order in these places indicates his conception of an international cause linking cities across Europe. His patriotism of the late 1880s gave way to a metropolitanism and interna-tionalism by the 1900s: 'We [those involved in the cause] have no nation', he insisted.[92] He thus turned the rhetoric about foreign 'vice' on its head and suggested a transnational identity and bond, rather as Carpenter did through the shifts around the globe in *Towards Democracy*.

The actual membership of the Order remains obscure, as the first chapter observed, but Ives' accounts of chance and planned meetings suggests it involved a fairly large number of men. Individuals were considered for membership on account of their position or expertise. Ives commented on one unnamed man: 'Being a learned figure we had thought he might have been of use to the Order, but so far as I know, he was never in it'.[93] In 1893 he wrote: 'I am hopeful [of the character of several London workers] but they are so far as I know untried and some are too apathetic for Us at present.'[94] He observed on another occasion the necessity of teaching 'workers' 'the faith'.[95] The context of both comments suggests the potential recruitment of working-class men to the Order and indicates a desire to attenuate the elitism of the group. He shrewdly observed, however, that the rich and powerful had the scope to act without the same threat of le-gal action: 'The helpless and the wage earners dare not, must not, move or speak unless they wish for martyrdoms.'[96] Ives treated the reformist task with the utmost seriousness and imagined a kind of Athenian social contract in the face of apparently more self-indulgent explorations of the city. He was damning of those whom he felt used the Order frivolously. Just before the 1914–18 war he wrote: 'met accidentally a member of the Order who ought never to have been elected. He does nothing save amuse himself…I do regret he ever heard our first service. X is another feeble creature who is not worthy of our movement.'[97] John Stokes is right in his observation that Ives 'found it a challenge to reconcile the variety of homosexual personalities with his own sombre ideals and retiring nature'.[98]

Like some of the writers considered earlier, Ives drew on the pastoral tradition to cleanse and redeem homosexuality in the city. He advocated ruralisation and the fostering of spaces where people could retreat from the streets and find privacy at night, areas he called 'spoonitoria'. 'In the future', he wrote, 'such places will be provided and there will be no spies or restrictions.'[99] He wrote a piece for the *Saturday Review* insisting that London's parks should not be lit after dark and was outraged by a pro- posal to close Hyde Park at night.[100] He consequently compared London unfavourably to Berlin, where he admired the Thiergarten, with its 'mean- dering paths, thick trees and waterways right in the middle of the capital!' It was, he wrote: 'unfenced and open as a spoonitorium at all times…much more free than London'.[101] He saw in Berlin a wholesomeness, freedom and unpretentiousness that both London and Paris lacked for him. He found something similar in Sydney, Australia, and Portsmouth. To Ives each of these cities had a compact with nature, and, partly in consequence, an ap- parent toleration of 'natural' desires. By contrast he characterised London as especially dangerous in terms of arrests and blackmail. It was nonetheless the centre of his social life, support network and campaigning work, and Ives also noted its cosmopolitanism and liberalism. There were – or had been – a number of groups dedicated to more open discussion of sex based in the city, including the Men and Women's Club of the 1880s, the Legit- imation League of the 1890s and the British Society for the Study of Sex Psychology from 1913.[102] 'I renounce nature', he wrote melodramatically in 1894, 'to live among friends, among the faithful – I wouldn't care to be alone, no, not in paradise, so I must needs live in London, and besides I can do much work there.'[103]

Ives appreciated the metaphorical power of the city – the prominence of Whitman in the Service of Initiation indicates that clearly – but it was also for him the practical hub through which support could be offered and pressure exerted. Though caution incarnate, it was there that Ives lobbied, established contacts, built up the Order and supported friends and associates. The nostalgia of the solitary observer and the eroticism associated with the bathing youth were supplemented in Ives' diary and scrapbook with images of active fraternity and political, sexual and social consciousness. It was these images and potentialities that underpinned Ives' campaign and, despite the familiar appeals to the pastoral, it was the city as a symbol, and London as a material reality, which compelled him both in his personal and political life.

The writers considered here and in the last chapter were reacting in particular to images of the sexualised and dangerous city in the newspaper press, and to ideas of urban sexual pathology emerging from early sexology, with which they were all familiar. They were also responding to a legacy of sexual possibility, adventuring and difference, a history of urban resistance and protest, and to the scope for both anonymity and community in London. In their published or private writing they charted a response to the city and to some of the complex issues it threw up, and in so doing they reshaped it to accommodate their hopes and longings, often by drawing on other times and places. They each indicated the importance of London to late-nineteenth century understandings and experiences of homosexual desire, selfhood and community, and, as we have seen through the work of Ives and Carpenter in particular, the city also emerged as the crucible through which an overt homosexual politics was forged.

Epilogue: public spaces/private lives

George Ives, the earnest twenty-six-year-old we first encountered being courted on a train to France, served as a lodestone as I was writing this book. He guided me through the diverse material it has considered and showed me how it affected the thinking and behaviour of one individual in the city. He was certainly not typical. He was the illegitimate son of Gordon Maynard Ives and the Baroness de Molarti of Spain, and was brought up by his paternal grandmother, the Hon. Emma Ives. His privileged background allowed him to live on a private income in London all his adult life. He devoted his time to research and writing,[1] prison reform and, as we have seen, to the legitimisation of homosexual relations. The Order of the Chaerona, which he established, was the first group of its kind in Britain, bringing together men who were seeking to find an affirmative framework within which to live out their desires and relationships. For this alone he is a highly significant figure; in its radical agenda and metropolitan focus the Order prefigured much lesbian and gay political organising of the twentieth century. He also left an immense archive, which is split between Yale and the University of Texas at Austin in the USA. His diary covers the period from 1886 to 1950 and runs to 122 volumes and around three million words. It includes extensive notes on his reading and campaign work, details of his friendships with Carpenter, Wilde, Lord Alfred Douglas, Havelock Ellis and Magnus Hirschfeld – amongst many others – and commentary on scandals, major public events and his own daily life in London. The forty-five-volume scrapbook – or casebook as he called it – is equally remarkable, and includes indexed clippings from a range of newspapers and periodicals as well as personal photographs and ephemera. He religiously collected accounts of court proceedings involving homosexuality, and these have led me to many of the cases the book has considered. Alongside these are reports of cricket matches and chess games (his two sporting passions), eccentric human and animal behaviour, cross-dressing men and women, injustice and prison conditions and all things Greek. The scrapbook was privately owned until the late 1990s and though an edited selection appeared in 1980, this stressed Ives' eccentricity and did scant justice to his reformist zeal, which is evident on virtually every page.[2] That most of the volumes have been out of reach of researchers until recently, and that his diary is both difficult to read and punctuated by sections of sometimes impenetrable numerical and alphabetic code, partially explains the limited attention Ives and his work have received.[3] Taken together, however, the diary and scrapbook constitute a hugely valuable resource and give an insight into the ways in which one man assembled a distinctive sense of self, desire and the city in part through the bricolage of ideas considered in this book. The scale of his public and private output and his mammoth reading schedule vividly indicates the importance of rhetorical practice in this process.[4] The eclecticism of the diary and scrapbook, moreover, reflects and constitutes the challenge of achieving a coherent sense of place and subjectivity when there was no unequivocal way of understanding either the city or homosexual desire and identity.[5]

Ives began his diary when he was nineteen. He was dividing his time largely between Magdalene College, Cambridge, and his 'den' at his grandmother's London home in Park Road, to the south-west of Regent's Park. In an entry of 1889 he mentioned retreating to London to escape some 'ragging and teasing' at Cambridge and in a verso note added in 1925 described the compulsion at college to be part of a 'pack' of 'young fools'. 'I never took to it', he wrote, 'and when I settled in London I dropped it all very thankfully.'[6] In London he developed a new circle of friends and also a strong sense of his own independence. His relationship with the city was nevertheless an uneasy one. He testified to feelings of isolation and loneliness, a fear of the blackmailer and the police in the metropolis, and a yearning for the countryside and for retreat to the family's country home at Bentworth, Hampshire, or their villa at Nice in the South of France. Page after page of clippings detailed prosecutions, blackmails and suicides, sustaining for Ives the sense of danger and tragedy which braced his life and work in London. His desire for seclusion, the closely guarded Order of the Chaerona, the codes and abbreviations in his diary, his relish of night-time in the city, his dreams of confinement[7] and his reticence about casual encounter all constituted a response to the perils of revelation. The reports he collected pressed him towards privacy in his London life, yet they also intersected with alternative languages and ideas which enabled Ives to engage with the city in other ways and to negotiate the prevailing pejorative images of homosexual activity there. He described the excitement of exchanged glances in the streets and relished the scope for both anonymity and communal bonds. The reformist activity he undertook in London also showed him how struggle might be a defining component of homosexual identity and a consolidating factor in homosexual community. These parallel feelings of alienation and belonging have been identified in several of the works discussed in this book and in this sense Ives depicted a familiar gamut of hope and despair. London offered 'homosexual' men much but it could never be an unproblematic site of liberation – in part because of its own diversity and contradictions. These final pages look briefly at how the aspirations and fears evident in Ives' reading and writing affected his relationship with, and negotiation of, the city.

In the late 1880s and early 1890s Ives self-consciously assumed the mantle of independent West End bachelor. He kitted himself out with a malacca cane from the Burlington Arcade, a new pin, studded with opal, garnet rubies and diamonds, and a dressing case, 'fitted with ebony and silver', which was 'quite enough for a bachelor'.[8] He visited friends in Half Moon Street, just off Piccadilly, ate with others at the Savoy and went to performances at the Empire in Leicester Square. In July 1891 he took chambers at 56 St James' Street, just round the corner from Jermyn Street, where, he noted, 'I can be left entirely to myself.'[9] He 'admit[s] never to have been to the East End', an area he associated with a political agenda he did not yet share: 'I am no socialist', he insisted.[10]

Ives' social circuit expanded when he met Wilde shortly after his move to St James'. London, he said in October 1891, was a 'grand place',[11] and he enjoyed the company of Wilde and his circle in some of the new continental cafés and at the Authors' Club, the Lyric Club and the New Travellers' Club, where Wilde once kissed him 'passionately' goodbye.[12] He yearned for more independence so that he could, in aesthetic manner, 'get a glimpse now and then of the beauty still in life' – 'so long', he added cautiously, 'as it does not hurt the cause'.[13] He looked for a permanent West End apartment and in 1894 moved into Flat E4, the Albany. The journal *Leisure Hour* had previously reported that the 'bachelor of the Albany was a recognised variety of the man about town'[14] and it was the address Wilde later gave to Jack Worthing in the original four-act version of *The Importance of Being Earnest*, as has already been noted. On Wilde's advice – and once he had gained his grandmother's permission – he also shaved off his moustache, noting that it was 'anti-Hellenic' and 'bad art', an offence both to his ascetic sense of the Hellenic masculine ideal and to his aestheticism.[15] In removing it he keyed into an urban trend and West End fashion which was at

Figure 9 George Ives in old age.

least mildly suggestive of sexual dissidence. Ives shared his new home, and sometimes his bed, with James Goddard (Kit), the son of one of his father's employees, and Harold Holt (Cubby), his grandmother's former secretary. It was also here that he spent the night with Lord Alfred Douglas, though he refused to allow a third party to join them because he 'thought it wouldn't do in the Albany'.[16] The episode reveals Ives' enduring sense of propriety and reservation. He could not embrace Douglas' more abandoned lifestyle and worried about the consequences of the young lord's indiscretions. 'I warned Lord A more than once that he was indulging in homosexuality to a reckless and highly dangerous degree. For tho' I had no objection to the thing itself we were all afraid he would get arrested any day.'[17] This concern evaporated when Douglas turned on Wilde: Ives added the words 'traitor' to any mention of him in the diary.

During this period Ives read Carpenter's *Civilisation: Its Cause and Cure* and made extensive notes on the section discussing the Theban Bands; he also visited poorer parts of the city, making 'acquaintance among the youthful denizens of the Borough'.[18] His daily life now took him frequently between the West and East Ends, incorporating the swimming baths in Whitechapel and a visit to Wilde in St James' on one day in the summer of 1892, for example.[19] He developed a keen interest in the potential of homoerotic bonds to foster a new social and moral order, and when he overheard two working-class men having sex in a changing cubicle at the Polytechnic baths in Regents Street in 1893 he concluded that, removed from 'mercantile surroundings', a new potential had been unleashed by these men, who were apparently able to flout convention and the common conflation of monetary exchange with homosexual sex. 'How much', he wrote, 'might this be but a type of the rising generation, may these two but be specimens and samples of the millions and we shall do well.'[20] Influenced by Carpenter's insights and his own experiences in the East End Ives put a utopian and reformist gloss on the swimming pool encounter.

Buoyed by his expanding circle of friends, his developing sense of liberalism in London and the growing body of affirmative writing about homosexuality, Ives decided to enter the debate more publicly in October 1894 and submitted – this time against Wilde's advice – his outspoken justification of same-sex love to *The Humanitarian*.[21] He 'tried for a Humanitarian' at Charing Cross on 6 October 1914 and was pleased to find that it had sold out. 'I hope the light has been spread', he wrote, adding that 'a friend – not sympathetic – said yesterday that our Ideal is in the air'.[22] The piece was roundly attacked in the *Review of Reviews*,[23] and though Ives felt he had done his 'duty' and seems to have enjoyed the fray, he was more reticent in print thereafter.

His interest in the West End waned around this time. He chose to visit Ashbee at the Guild of Handicrafts in Mile End Road rather than attend a dinner with Wilde after the premiere of *The Importance of Being Earnest*, for example,[24] and claimed to like the main streets of the East End better than 'the horrid West Central district'. After a trip to a pantomime and dinner at the Savoy in 1906 Ives proclaimed irritably, 'I can't stand society and its amusements.'[25] Rather than seeing the West End as a permissive space for homosexual experimentation and expression he felt it detracted from the

serious business of reform.[26] For him it represented a version of homosexuality which was allied too closely to the prevailing social and cultural order.
From the mid-1890s he became more actively involved in the Rugby House
and Magdalene settlements, in Notting Hill and Camberwell respectively,
and this expanded topographical frame of reference both indicated and
fostered a strong commitment to ideas of homosocial and cross-class comradeship, a greater sympathy for socialism and an interest in anarchy. His
attachment to the city was increasingly related to the streets, the settlements, his associates in the Order of the Chaerona and various meetings
and conferences, including from 1913 events organised by the British Society
for the Study of Sex Psychology. This shift in his engagement with London
was shaped by the interplay of Hellenism, sexology and socialism in his
thinking, whilst the presence of these institutions, networks and organisa-
tions in the city sustained his vision of reform and made it sometimes feel
almost achievable.

At the close of the 1890s Ives moved from Piccadilly; first to his former
home in Park Road and then, in 1905, to Adelaide Road in Primrose Hill.
Adelaide Road was, according to historian Donald Olsen, 'the essence of
suburbia',[27] and in the diary for the post-1905 period there is a sense
of Ives settling down – not to a 'conventional' family, but with a series of
working- and lower-middle-class men whom he paternalistically referred
to as his 'children'. Kit brought his wife and children to live there for a
while, and in 1909, Harold Bloodworth, a teenage footballer, moved in
and stayed until Ives' death in 1950. Ives' aim at Adelaide Road was seclusion for himself and his housemates. 'I am laying plans to keep people
out', he wrote in 1905, though in a verso note of 1927 he noted that his
'precautions and locks [had] never been necessary'.[28] Despite the communal
surveillance and gossip associated with suburbia, suburban architecture also
fostered separation and privacy, adequately fulfilling Ives' requirements for
his unconventional household.

Throughout his diary Ives maintained an anthropological and analytical
stance redolent of the sexologists and the broader Victorian empirical and
typological tradition. He measured himself against the sexologist's schema –
commenting, for example, on his relative hairlessness and lack of taut
muscle despite being a regular swimmer. 'Like most of my species', he noted
in another entry, 'I always had a very keen aesthetic sense.'[29] He associated
his 'strong tendency to orientalisms' directly to his desires.[30] Aside from this
self-examination, Ives described himself as 'the Sherlock Homes of a 1000
little peculiarities'.[31] He recorded what he saw and heard as he wondered

around the streets of London, often late at night, and noted seeing inverts, fellow members of the Order and even plainclothes policemen around the city. He also monitored opinion about homosexuality in the gentlemen's clubs and from men he met in the streets, on a train and at the Serpentine. Through the scrapbook he indicated sites in the city which were important to him, and he compiled images of boys and men swimming in the Thames and the pond at Victoria Park as well as places and monuments which had homosexual resonances. These included the statue of educationalist and pioneer of the polytechnic movement Quentin Hogg, which was unveiled in Portland Place in 1906.[32] In a parallel entry in his diary he noted the inspirational impact of Hogg's 'homogenic spirit'.[33]

Ives was keen to figure homosexuality within London's monumental topography and the mainstream of the city's social, cultural and sporting life, yet his engagement with London was individualistic and he conceived of a distinctive and secretive identity there. He explored by bike and foot rather than by public transport, and relished secret signs and hidden meanings. He wanted Hyde Park to be publicly redesignated a spoonitorium – for it to be open to lovers at all times and for the authorities to ensure the gates remained unlocked – but also imagined it cloaked in darkness so that the configuration of those lovers, what they did, and precisely where they went, remained a secret. This drive to secrecy was a means of resisting domineering interpretations of and reactions to homosexual activity. But it also maintained a space for self-determination and for developing patterns of behaviour which were distinct and exclusive. For the same reason, and in a reflection of this approach to the city, Ives' engagement with public discourse on homosexuality largely took place at closely guarded meetings of the Order and in a private diary with codes designed to confuse 'prying eyes'. Ives' fight for public space and recognition for the invert was thus marked by what Wilde called his 'silly mania for secrecy'.[34] H. G. Cocks convincingly argues that the unspeakable nature of homosexuality 'produced paradoxical opportunities for self-making', and this relates closely to the impulse to inscribe a personal mapping of the city as part of the quest for a distinctive sense of self and mode of resistance.[35] Ives felt compelled to secrecy because of the dangers associated with homosexuality in the metropolis but he also found the exclusivity it brought appealing since it related closely to his conception of an enlightened and heroic elite in the city akin to the Theban Bands and the Athenian citizenry.

The dynamic between public spaces with their domineering associations on the one hand, and personal mappings and meanings on the other, was certainly not particular to Ives or the homosexual condition.[36] Clearly, however, inscribing an independent mapping of, and presence within, the city was especially pressing for those whose lifestyles and relationships were censured and who were seeking, partly in reaction, to outline a sustaining identity, history and culture. Men exploring London's homosexual possibilities each had their own conceptions and experience of the city, as chapter 1 concluded, and these often overlapped, consolidating a subcultural network of places and affirming the presence and endurance of homosexuality. Such communal networks and understandings should not obscure the individual, however, and it is useful to observe the ways in which the particular value of a place shifted from man to man and account to account. Hyde Park, for example, prompted Wilde's fictional Dorian in his quest for new sensation; it was a place of comfort for Symonds where he could fantasise about Hellenic and pastoral muscularity; Carpenter conceived of it as a key site in the evolution of democratic bonds fuelled by desire; some guardsmen saw it as a venue for both sexual and economic transaction; Ives yearned for its recreation as a spoonitorium. The newspapers' pronouncements about homosexual activity in the park did not – and could not – wholly account for these other understandings, associations and experiences. A range of ways of comprehending homosexuality and its place in London were circulating during this period and men found different ways of negotiating them and operating within the metropolis. What Ives' work and account of his life in London show us are some of the possibilities and restrictions associated with these competing and overlapping frameworks – and the difficulty of achieving subjective composure within them. This complex intersection of discourses of identity, desire and the city ultimately prevent us from discerning either a unitary urban type or a coherent culture of homosexuality in the city, even though there were established networks, sustaining groupings and recognisable types. What we can do, however, is to mark the persistent connection of homosexuality and urban life in writing and debate from this period. Despite the complexities of Ives' relationship with the city and his own desires, it was surely the insistence on this connection which underpinned his feeling that he 'ha[d] always been [him]self' in London. It was there, he realised, that 'the attack' would 'commence'.[37]

Appendix

Table 1. *Arrest (arr.) and conviction (con.) figures for 'sodomy', 'intent to commit sodomy' and 'gross indecency between males', 1880–1915*

Year	Sodomy (see note 1)		Intent to commit sodomy (see note 1)		Gross indecency with males		Total	
	arr.	con.	arr.	con.	arr.	con.	arr.	con.
1880	7	1	4	0	n/a	n/a	11	1
1881	1	0	5	1	n/a	n/a	6	1
1882	1	0	8	5	n/a	n/a	9	5
1883	7	5	see note 2		n/a	n/a	7	5
1884	1	1	3	3	n/a	n/a	4	4
1885	4	2	4	1	2	0	10	3
1886	3	1	see note 2		18	5	21	6
1887	2	1	3	2	11	5	16	8
1888	2	0	2	0	8	5	12	5
1889	1	0	3	1	17	3	21	4
1890	7	1	10	8	20	12	37	21
1891	13	5	4	3	27	13	44	21
1892	5	3	3	2	24	11	32	16
1893	8	2	7	5	42	21	57	28
1894	2	0	3	1	35	7	40	8
1895	3	1	6	3	35	28	44	32
1896	6	0	9	7	27	10	42	17
1897	2	2	14	7	32	17	48	26
1898	6	4	5	2	52	30	63	36
1899	9	1	10	6	39	19	58	26
1900	7	4	15	6	28	12	50	22
1901	8	2	12	5	39	15	59	22
1902	4	3	12	5	38	14	54	22
1903	3	1	8	5	41	12	52	18
1904	9	5	7	3	38	18	54	26
1905	5	3	5	4	40	14	50	21
1906	8	3	15	14	44	20	67	37
1907	4	0	19	15	30	10	53	25

Table 1. *(cont.)*

Year	Sodomy (see note 1) arr.	con.	Intent to commit sodomy (see note 1) arr.	con.	Gross indecency with males arr.	con.	Total arr.	con.
1908	9	2	15	6	35	11	59	19
1909	7	5	12	4	45	23	64	32
1910	2	2	20	9	35	12	57	23
1911	6	4	18	4	44	21	68	29
1912	5	4	20	6	46	16	71	26
1913	3	2	52	14	35	15	90	31
1914	6	4	42	13	46	13	94	30
1915	3	0	38	14	73	32	114	46

Source: Compiled from the annual reports to parliament from the Commissioner of the Metropolitan Police.
Note 1. There are some anomalies in the categorisation of crimes. In 1895 'sodomy' changed to 'unnatural offences', and 'intent to commit sodomy' to 'intent to commit unnatural offences'. There is no accompanying explanation but it seems that the only additional crime included in this category is bestiality. There is no listing for arrests and prosecutions for bestiality after 1885, but in the preceding five years there were three convictions and an average of 3.4 arrests per year. This causes a problem in the analysis of statistics after 1895, and means that the figures for 'sodomy' and 'intent to commit sodomy' as listed here may include bestiality cases.
Note 2. In these years figures for sodomy and intent to commit sodomy were combined without explanation.

Table 2. *Annual arrest (arr.) and conviction (con.) figures for 'sodomy', 'intent to commit sodomy' and 'gross indecency between males', averaged over five-year periods, 1880–1914*

Year	Sodomy		Intent to commit sodomy		Gross indecency between males		Total	
	arr.	con.	arr.	con.	arr.	con.	arr.	con.
1880–1884	3.4	1.4	4	1.8	n/a	n/a	7.4	3.2
1885–1889	2.4	0.8	2.4	0.8	11.2	3.6	16	5.2
1890–1894	7	2.2	5.4	3.8	29.6	12.8	42	20.6
1895–1899	5.2	1.6	12	5	37	20.8	51	27.4
1900–1904	6.2	3	10.8	4.8	36.8	14.2	53.8	22
1905–1909	6.6	2.6	13.2	8.6	38.8	15.6	58.6	26.8
1910–1914	4.4	3.2	30.4	9.2	41.2	15.4	76	27.8

Source: Compiled from the annual reports to parliament from the Commissioner of the Metropolitan Police.

Note. Usually figures for each year appear in the police commissioners' report of the succeeding year, so figures for 1880 appear in the report of 1881. There are anomalies, however, and in some years reports are included for the preceding two years. Page references refer to the beginning of the 'Report from the Commissioner of the Police of the Metropolis', *Report from the Commissioners: Police*, vol. 51 (London, 1881), p. 14; vol. 33 (1882), p. 14; vol. 31 (1883), p. 15; vol. 42 (1884), p. 17; vol. 37 (1885), p. 13; vol. 34 (1886), pp. 20–1; vol. 40 (1887), p. 21; vol. 57 (1888), pp. 26–7; vol. 40 (1889), pp. 26–7; vol. 42 (1890–1), pp. 28–9; vol. 41 (1892), p. 28; vol. 45 (1893–4), pp. 26–7; vol. 42 (1894), p. 32; vol. 42 (1895), p. 32; vol. 42 (1896), p. 34; vol. 39 (1897), p. 35; vol. 46 (1898), p. 38; vol. 42 (1899), p. 46; vol. 40 (1900), p. 49; vol. 42 (1902), pp. 51–2; vol. 34 (1904), p. 52; vol. 36 (1905), p. 56; vol. 49 (1906), 56; vol. 51 (1908), pp. 50 and 56; vol. 36 (1909), p. 60; vol. 45 (1910), p. 50; vol. 43 (1912–13), pp. 39 and 47; vol. 44 (1914), p. 39; vol. 32 (1914–16), p. 39; vol. 14 (1916), p. 16.

Notes

INTRODUCTION

1. 'Middlesex Sessions Appeals', *Reynolds*, 9 May 1896: p. 8.
2. Roger Casement, *The Black Diaries*, eds. Peter Singleton-Gates and Maurice Girodias (London, 1959), p. 561. There has been debate about the authenticity of the Casement diaries, though the weight of evidence suggests that they are genuine. For discussion of the controversy see Brian Inglis, *Roger Casement* (Belfast, 1993), pt. 7, ch. 1; and Adrian Weale, *Patriot Traitors: Roger Casement, John Amerty and the Real Meaning of Treason* (London, 2001), ch. 13.
3. Alan Crawford, *C. R. Ashbee: Architect, Designer and Romantic Socialist* (London, 1985), p. 161.
4. George Ives, 'Diary', vol. XVIII, 27 December 1893, p. 83, George Ives papers, Harry Ransom Humanities Research Center, University of Texas at Austin.
5. The railways were, Lynda Nead writes, 'the most significant player in the demolition and transformation of Victorian London'. Lynda Nead, *Victorian Babylon: People, Street and Images in Nineteenth-Century London* (New Haven, 2000), p. 34
6. See Donald Olsen, *The Growth of Victorian London* (London, 1976), pp. 220 and 240; H. J. Dyos, 'Speculative Builders and Developers of Victorian London' and 'A Victorian Speculative Builder: Edward Yates', in David Cannadine and David Reeder (eds.), *Exploring the Urban Past: Essay in Urban History by H. J. Dyos* (Cambridge, 1982).
7. By 1910 the central London Underground we know today, with the exception of the Jubilee and Victoria lines, was in place.
8. This sense is communicated particularly strongly by Ford Maddox Ford (*né* Hueffer) in *The Soul of London: A Survey of a Modern City* (London, 1905). See also Marshall Berman, *All That Is Solid Melts into Air: The Experience of Modernity* (New York, 1982); Stephen Kern, *The Culture of Time and Space, 1880–1918* (London, 1983).
9. George Sims, *Living London*, vol. 1 (London, 1901), p. 94; George Sala, *London Up to Date* (London, 1894), pp. 347–51; Robert Machray, *The Night Side of London* (London, 1902), p. 31.
10. Henning Bech, *When Men Meet: Homosexuality and Modernity*, trans. Teresa Mesquit and Tim Davies (Cambridge, 1997), pp. 158–9.

11. *Ibid.*
12. Charles Féré, *The Evolution and Dissolution of the Sexual Instinct* (1899; Paris, 1904), p. 226.
13. On this point see also Eve Sedgwick, *The Epistemology of the Closet* (Berkeley, 1990), p. 25; and Jeffrey Weeks, *Coming Out: Homosexual Politics from the Nineteenth Century to the Present* (1979; London, 1990), pp. 33–5.
14. See Sims, *Living London*, pp. 94–100.
15. The population almost trebled between 1851 and 1911 from 2.5 million to just over 7 million people. Christopher Hibbert and Ben Weinreb (eds.), *The London Encyclopaedia* (London, 1995), p. 632. Figures are for Greater London, as defined by the London Government Act, 1963, and compiled from the decennial census.
16. Michel Foucault, *The History of Sexuality*, vol. 1, *An Introduction*, trans. Robert Hurley (1976; London, 1990); Weeks, *Coming Out* and *Sex, Politics and Society: The Regulation of Sexuality Since 1800* (London, 1981). See also David Greenberg, *The Construction of Homosexuality* (Chicago, 1988); Richard Davenport-Hines, *Sex, Death and Punishment: Attitudes to Sex and Sexuality in Britain Since the Renaissance* (London, 1990); Leslie Moran, *The Homosexual(ity) of Law* (London, 1996); Ed Cohen, *Talk on the Wilde Side: Towards a Genealogy of a Discourse on Male Sexualities* (London, 1993); Harry Oosterhuis, *Stepchildren of Nature: Krafft-Ebing, Psychiatry and the Making of Sexual Identity* (Chicago, 2000); Linda Dowling, *Hellenism and Homosexuality in Victorian Oxford* (New York, 1994); Alan Sinfield, *The Wilde Century: Effeminacy, Oscar Wilde and the Queer Moment* (London, 1994); Regenia Gagnier, *Idylls of the Marketplace: Oscar Wilde and the Victorian Public* (Aldershot, 1987); Eve Sedgwick, *The Epistemology of the Closet* and *Between Men: English Literature and Male Homosocial Desire* (New York, 1985); and Elaine Showalter, *Sexual Anarchy: Gender and Culture at the Fin de Siècle* (London, 1990).
17. See, for example, Steve Pile, *The Body and the City: Psychoanalysis, Space and Subjectivity* (London, 1996); David Bell and Gill Valentine (eds.), *Mapping Desire: Geographies of Sexualities* (London, 1995); Beatriz Columina (ed.), *Sexuality and Space* (New York, 1992); David Harvey, *Consciousness and the Urban Experience* (Oxford, 1985); Henri Lefebvre, *Everyday Life in the Modern World*, trans. Sacha Rabinovitch (New Brunswick, 1990); Doreen Massey, 'Politics of Space/Time', in Michael Keith and Steve Pile (eds.), *Place and the Politics of Identity* (London, 1993); Edward Soja, *Post-modern Geographies: The Reassertion of Space in Critical Social Theory* (London, 1989); and Michel de Certeau, *The Practice of Everyday Life*, trans. Steven Rendell (Berkeley, 1988). See also Michel Foucault, 'Of Other Spaces', *Diacritics*, 16 (1986): 22–7.
18. Tony Tanner, *Venice Desired* (London, 1992); Catherine Edwards, *Writing Rome: Textual Approaches to the City* (Cambridge, 1996); Christopher Prendergast, *Paris and the Nineteenth Century* (Oxford, 1992); Deborah Epstein Nord, *Walking the Victorian Streets: Women, Representation and the City* (Ithaca, NY, 1995); Judith Walkowitz, *City of Dreadful Delight: Narratives of Sexual Danger in Late Victorian London* (London, 1992); Elizabeth Wilson, *The Sphinx*

and the City: Urban Life, the Control of Disorder, and Women (London, 1991); Nead, *Victorian Babylon*; Erica Rappaport, *Shopping for Pleasure: Women in the Making of London's West End* (Princeton, 2000).

19. Gillian Beer, *Open Fields: Science in Cultural Encounter* (Oxford, 1996), p. 178; see also Beer, *Forging the Missing Link: Interdisciplinary Stories* (Cambridge, 1991).

20. Despite an apparently radical shift in the conceptualisation and treatment of pauperism and poverty in the 1830s, for example, Mary Poovey shows how these changes retained 'traces' of previous conceptualisations. Mary Poovey, *Making a Social Body: British Cultural Formation, 1830–1864* (Chicago, 1995).

21. On this point see Alan Sinfield, *Faultlines: Cultural Materialism and the Politics of Dissident Reading* (Berkeley, 1992).

22. Kaja Silverman, *Male Subjectivity at the Margins* (London, 1992), p. 23.

23. Barbara H. Rosenwein, 'Worrying About Emotions in History', *American Historical Review*, 107, 3 (June 2002): 821–45, p. 842.

24. Lyndal Roper, *Oedipus and the Devil: Witchcraft, Sexuality and Religion in Early Modern Europe* (London, 1994), p. 26.

25. H. Montgomery Hyde, *The Other Love: An Historical and Contemporary Survey of Homosexuality in Britain* (London, 1970); Rupert Croft-Cooke, *Feasting With Panthers: A New Consideration of Some Late Victorian Writers* (London, 1967).

26. Neil Bartlett, *Who Was That Man? A Present for Mr Oscar Wilde* (London, 1988).

27. See, for example, Stephen White (ed.), *The Margins of the City: Gay Men's Urban Lives* (Aldershott, 1994); Davina Cooper, *Sexing the City: Lesbian and Gay Politics within the Activist State* (London, 1994); George Chauncey, *Gay New York: The Making of the Gay Male World, 1890–1940* (London, 1995); Garry Wotherspoon, *City of the Plain: History of a Gay Subculture* (Sydney, 1991); David Higgs (ed.), *Queer Sites: Gay Urban Histories Since 1600* (London, 1999); and Bech, *When Men Meet*. For accounts of homosexuality in London in earlier periods see Alan Bray, *Homosexuality in Renaissance England* (London, 1982); Davenport-Hines, *Sex, Death and Punishment*; Rictor Norton, *Mother Clap's Molly House: The Gay Subculture in England, 1700–1830* (London, 1992); Randolph Trumbach, 'London's Sodomites: Homosexual Behaviour and Western Culture in the Eighteenth Century', *Journal of Social History*, 11, 1 (Fall 1977): 1–31; and Trumbach, 'Sodomitical Subcultures, Sodomitical Roles, and the Gender Revolution of the Eighteenth Century: The Recent Historiography', in Robert MacCubbin (ed.), *'Tis Nature's Fault: Unauthorised Sexuality During the Enlightenment* (Cambridge, 1987). For London later in the twentieth century see: Frank Mort, *Cultures of Consumption: Masculinity and Social Space in Twentieth-Century Britain* (London, 1996); Matt Houlbrook, 'Soldier Heroes and Rent Boys: Homosex, Masculinities and Britishness in the Brigade of Guards: c.1900–60', *Journal of British Studies*, forthcoming, July 2003; Houlbrook, 'Lady Austin's Camp Boys: Constituting the Queer Subject in 1930s London', *Gender and History*, 14, 1 (2002): 31–61; Houlbrook, 'Towards a Historical Geography of Sexuality', *Journal of Urban History*, 2, 4 (2001): 497–504;

Houlbrook, 'For Whose Convenience? Gay Guides, Cognitive Maps and the Construction of Homosexual London: 1917–67', in Simon Gunn and R. J. Morris (eds.), *Identities in Space: Contested Terrains in the Western City since 1850* (Aldershot, 2001); and Houlbrook, 'The Private World of Public Urinals: London 1918–57', *London Journal*, 25, 1 (2000): 52–70.

28. See Morris B. Kaplan, 'Who's Afraid of Jack Saul? Urban Culture and the Politics of Desire in Late Victorian London', *Gay and Lesbian Quarterly (GLQ)*, 5, 3 (1999): 267–314; Kaplan, 'Did My Lord Gomorrah Smile? Social Class, Prostitution, and Sexuality in the Cleveland Street Affair', in Nancy Erber and George Robb (eds.), *Disorder in the Court: Trials and Sexual Conflict at the Turn of the Century*, Basingstoke, 1999; Kaplan, '"Men in Petticoats": the Queer Case of Mr Boulton and Mr Park', in Pamela Gilbert (ed.), *Imagined Londons* (New York, 2002). See also *Sodom by the Thames: Love, Lust and Scandal in Wilde Times*, forthcoming with Cornell University Press.

29. H. G. Cocks, 'Nameless Offences: Homosexual Desire in the Nineteenth Century', ts, forthcoming (London, 2003).

30. The supposition has a long history. Holbrook Jackson noted in 1913 that after 1895 'Bohemians cut off their locks, shed their soft collars and fell back upon suburbia.' More recent work on homosexuality tends to highlight the early 1890s as a period of activity and transition, whilst the first fourteen years of the twentieth century are largely sidelined or bypassed. Sinfield, Weeks and Jonathan Dollimore, for example, each emphasise the pre-1900 and post-1914 periods in their respective examinations of homosexual sensibility, identity and politics. Holbrook Jackson, *The 1890s: A Review of Art and Ideas* (1913; London, 1927), p. 116; Sinfield, *The Wilde Century*; Weeks, *Coming Out*; Jonathan Dollimore, *Sexual Dissidence: Augustine to Wilde, Freud to Foucault* (Oxford, 1991).

1 LONDON AND THE CITIES OF THE PLAIN

1. Michel Foucault, *The History of Sexuality*, vol. 1, *An Introduction*, trans. Robert Hurley (1976; London, 1990), p. 43.

2. Foucault's work, David Halperin argues, did not discount the possibility of such earlier identities and subcultures, as historians and critics have tended to suggest. See David Halperin, 'Forgetting Foucault: Acts, Identities, and the History of Sexuality.' *Representations*, 63 (Summer 1998): 93–120. For accounts of pre-1800 homosexual activity in London see Alan Bray, *Homosexuality in Renaissance England* (London, 1982); Richard Davenport-Hines, *Sex, Death and Punishment: Attitudes to Sex and Sexuality in Britain Since the Renaissance* (London, 1990); Rictor Norton, *Mother Clap's Molly House: The Gay Subculture in England, 1700–1830* (London, 1992); Alan Sinfield, *The Wilde Century: Effeminacy, Oscar Wilde and the Queer Moment* (London, 1994); Randolph Trumbach, 'London's Sodomites: Homosexual Behaviour and Western Culture in the Eighteenth Century', *Journal of Social History*, 11, 1 (1978): 1–31; Trumbach, 'Sodomitical Subcultures, Sodomitical Roles, and the Gender

Revolution of the Eighteenth Century: The Recent Historiography', in Robert MacCubbin (ed.), *'Tis Nature's Fault: Unauthorised Sexuality During the Enlightenment* (Cambridge, 1987); and Trumbach, 'Gender and the Homosexual Role in Modern Western Culture: The Eighteenth and Nineteenth Centuries Compared', in D. Altman (ed.), *Homosexuality, Which Homosexuality?* (London, 1989).

3. Bray, *Homosexuality*, p. 78. Trumbach modifies Bray's claims, suggesting that urban sodomitical subcultures did exist before this time. He also argues, however, that they became more concerted and visible during the 1700s. See Trumbach, 'Sodomitical Subcultures', pp. 116–18.

4. Bray, *Homosexuality*, p. 75.

5. Davenport-Hines, *Sex, Death and Punishment*, pp. 66–8.

6. Sinfield, *The Wilde Century*, p. 43.

7. *Hell Upon Earth, or the Town in Uproar* (London, 1729), pp. 33–5 and 41.

8. See Trumbach, 'Sodomitical Subculture', pp. 116–17; G. S. Rousseau, 'The Pursuit of Homosexuality in the Eighteenth Century: Utterly Confused Category and/or Rich Repository', in MacCubbin, *'Tis Nature's Fault*, p. 145; Ian McCormick (ed.), *Secret Sexualities: a Sourcebook of Seventeenth and Eighteenth Century Writing* (London, 1997), p. 63.

9. Ned Ward, *Satyrical Reflections on Clubs in 29 Chapters* (London, 1710), p. 284.

10. Holloway, *The Phoenix of Sodom*, p. 17 (original emphasis).

11. For accounts of the trials of some of those arrested at Margaret Clap's house see *Select Trials*, vol. II (1735), pp. 193–7; for Clap's own trial see *Select Trials*, vol. III (London, 1742), p. 37. For further discussion of the case see Norton, *Mother Clap's Molly House*, ch. 3.

12. George Parker, *A View of Society and Manners in High and Low Life*, vol. II (London, 1781), pp. 87–8.

13. *Select Trials*, vol. II (London, 1735), p. 211. For a discussion of the case see Norton, *Mother Clap's Molly House*, p. 58.

14. *Hell Upon Earth*, p. 43.

15. Holloway, *The Phoenix of Sodom*, p. 13.

16. *Ibid.* The citation is from an unreferenced newspaper clippings pasted into the British Library copy of the text (callmark: cup 3e4.p. 12).

17. See Christopher Hibbert and Ben Weinreb (eds.), *The London Encyclopaedia* (London, 1995), p. 630.

18. 'A Full and True Account of the Discovery and Apprehending of A Notorious Gang of Sodomites' (1709), in MacCubbin, *'Tis Nature's Fault*, p. 66; *Select Trials*, vol. III (London, 1742), p. 36.

19. *Hell upon Earth*, p. 42; Parker, *A View of Society and Manners*, pp. 87–8; see also *A View of the Town in an Epistle to a Friend in the Country: A Satire* (London, 1735), p. 19.

20. Humphrey Nettle, *Sodom and Onan: A Satire* (London, 1772). Nettle's satire focuses on the arrest, trial and subsequent acquittal of Samuel Foote, an actor – and possibly also the proprietor – of the Little Theatre, Haymarket. The

British Library copy includes newspaper clippings about the case (callmark: 11642.g.15). For the Star and Garter case see the clipping pasted in the British Library copy of Holloway's *The Phoenix of Sodom*.

21. Cited in Davenport-Hines, *Sex, Death and Punishment*, p. 86.
22. *Ibid.*
23. *Ibid.*
24. *Select Trials*, vol. III (London, 1742), p. 197.
25. Holloway, *The Phoenix of Sodom*, newspaper clippings.
26. 'The Trial and Conviction of Several Reputed Sodomites, Before the Right Honourable Lord Mayor and Recorder of London, at Guildhall, the 20th day of October, 1707', in MacCubbin, *'Tis Nature's Fault*, p. 64; *Hell Upon Earth*, p. 42.
27. *Select Trials*, vol. I (London, 1764), p. 67.
28. *Hell Upon Earth*, p. 43.
29. *Select Trials*, vol. III (London, 1735), p. 36.
30. Holloway, *The Phoenix of Sodom*, p. 30.
31. *Select Trials*, vol. II (London, 1742), p. 193.
32. Holloway, *The Phoenix of Sodom*, p. 22.
33. *Ibid.*, newspaper clippings.
34. In coverage of the case the press called for the imposition of the death penalty for attempted sodomy as well as sodomy. See Louis Crompton, *Byron and Greek Love: Homophobia in Nineteenth-Century England* (London, 1984), p. 168.
35. Davenport-Hines, *Sex, Death and Punishment*, p. 101.
36. *Satan's Harvest Home, or the Present State of Whorecraft, Pimping, Adultery, Fornication, Sodomy, Procuring and the Game of Flats* (London, 1749), p. 52; Parker, *A View of Society and Manners*, p. 87; Holloway, *The Phoenix of Sodom*, p. 26; *Morning Chronicle*, cited in Crompton, *Byron and Greek Love*, p. 167.
37. *A View of the Town*, p. 19.
38. Holloway, *The Phoenix of Sodom*, p. 11.
39. *Select Trials*, vol. II, (London, 1735), p. 211; *Select Trials*, vol. III (London, 1742), p. 39; Norton, *Mother Clap's Molly House*, pp. 44–59; Davenport-Hines, *Sex, Death and Punishment*, pp. 69–72.
40. Norton, *Mother Clap's Molly House*, pp. 221–6. The son of the wealthiest man in England, William Beckford (1760–1844) became the subject of newspaper gossip over his friendship with William Courtney, later 9th Earl of Devon, in the 1780s. He subsequently lived largely outside London society at his estate at Fonthill, near Exeter, but Norton shows that he nevertheless continued to explore the homosexual possibilities London offered. See Norton, *Mother Clap's Molly House*, pp. 221–31.
41. See *ibid.*, pp. 216–21; Crompton, *Byron and Greek Love*, p. 300.
42. For details see H. G. Cocks, 'Nameless Offences: Homosexual Desire in the Nineteenth Century', ts, forthcoming (London, 2003), p. 109.
43. Norton, *Mother Clap's Molly House*, p. 228.
44. *Ibid.*

45. Cocks, 'Nameless Offences', chapter 2.
46. *Yokel's Preceptor or More Sprees in London!* (London, *c.*1855), pp. 5–7.
47. *Ibid.*, p. 6.
48. 'Lord Byron', *Don Leon* (London, 1866), pp. 1, 32 and 17. In the encyclopaedia of erotic writing, *Index Librorum Prohibitorum*, Pisanus Fraxi (the alias of Henry Spenser Ashbee) observed that the notes in *Don Leon* 'are copious, curious, frequently erudite, and give much information about the scandalous doings of the times'. Pisanus Fraxi, *Index Librorum Prohibitorum* (London, 1877), p. 189. For discussion of the poem and its authorship see Crompton, *Byron and Greek Love*, pp. 343–86.
49. *Ibid.*, p. 33.
50. Erica Rappaport, *Shopping for Pleasure: Women in the Making of London's West End* (Princeton, 2000).
51. Michael Miller, *The* Bon Marché: *Bourgeois Culture and the Department Store, 1869 –1920* (London, 1981), p. 167.
52. See Rappaport, *Shopping for Pleasure*; Lynda Nead, *Victorian Babylon: People, Streets and Images in Nineteenth-Century London* (New Haven, 2000), esp. part 1, section 4; Judith Walkowitz, *City of Dreadful Delight: Narratives of Sexual Danger in Late Victorian London* (London, 1992), ch. 2.
53. 'Piccadilly', *Chambers Journal of Popular Literature, Science, and Art*, 9, 444 (2 July 1892): 418.
54. Alison Adburgham, *Shopping in Style: London from the Restoration to Edwardian Elegance* (London, 1979), p. 101.
55. The case has been discussed extensively by historians and critics. See Neil Bartlett, *Who Was that Man? A Present for Mr Oscar Wilde* (London, 1988), pp. 128–43; Cocks, 'Nameless Offences', pp. 166–81; Sinfield, *The Wilde Century*, pp. 6–8; William Cohen, *Sex Scandal: The Private Parts of Victorian Fiction* (Durham, NC, 1996), ch. 3; Morris B. Kaplan, ' "Men in Petticoats": The Queer Case of Mr Boulton and Mr Park', in Pamela Gilbert (ed.), *Imagined Londons* (New York, 2002); Charles Upchurch, 'Forgetting the Unthinkable: Cross-dressers and British Society in the Case of the Queen vs Boulton and Others', *Gender and History*, 12, 1 (2000): 127–57.
56. 'The Trial of Boulton and Park', *Reynolds*, 14 May 1871: p. 7.
57. *The Lives of Boulton and Park: Extraordinary Revelations* (London, *c.*1870), p. 3. The broadsheet was also published as *Men in Petticoats*.
58. 'The Queen v. Boulton and Others', *The Times*, 10 May 1871: p. 11.
59. Cited in Bartlett, *Who Was That Man*, p. 132.
60. *The Lives of Boulton and Park*, p. 6.
61. 'The Boulton and Park Prosecution', *Telegraph*, 10 May 1871: p. 5.
62. 'The Trial of Boulton and Park', *Reynolds*, 14 May 1871: p. 6.
63. *The Lives of Boulton and Park*, p. 3.
64. Cocks, 'Nameless Offences', p. 174.
65. 'The Boulton and Park Case: The Verdict', *Reynolds*, 21 May 1871: p. 6.
66. Bartlett, *Who Was that Man?*, p. 138.

67. *The Lives of Boulton and Park*, p. 3
68. Bartlett, *Who Was that Man?*, p. 133. Kaplan develops a similar argument, noting that the case 'conveys a complex picture of distinctively urban forms of life. London is revealed as a site of individual freedom, public performance and social surveillance'. Kaplan, '"Men in Petticoats"', p. 52.
69. 'The Trial of Boulton and Park', *Reynolds*, p. 6
70. On this point see Upchurch, 'Forgetting the Unthinkable'.
71. *The Lives of Boulton and Park*, p. 7.
72. *Ibid.*
73. 'The Boulton and Park Prosecution', *Telegraph*, 10 May 1871; 'The Trial of Boulton and Park', *Reynolds*.
74. Bartlett, *Who Was That Man?*, p. 142; Sinfield, *The Wilde Century*, p. 8.
75. Cocks, 'Nameless Offences', p. 179.
76. Peter Mendes, *Clandestine Erotic Fiction in English 1800–1930* (Aldershot, 1993), p. 216.
77. Pisanus Fraxi, *Catena Librorium Tacendorum* (London, 1885), p. 195.
78. *Sins of the Cities of the Plain, or Recollections of a Mary-Ann, with Short Essays on Sodomy and Tribadism* (London, 1881), p. 89.
79. *Ibid.*, p. 9.
80. John Addington Symonds, *The Memoirs of John Addington Symonds*, ed. Phyllis Grosskurth (London, 1984), pp. 186 and 253.
81. For details of Beckford's scrapbooks see Norton, *Mother Clap's Molly House*, pp. 221–31. George Ives' 'Casebooks' are held at the Beinecke Rare Book and Manuscript Library, Yale University, MSS 14.
82. On this point see Lisa Z. Sigel, *Governing Pleasures: Pornography and Social Change in England, 1815–1914* (New Brunswick, 2002), p. 2; and Cohen, *Sex Scandal*, p. 124.
83. *Sins of the Cities*, pp. 38–9.
84. On this point see Rudi Bleys, *The Geography of Perversion: Male to Male Sexual Behaviour Outside the West and the Ethnographic Imagination, 1750–1918* (London, 1996).
85. *Ibid.*, p. 75. See Seth Koven's incisive account of the novel in relation to works of urban exploration, the settlement movement and cross-class erotics. Seth Koven, 'From Rough Lads to Hooligans: Boy Life, National Culture and Social Reform,' in Andrew Parker, Mary Russo, Doris Sommer and Patricia Yaeger (eds.), *Nationalisms and Sexualities* (London, 1992).
86. *Sins of the Cities*, p. 60.
87. On this point see Laurence Senelick, 'Boys and Girls Together: Subcultural Origins of Glamour Drag and Male Impersonation on the Nineteenth Century Stage', in Lesley Ferris (ed.), *Crossing the Stage: Controversies in Cross-Dressing* (London, 1993), p. 88.
88. Morris B. Kaplan, 'Who's Afraid of Jack Saul?: Urban Culture and the Politics of Desire in Late Victorian London', *GLQ*, 5, 3 (1999): 267–314, p. 285.
89. *Sins of the Cities*, p. 54.

90. The limerick read: 'There was a person of Sark / Who buggered a pig in the dark; / The swine in surprise / Murmured: "God blast your eyes, / Do you take me for Boulton or Park?"' Cited by Colin Simpson, Chester Lewis and David Leitch, *The Cleveland Street Affair* (Boston, 1976), p. 59. See also: 'Male Prostitution', *Reynolds*, 26 May 1895: p. 1; 'In Male Attire: No Law Against Masquerade', *Globe*, 27 July 1910, in Ives, 'Casebook', vol. VII, p. 89.

91. Pisanus Fraxi, *Index Librorum Prohibitorum*; *Centuria Librorum Absconditorum* (London, 1879); *Catena Librorum Tacnedorum* (London, 1885).

92. Subheading from: Lord Alfred Douglas, *The Rossiad* (1914; London, 1916), p. 10; Carl Baedeker, *London and its Environs* (London, 1885), pp. 5–15; Baedeker, *London and its Environs* (London, 1911), pp. 1–17.

93. Donald Olsen, *The Growth of Victorian London* (London, 1976), p. 114.

94. *Parliamentary Papers: Reports from the Commissioners*, vol. 57 (London, 1888), p. 49; Susan Pennybacker, *A Vision for London, 1889–1914: Labour, Everyday Life and the London County Council Experiment* (London, 1995), pp. 212–13 and 225.

95. Walkowitz, *City of Dreadful Delight*, p. 46.

96. George Sims, *Living London*, vol. 1 (London, 1901–3), p. 4; Arthur Ransome, *Bohemia in London* (London, 1907), p. 114.

97. Ransome, *Bohemia in London*, p. 122.

98. Oscar Wilde, 'The Decay of Lying' (1889), in *De Profundis and Other Writings* (London, 1986), p. 82.

99. Fergus Hume, *The Piccadilly Puzzle: A Mysterious Story* (London, 1889), p. 6.

100. *Tempted London* (London 1889), p. 199. See also Percy Fitzgerald, *Music Hall Land* (London, 1890), p. 11.

101. George Gissing, *In the Year of Jubilee* (1894; London, 1994), p. 58.

102. Fashion, appearance and locale were used repeatedly in literature of the second half of the nineteenth century to fix the random subject and to assign a biography. See, for example, Henry Mayhew, *London Labour and London Poor* (London, 1861); W. E. Henley and William Nicholson, *London Types* (London, 1898); and Sims, *Living London*. See also Christopher Breward, *The Hidden Consumer: Masculinities, Fashion and City Life, 1860–1914* (Manchester, 1999); and Mary Cowling, *The Artist as Anthropologist: The Representation of Type and Character in Victorian Art* (Cambridge, 1989).

103. *Tempted London*, p. 206.

104. Ives' scrapbook gives a good indication of Piccadilly's reputation. See, for example, 'Man in Woman's Attire: A Struggle in Piccadilly', *Echo*, 14 April 1897, in Ives, 'Casebook', vol. I, p. 95; 'Perils of Piccadilly', *Star*, 19 July 1902, in 'Casebook', vol. III, p. 52; 'Remarkable Blackmail Charge', *Daily Chronicle*, 18 January 1906, in 'Casebook', vol. V, p. 108; and 'Prison and a Whipping', 23 October 1906, in 'Casebook', vol. VI, p. 41 (newspaper not cited).

105. 'Man in Woman's Dress', *Daily Mail*, 22 August 1906, in Ives, 'Casebook', vol. VI, p. 36.

106. Roger Casement, *The Black Diaries*, eds. Peter Singleton-Gates and Maurice Girodias (London, 1959).

107. See, for example, 'The Curse of Marylebone Yet Again', *Marylebone Advertiser*, 21 September 1901, in Ives, 'Casebook', vol. III, p. 21; 'Serious Charge of Blackmailing: Strange Case at the West End', *Daily Chronicle*, 8 May 1895: p. 9; *The Law Reports: King's Bench Division* (London, 1913), p. 155–8. See also H. Montgomery Hyde, *The Other Love: An Historical and Contemporary Survey of Homosexuality in Britain* (London, 1970), p. 206; and Matt Houlbrook, 'The Private World of Public Urinals: London, 1918–57', *London Journal*, 25, 1 (2000): 52–70.

108. Hyde, *The Other Love*, p. 208.

109. Rupert Croft-Cooke, *Feasting With Panthers: A New Consideration of Some Late Victorian Writers* (London, 1967), pp. 262, 268 and 270.

110. George Ives, 'Diary', vol. XXXIX, 30 May 1901, p. 30, George Ives Papers, Harry Ransom Humanities Research Center, University of Texas of Austin.

111. See 'Suspects on the Embankment', *Evening News*, 7 May 1905, in Ives, 'Casebook', vol. V, p. 43; 'Serious Allegations Against Two Constables', *Evening Mail*, 21 April 1903, in 'Casebook', vol. III, p. 97; 'Prosecutor Commits Suicide', *Daily Chronicle*, 13 May 1904, in 'Casebook', vol. IV, p. 68; 'Hyde Park Incident', *Reynolds*, 16 July 1906, in 'Casebook', vol. V, p. 78; 'Met in Hyde Park', *News of the World*, 22 November 1908, in 'Casebook', vol. VII, p. 85; 'West End Blackmailers', *Star*, 12 January 1898: p. 3. The parks also feature repeatedly in Casement's diaries.

112. Two weeks later the *Express* printed complaints from guardsmen that they feared to look in a shop window for two minutes for fear of being arrested by the military police. 'Law for Loitering Soldiers', *Star*, 28 September 1903, in Ives, 'Casebook', vol. IV, p. 17; 'Many Soldiers Arrested', *Express*, 12 October 1903, in 'Casebook', vol. IV, p. 20.

113. See Matt Houlbrook, 'Soldier Heroes and Rent Boys: Homosex, Masculinities and Britishness in the Brigade of Guards, *c*.1900–60', *Journal of British Studies*, forthcoming, July 2003.

114. Symonds, *Memoirs*, p. 254; Casement, *Black Diaries*, 7 February 1911, p. 547; 10 February 1911, p. 548; 25 July 1911, p. 598; and 3 August 1911, p. 602; A. E. Housman, 'The Shropshire Lad', Poem xxxvii, in *Collected Poems and Selected Prose*, ed. Christopher Ricks (London, 1988); Ives, 'Diary', vol. XLIII, 6 December 1903, p. 61.

115. Croft-Cooke, *Feasting With Panthers*, p. 246: Casement, *Black Diaries*, 12 February 1911, p. 549; 'To Defeat the Blackmailer', *Daily Chronicle*, 12 April 1901, in Ives, 'Casebook', vol. III, p. 43; 'Impropriety on a Bus', *c*.March 1904, in 'Casebook', vol. IV, p. 64; and 'Charge Against Dr Stanton Coit', *Daily Telegraph*, 25 March 1908, in 'Casebook', vol. VII, p. 3.

116. John Gambril Nicholson, 'Your City Cousins', in *Love in Earnest: Sonnets, Ballades, and Lyrics*, (London, 1892), pp. 331–2

117. Jeffrey Weeks notes that in Casement's diary 'there is no sense . . . of his seeing the possibility of a full homosexual lifestyle'. Jeffrey Weeks, *Sex, Politics and Society* (London, 1981), p. 110.

118. Theo Aronson, *Prince Eddy and the Homosexual Underworld* (London, 1994), p. 24; Croft-Cooke, *Feasting With Panthers*, pp. 260–70; Hyde, *The Other Love*, p. 163.
119. Ives, 'Diary', vol. xlvii, 15 June 1905, p. 38.
120. Sims, *Living London*, vol. ii, p. 288.
121. Their operations came to light when their landlady called the police, but they were not prosecuted. They were later implicated in the Wilde trials. See Croft-Cooke, *Feasting with Panthers*, pp. 264–6.
122. Ives, 'Diary', vol. xvii, 15 October 1893, p. 119.
123. Robert Machray, *The Night Side of London* (London, 1902), p. vi.
124. Charles Hirsch, '*Notice Bibliographique*', in *Teleny: Étude Physiologique (traduit de l'anglais sur le manuscrit original révisé par l'auteur)* (Paris, 1934), p. 9.
125. For details see Mendes, *Clandestine Erotic Fiction*, pp. 3–23.
126. For discussion of the Holywell Street book trade see Nead, *Victorian Babylon*, pt 3, sec. 2.
127. Mendes, *Clandestine Erotic Fiction*, p. 215; Morris B. Kaplan, 'Did My Lord Gomorrah Smile? Social Class, Prostitution, and Sexuality in the Cleveland Street Affair', in Nancy Erber and George Robb (eds.) *Disorder in the Court: Trials and Sexual Conflict at the Turn of the Century* (Basingstoke, 1999).
128. Croft-Cooke, *Feasting with Panthers*, p. 268.
129. *Ibid.*, p. 270.
130. Hirsch, '*Notice Bibliographique*', p. 11. The translation is taken from Mendes, *Clandestine Erotic Fiction*, appendix D, p. 449.
131. See Robert Hichens *Yesterday* (London, 1947), pp. 69–70; Regenia Gagnier, *Idylls of the Marketplace: Oscar Wilde and the Victorian Public* (Aldershot, 1987), pp. 164–5; Bartlett, *Who Was That Man?*, p. 50.
132. 'West-End Flat Scandal', *Reynolds*, 15 April 1906: p. 5; 'Recorder's Regret. One of A Dangerous Gang', *Reynolds*, 5 May 1906: p. 4. Mellors was sentenced to eighteen months' hard labour under the Criminal Law Amendment Act.
133. Kerry Powell, *Oscar Wilde and the Theatre of the 1890s* (Cambridge, 1990), p. 2 and ch. 5.
134. See Christopher Innes, *A Sourcebook on Naturalistic Theatre* (London, 2000), esp. chs. 4 and 6; Holbrook Jackson, *The 1890s: A Review of Art and Ideas* (1913; London, 1927), ch. 15; James Roose-Evans, *London Theatre, from the Globe to the National* (Oxford, 1977), ch. 7.
135. On this point, see Gagnier, *Idylls of the Marketplace*, pp. 105–6 and ch. 3.
136. Susan Pennybacker and Gareth Stedman Jones both detail this conservatism, though Peter Bailey argues that whilst the bare lyrics and turns suggest a reactionary repertoire, the performers and audience often shared 'a sense of complicit mischief', with silences, gesture and banter indicating hidden meaning. Pennybacker, *A Vision for London*, pp. 212–13 and 225; Gareth Stedman Jones, *Languages of Class* (Cambridge, 1983), ch. 4; Peter Bailey, 'Conspiracies of Meaning: Music Hall and the Knowingness of Popular Culture', *Past and Present*, 144 (August 1994): pp. 138–71.

137. Martha Vicinus, 'Male Impersonation and Lesbian Desire', in Billie Melman (ed.) *Borderlines: Genders and Identities in War and Peace, 1870–1930* (London, 1998), p. 165. See also Laurence Senelick, 'Boys and Girls Together'.
138. On the importance of impersonation, 'passing' and performance to understandings of homosexuality during this period see Vicinus, 'Male Impersonation'; and Cocks, 'Nameless Offences', p. 150.
139. Hyde, *The Other Love*, p. 110.
140. H. Montgomery Hyde, *The Cleveland Street Scandal* (London, 1976), p. 88.
141. Ives, 'Diary', vol. XLI, 18 September 1902, p. 112.
142. *Ibid.*, vol. XXIX, 24 October 1896, p. 49.
143. *Ibid.*, vol. XXXVIII, 30 September 1900, p. 30.
144. Alan Crawford, *C. R. Ashbee: Architect, Designer and Romantic Socialist* (London, 1985), p. 4.
145. See Ives, 'Diary', vol. XVII, 26 October 1893, p. 129.
146. Karl Beckson, *London in the 1890s: A Cultural History* (New York, 1992), p. 210.
147. G. S. Street, *The Autobiography of a Boy* (London, 1894), p. xiii; Roy Porter, *London: A Social History* (London, 1994), p. 282.
148. Vernon Lee, 'Lady Tal', in Elaine Showalter (ed.), *Daughters of Decadence* (New Brunswick, 1993), p. 195.
149. *Ibid.*, p. 231.
150. *Ibid.*, p. 232.
151. Ellen Moers, *The Dandy: Brummel to Beerbohm* (Lincoln, NE, 1978), p. 314.
152. H. Montgomery Hyde, *The Trials of Oscar Wilde* (New York, 1973), p. 189.
153. There was also a broader interest in the bohemian and his position on the fringes of respectability during this period. George Du Maurier and Giacomo Puccini's popular depictions of bohemian life – in *Trilby* (1894) and the opera *La Bohème* (1896) – both date from the 1890s.
154. Ives, 'Diary', vol. XXI, 28 August 1894, p. 48 (verso note); vol. XVII, 9 July 1893, p. 1; vol. XVII, 17 July 1893, p. 2; vol. XX, 5 July 1894, p. 108.
155. See Jeffrey Weeks, *Coming Out: Homosexual Politics from the Nineteenth Century to the Present* (1979; London, 1990), pp. 122–4. Laurence Housman is also named as a member by Weeks but a letter from Housman to Janet Ashbee suggests that although Ives promised to bequeath his sacred ring to Housman if he joined the order, he refused: 'I hadn't the faith for it', he said. Fiona MacCarthy, *The Simple Life: C. R. Ashbee in the Cotswolds* (Berkeley, 1981), p. 144. I am grateful to Anna Davin for directing me to this reference.
156. Laurel Brake, *Print in Transition, 1850–1910: Studies in Media and Book History* (Basingstoke, 2001), p. 119.
157. 'The New Chivalry', *The Artist and Journal of Home Culture*, 14/15 (April 1893): 102–3.
158. Michael Holroyd (ed.), *Lytton Strachey By Himself: A Self Portrait*, (London, 1994), 24 March 1910, p. 128,
159. A. C. Whitmore, MP, 'Architecture: London', *The Artist*, 8/9 (July 1888): p. 212. 'The British Museum', *The Artist*, 14/15 (February 1893): p. 41.

160. Walter Pater, *The Renaissance: Studies in Art and Poetry* (1873; Oxford, 1986), p. 140.
161. Walter Pater, 'The Age of Athletic Prizemen', in *Greek Studies* (1895; London, 1901), p. 288.
162. Cited in P. N. Furbank, *E. M. Forster: A Life* (London, 1978), p. 110.
163. Housman, *Collected Poems*, Poem li, p. 77.
164. Pygmalion was the subject of Edward Burne-Jones' Pygmalion series of paintings (1868–78); William Morris' poem *The Earthly Paradise* (1868); W. S. Gilbert's comedy *Pygmalion and Galatea* (1872); and later George Bernard Shaw's play *Pygmalion* (1912). Once again a popular contemporary motif was being used to homoerotic effect.
165. E. M. Forster, *Maurice* (1914; London, 1972), p. 197.
166. *Tempted London*, p. 218.
167. Ives, 'Diary', vol. XLVIII, 19 October 1905, p. 4.
168. Philip Hoare, *Wilde's Last Stand: Decadence, Conspiracy and the First World War* (London, 1997), p. 21.
169. Pater, for example, compared the discobus to the English cricketer, and Richard Livingstone was confident that the ancient Greeks would feel at home at Oxford or Cambridge, among people 'mainly young, active, well-developed in body and mind'. Pater, 'The Age of Athletic Prizemen', pp. 282 and 296; Livingstone, cited in Richard Jenkyns, *The Victorians and Ancient Greece* (Oxford, 1980), p. 221. On the LCC see also Chris Waters, 'Progressives, Puritans and the Cultural Politics of the Council, 1889–1914', in Andrew Saint (ed.), *Politics and the People of London: the London County Council, 1889–1965* (London, 1989), p. 69.
170. Ives, 'Diary', vol. XVI, 9 September 1911, p. 44.
171. Sims, *Living London*, vol. I, p. 139. Carl Baedeker, *London and its Environs* (London, 1911), p. 262.
172. Symonds, *Memoirs*, p. 166.
173. Ives, 'Diary', vol. XXII, 27 August 1894, p. 57.
174. *Ibid.*, vol. LII, 20 June 1908, p. 9; vol. XLVII, July 8, 1905, p. 50.
175. See J.Cooper, *Victorian and Edwardian Furniture and Interiors* (London, 1987), p. 187.
176. Novels included Walter Besant's *All Sorts and Conditions of Men* (London, 1882), George Gissing's *The Nether World* (Oxford, 1889), Israel Zangwill's *Children of the Ghetto* (London, 1892) and Arthur Morrison's *A Child of the Jago* (London, 1896). Amongst the journalism and survey work: Charles Booth's *Life and Labour of the People of London* (London, 1889–1905), James Greenwood's *In Strange Company* (London, 1873–83), Andrew Mearns' pamphlet *The Bitter Cry of Outcast London* (London, 1883), George Sims' *How the Poor Live* (London, 1883), Charles Masterman's *The Heart of Empire* (London, 1901) and Jack London's *The People of the Abyss* (London, 1903).
177. On these crises see especially Gareth Stedman Jones, *Outcast London: A Study in the Relationship Between Classes in Victorian Society* (Oxford, 1971) and

Daniel Pick, *Faces of Degeneration: A European Disorder, c.1848–1918* (Cambridge, 1989).

178. C. R. Ashbee, 'Memoirs' (unpublished), cited in Jonathan Rose, *The Edwardian Temperament, 1895–1919* (Ohio, 1986), p. 65.
179. Walkowitz, *City of Dreadful Delight*, p. 59.
180. Edward Carpenter, 'The Intermediate Sex'(1908), in *Selected Writings: Sex* (London, 1984), p. 236.
181. Edward Carpenter, *Towards Democracy* (1883–1902; London, 1985), p. 325.
182. 'Immorality at Public Schools. Striking Correspondence', *Reynolds*, 2 June 1895: p. 5.
183. See Sinfield, *The Wilde Century*, ch.6; Croft-Cooke, *Feasting with Panthers*, pt. 2; Koven, 'From Rough Lads to Hooligans'.
184. The Cleveland Street scandal and the cases of James Smith (1877, 1897) and Edward Lovell (1906) each involved telegraph boys. On Smith's prosecution see 'Corrupting the Youth of the Country', *c.*February 1897, in Ives, 'Casebook', vol. I, p. 44, and Ives, 'Diary', vol. XLVIII, 20 December 1905, p. 38. On Lovell see 'Aristocratic Rogues. Abominable Conduct, Ex-University Student Sentenced', *Reynolds*, *c.*July/August 1906, in Ives, 'Casebook', vol. VI, p. 28. Each mention of telegraph boys in the article was underlined by Ives.
185. Casement, *Black Diaries*, 15 December 1903, p. 185; 3 February 1911, p. 545; and 18 February 1911, p. 551.
186. Eve Sedgwick, *Between Men: English Literature and Male Homosocial Desire* (New York, 1985), pp. 172–3.
187. Weeks, *Coming Out*, p. 43.
188. Sinfield, *The Wilde Century*, ch. 2.
189. 'Retribution', *Evening News*, 27 May 1905: p. 2.
190. Carpenter referred to the homosexual lives of working-class men in *Towards Democracy*; Ives reported hearing two 'workers' having sex in a changing cubicle at the Westminster baths; and in the Cleveland Street case the telegraph boys had been having sex with each other in the toilets at the Post Office headquarters before they started working at the brothel. See Carpenter, *Towards Democracy*, pp. 323–6; Ives, 'Diary', vol. XVII, 29 July 1893, p. 18; Kaplan, 'Did My Lord Gomorrah Smile', p. 86.
191. 'The Dandy's Toilet', *Modern Man*, 28 November 1908: p. 22. For discussion of *Modern Man*, masculinity and fashion see Breward, *The Hidden Consumer*, pp. 180–1, 192–3.
192. Captain L. H. Saunders, 'The Outer Man', *Modern Man*, 12 December 1908: p. 24 and 13 March 1909: p. 24.
193. C. D. Witton, 'Judging a Man by His Button Hole', *Modern Man*, 15 January 1910: p. 22.
194. Stuart Freeman, 'London Hell: Vampires', *Modern Man*, 12 December 1908: p. 10.
195. Freeman, 'London Hell: Blackmailers', *Modern Man*, 21 November 1908: p. 10.

196. For discussion of middle-class masculinity under threat see A. James Hammerton, 'The English Weakness? Gender, Satire and Moral Manliness in the Lower-Middle Classes, 1870–1920', in Alan Kidd and David Nicholls (eds.), *Gender, Civic Culture and Consumerism* (Manchester, 1999); Angus McLaren, *The Trials of Masculinity: Policing Sexual Boundaries, 1870–1930* (Chicago, 1997); Michael Roper and John Tosh (eds.), *Manful Assertions: Masculinities in Britain Since* 1800 (London, 1991); Christopher Breward, 'Fashion and the Man, From Suburb to City Street: The Cultural Geography of Masculine Consumption, 1870–1914', *New Formations*, 37 (Spring 1999): 47–70.

197. See, for example, H. Barton-Baker, *Stories of the Streets of London* (London, 1899); Richard Tames, *Soho Past* (London, 1894); E. F. Rimbault, *Soho and its Associations* (London, 1895); Walter Thornbury, *Old and New London* (London, 1873–8 and 1897); and E. Beresford Chancellor, *Wanderings in Piccadilly, Mayfair and Pall Mall* (London, 1907). Stephen Kern suggests that these years were also characterised by a more general interest in heritage and history, which can be related to mounting anxieties about what the city and modern society 'meant'. See Stephen Kern, *The Culture of Time and Space, 1880–1918* (London, 1983), pp. 38–9.

198. Peter Bailey, 'Conspiracies of Meaning'.

2 THE GROSSLY INDECENT CITY

1. *Public General Acts, 44 and 45 Vict.* (London, 1861), p. 833, sec. 61 and 62. The legal theorist Leslie Moran observes that these pieces of legislation organised the crime of sodomy in thematic relation to other criminal acts, and so connected it to both paedophilia and rape. Leslie Moran, *The Homosexual(ity) of Law* (London, 1996), p. 79.

2. *Public General Acts, 48–49 Vict.* (London, 1885), p. 6, sec. 11.

3. Ed Cohen, *Talk on the Wilde Side: Towards a Genealogy of a Discourse on Male Sexualities* (London, 1993), p. 91–2; Jeffrey Weeks, *Coming Out: Homosexual Politics from the Nineteenth Century to the Present* (1979; London, 1990), p. 10–11. On this point see also H. G. Cocks, 'Nameless Offences: Homosexual Desire in the Nineteenth Century', ts, forthcoming (London, 2003), pp. 18–25.

4. This apparent domestic self-determination was carefully controlled through 'ideological directives and constraints', as Zedner goes on to argue. Lucia Zedner, 'Regulating Sexual Offences Within the Home', in Ian Loveland (ed.) *Frontiers of Criminality* (London, 1995), p. 176. See also Roy Porter and Lesley Hall, *The Facts of Life: The Creation of Sexual Knowledge in Britain, 1650–1950* (London, 1995), part II.

5. Henry Labouchere, *Truth*, 28 November 1889: p. 983.

6. *Public General Acts, 61–62 Vict.* (London, 1898), p. 221, sec. 1b.

7. *Public General Acts, 4 Geo.* (London, 1824), p. 698, sec. 3; *Public General Acts, 2–3 Geo. V* (London, 1912), p. 91–91, secs. 5 and 7.

8. George Ives, *The Continued Extension of the Criminal Law* (London, 1922), p. 8.

9. 'Perils of Piccadilly', *Star*, 19 July 1902, in George Ives, 'Casebook', vol. III, p. 52, Beinecke Rare Book and Manuscript Library, Yale University, MSS 14.

10. 'Marlborough Street Rogues and Vagabonds', *Illustrated Police News*, 15 June 1912: p. 14.

11. *The Law Reports: King's Bench Division* (London, 1913), p. 155–8. Les Moran also discusses this case. See Moran, *The Homosexual(ity) of Law*, pp. 135–6.

12. George Ives, 'Diary', vol. LXI, 15 July 1914, p. 4, George Ives papers, Harry Ransom Humanities Research Center, University of Texas at Austin.

13. See François Lafitte, 'Homosexuality and the Law', *British Journal of Delinquency*, 9, 1 (July 1958): 8–19, p. 12.

14. Henry Havelock Ellis and John Addington Symonds, *Studies in the Psychology of Sex*, vol. I, *Sexual Inversion* (London, 1897), p. 155.

15. Ives, 'Diary', vol. XXXVII, 18 July 1900, p. 81; vol. X, 10 January 1891, p. 2.

16. Jeffrey Weeks and Alan Sinfield both show how the 1885 Act was passed in an atmosphere of general concern about incontinent male lust and note the legislative links made between homosexuality and prostitution by the 1885 and 1898 Acts. Weeks, *Coming Out*, pp. 16–17; Weeks, *Against Nature: Essays on History, Sexuality and Identity* (London, 1991), pp. 52–3; Alan Sinfield, *The Wilde Century: Effeminacy, Oscar Wilde and the Queer Moment* (London, 1994), p. 14.

17. Henry Labouchere, *Truth*, 11 April 1895: p. 1331. The historian F. B. Smith also indicates the importance of Labouchere's character and public profile. F. B. Smith, 'Labouchere's Amendment to the Criminal Law Amendment Bill', *Historical Studies*, 17 (October 1976): 165–73.

18. *Parliamentary Debates*, vol. 64 (London, 1898), col.747–58.

19. *Parliamentary Papers: Reports from the Commissioners: Police*, vol. 57 (London, 1888), p. 49.

20. *Parliamentary Papers: Reports from the Commissioners*, vol. 46 (London,1898), p. 57. See also Stefan Petrow, *Policing Morals: The Metropolitan Police and the Home Office, 1870–1914* (Oxford, 1994), ch. 5

21. *Parliamentary Papers: Reports from the Commissioners: Police*, vol. 14 (London, 1916), p. 23.

22. 'Fitzroy Street Raid Decision', *Star*, 20 August 1894: p. 3.

23. 'Suspects on the Embankment', *Evening News*, 2 May 1905, in Ives, 'Casebook', vol. V, p. 43.

24. 'Prison and a Whipping', 23 October 1906, in Ives, 'Casebook', vol. VI, p. 41. Newspaper not specified.

25. For a discussion of the problems associated with the interpretation of this kind of crime data see V. A. C. Gatrell, 'The Decline of Theft and Violence in Victoria and Edwardian England', in V. A. C. Gatrell, Bruce Lenman and Geoffrey Parker (eds.) *Crime and the Law: the Social History of Crime in Western Europe since 1500* (London, 1980).

26. Cocks, 'Nameless Offences', p. 110.

27. Four police commissioners served during the period: General Sir Charles Warren (1886–8); James Munro (1888–90); Col. E. R. C Bradford (1890–1903); and Sir E. R. Henry (1903–18).
28. 'West End at Night: Police Indignation at MP's Imputation of Blackmail', *Reynolds*, 26 May 1912: p. 3.
29. *The Newspaper Press Directory: A Complete Guide to the Newspaper Press in Each County* (London, 1846; 1865; 1891; 1894).
30. See Laurel Brake, 'The Old Journalism and the New: Forms of Cultural Production in London in the 1880s', in Joel Wiener (ed.) *Papers for the Millions: The New Journalism in Britain 1850–1914* (New York, 1988), p. 2.
31. T. P. O'Connor, 'The New Journalism', *New Review*, 1, 5 (October 1889): 423–34, p. 434.
32. On this point see Judith Walkowitz, *City of Dreadful Delight: Narratives of Sexual Danger in Late Victorian London* (London, 1992), pp. 83–4.
33. Oscar Wilde, 'The Critic as Artist' (1891), in Richard Ellman (ed.) *The Artist as Critic: Critical Writings of Oscar Wilde* (London, 1970), p. 348. See also Richard Ericson, Patricia Baranek and Janet Chan, *Visualising Deviance: A Study of News Organisation* (Milton Keynes, 1987), p. 3; Nicola Lacey, 'Contingency and Criminalisation', in Ian Loveland (ed.), *Frontiers of Criminality* (London, 1995), p. 5.
34. 'The West End Scandals: Names of Some of the Distinguished Criminals Who Have Escaped', *North London Press*, 16 November 1889: p. 5.
35. For detailed accounts of the Cleveland Street scandal see H. Montgomery Hyde, *The Cleveland Street Scandal* (London, 1976), Colin Simpson, Chester Lewis and David Leitch, *The Cleveland Street Affair* (Boston, 1976) and Theo Aronson, *Prince Eddy and the Homosexual Underworld* (London, 1994). Morris Kaplan gives a sophisticated account of the class dynamics of the case: Morris B. Kaplan, 'Did My Lord Gomorrah Smile? Social Class, Prostitution, and Sexuality in the Cleveland Street Affair', in Nancy Erber and George Robb (eds.), *Disorder in the Court: Trials and Sexual Conflict at the Turn of the Century* (Basingstoke, 1999).
36. Hyde, *The Cleveland Street Scandal*, p. 207.
37. 'Other Cases: Horrible Condition of London', *Reynolds*, 28 April 1895: p. 1.
38. 'Other Serious Charges', *Reynolds*, 14 April 1895, p. 1; 'More Cases for the Old Bailey', *Reynolds*, 5 May 1895, p. 8.
39. 'In Women's Clothes', *Reynolds*, 21 April 1895: p. 8; 'In Women's Clothes', *Reynolds*, 28 April 1895: p. 6.
40. On this point see Walkowitz, *City of Dreadful Delight*, pp. 83–4.
41. *Reynolds*, 30 April 1891: p. 4; and 8 May, 1891: p. 14.
42. 'Middlesex Sessions Appeals', *Reynolds*, 9 May 1886: p. 8.
43. Lucy Brown, 'The Growth of the National Press', in Laurel Brake, Aled Jones and Lionel Madden (eds.) *Investigating Victorian Journalism* (London, 1990), p. 133.
44. Cocks, 'Nameless Offences', p. 143.
45. *Parliamentary Debates*, vol. 341 (London, 1890), col. 1585.

46. T. P. O'Connor, 'What We Think: A Word on the Scandals', *Star*, 25 November 1889: pp. 1–3.
47. Henry Labouchere, *Truth*, 6 March 1890: p. 473.
48. 'Euston Libel Case: A Witness for the Defence Tells a Sensational Story', *Star* 16 January 1890: p. 3.
49. *Parliamentary Debates*, vol. 341 (London, 1890), p. 1586.
50. Ives, 'Diary', vol. LVII, 16 July 1912, p. 101.
51. 'Recorder's Regret: One of a Dangerous Gang: An Actor's Penitence', *Reynolds*, 6 May 1906: p. 4.
52. 'The Cleveland Street Case', *Pall Mall Gazette*, 15 January 1890: p. 5; 'Another London Scandal' and 'The West End Scandals', *Reynolds*, 12 January 1890: p. 5; 'Fitzroy Square Raid', *Star*, 20, August 1894: p. 3; 'The West End Blackmailing Case', *Daily Chronicle*, 24 May 1895: p. 7; 'West End Blackmailers', *Star*, 12 January 1898: p. 3; 'West End Flat Scandal', *Reynolds*, 15 April 1906: p. 5; 'The Studio Murder', *The Times*, 25 May 1906: p. 9; and 'Met in Hyde Park', *News of the World*, 22 November 1908, in Ives, 'Casebook', vol. VII, p. 85.
53. 'What We Think', *Star*, 1 March 1890: p. 1.
54. 'Lord Euston's Case', *Reynolds*, 9 January 1890: p. 4.
55. *Parliamentary Debates*, vol. 341 (1890), col. 1541; 'West End Scandal Case: Severe Sentencing on Mr Parke', *Illustrated Police News, Law Courts and Weekly Record*, 25 January 1890: p. 1.
56. Cited in Hyde, *Cleveland Street*, p. 142.
57. *Ibid.*, p. 178.
58. 'Piccadilly', *Chambers Journal*, 9 (2 July 1892): 417–20, p. 419.
59. 'Retribution', *Evening News*, 27 May 1895: p. 2.
60. Cohen, *Talk on the Wilde Side*, p. 180.
61. H. Montgomery Hyde, *The Trials of Oscar Wilde* (London, 1973), p. 203. This cross-examination was also widely reported.
62. 'The Wilde Scandal', *Star*, 21 May 1895: p. 3.
63. Hyde, *Oscar Wilde*, p. 250.
64. 'Wilde: Judge's Summing Up', *Star*, 1 May 1895: p. 3.
65. Hyde, *Oscar Wilde*, p. 203.
66. 'Wilde: Cross-Examined for the Third Time', *Star*, 24 May 1895: p. 2.
67. 'Oscar Wilde', *Star*, 29 April 1895: p. 2.
68. 'Oscar Wilde: Charged this Morning at Bow Street', *Star*, 6 April 1895: p. 3.
69. Hyde, *Oscar Wilde*, p. 268.
70. 'Comment', *Chronicle*, 26 May 1895: p. 4. Correspondence in *Reynolds* after the trial further centred on the morality of public schools, and suggested they were a cause of urban vice. See, for example, 'Immorality at Public Schools: Remarkable Letters', *Reynolds*, 25 May 1895: p. 3; 'Immorality at Public Schools: Striking Correspondence', *Reynolds*, 2 June 1895: p. 5.
71. 'Dangerous Infiltration', *Telegraph*, 6 April 1895: p. 4.
72. 'Sale of Oscar Wilde's Effects', *Reynolds*, 28 April 1895: p. 1.
73. 'Corrupting the Youth of the Country', *c.*February 1897, in Ives, 'Casebook', vol. I, p. 44. Smith was sentenced to life imprisonment for sodomy with

telegraph boys in 1877 and his release in 1895 was on a ticket of leave. His prosecution in 1897 meant this ticket was revoked and his life sentence recommenced after he had served his two years with hard labour. He was released again in 1905 under the supervision of the Salvation Army in Bermondsey, but having committed another offence was sent back to prison in 1905. Ives commented: 'In the future they will be wondering what state of knowledge could then have prevailed, when such sentences were ever possible.' Ives, 'Diary', vol. XLVIII, 20 December 1905, p. 38.

74. Oscar Wilde to the Home Secretary, Sir Matthew White Ridley, 2 July 1896, in Rupert Hart-Davis (ed.), *Selected Letters of Oscar Wilde* (Oxford, 1979), pp. 142–5.

75. Cohen, *Talk on the Wilde Side*, p. 139.

76. *Morning Leader*, 4 and 5 April 1895; Cohen, *Talk on the Wilde Side*, pp. 139–41.

77. Marc-André Raffalovich, *Uranisme et Unisexualite*, cited in Chris White (ed.), *Nineteenth-Century Writing on Homosexuality* (London, 1999), p. 259.

78. 'Retribution', *Evening News*, 27 May 1895: p. 2.

79. 'Lord Euston's Case', *Reynolds*, 19 January 1890: p. 4; 'Euston Libel Case', *Star*, 16 January 1890: p. 3; 'What We Think', *Star*, 17 January 1890: p. 1.

80. Kaplan, 'Did My Lord Gomorrah Smile', p. 86.

81. 'Raid on Fitzroy Square', *Star*, 13 August 1894: p. 3.

82. 'In Woman's Clothes', *Reynolds*, 21 April 1895: p. 8; 'Man in Woman's Dress', *Daily Mail*, 22 August 1906, in Ives, 'Casebook', vol. VII, p. 36.

83. 'The Curse of Marylebone Yet Again', *Maylebone Advertiser*, 21 September 1901, in Ives, 'Casebook', vol. III, p. 21.

84. 'Met in Hyde Park', *News of the World*, 22 November 1908, in Ives, 'Casebook', vol. VII, p. 85.

85. Cited in Cohen, *Talk on the Wilde Side*, p. 198.

86. 'The Wilde Trial', *Star*, 27 April 1895: p. 3; 'Wilde and Taylor Committed for Trial', *Reynolds*, 21 April 1895: p. 4.

87. 'Oscar Wilde Charged this Morning at Bow Street', *Star*, 6 April 1895: p. 3.

88. 'Oscar Wilde: Brought Up at Bow Street this Morning', *Star*, 11 April 1895: p. 3; 'Wilde Case', *Star*, 19 April 1895: p. 3.

89. Gill Davies, 'Foreign Bodies: Images of the London Working Class at the End of the Nineteenth Century', *Literature and History*, 14, 1 (Spring 1988): 64–80, p. 69.

90. *Tempted London* (London 1889), p. 218

91. Allan Peterkin, *One Thousand Beards: A Cultural History of Facial Hair* (Vancouver, 2002), p. 66.

92. Cesare Lombroso, 'Atavism and Evolution', *Contemporary Review*, 68 (July 1895): 42–9, p. 46.

93. 'The West End Scandals', *Reynolds*, 12 January 1890: p. 5.

94. 'Masquerading as a Woman', 13 November 1908, in Ives, 'Casebook', vol. VII, p. 26; 'Blackmailers Letter', *People*, 3 July 1910, in 'Casebook', vol. VII, p. 85. Walters was ordered to be deported on completion of his five-month sentence.

95. 'Other Cases: Horrible Condition of London', *Reynolds*.
96. Rev. G. S. Reaney, 'The Moral Aspect', in Arnold White (ed.), *The Destitute Alien in Britain: A Series of Papers Dealing with the Subject of Foreign Pauper Immigration* (London, 1892), p. 75. See also Bernard Gainer, *The Alien Invasion: The Origin of the Alien's Act of 1905* (London, 1972).
97. 'Studio Crime', *Daily Chronicle*, 6 June 1906: p. 5. A trooper was suspected because of spur marks found on Wakley's thighs. Walker was tracked down through an address on a scrap of paper found in the studio but he had an alibi for the evening in question and was not charged.
98. See Anne Summers, 'Militarism in Britain Before the Great War', *History Workshop Journal*, 1, 2 (Autumn 1976): 104–23.
99. Cohen, *Talk on the Wilde Side*, p. 188.
100. 'Oscar Wilde at Bow Street', *Illustrated Police News*, 20 April 1895: p. 3.
101. 'What We Think: A Word on the Scandals', *Star*, 25 November 1895: p. 1. This rhetoric keys into what Daniel Pick has identified as 'a cross-disciplinary preoccupation with how we see and what we see' during the period. Daniel Pick, 'Stories of the Eye', in Roy Porter (ed.), *Rewriting the Self: Histories from the Renaissance to the Present* (London, 1997), p. 188.
102. 'Police Raid in Fitzroy Square: 20 Persons Arrested', *Globe*, 13 August 1894: p. 7.
103. Park by-laws included provisions against 'using indecent or improper language ... sleeping, sitting, or resting in an indecent posture, or being disorderly or wilfully or designedly doing any act which outrages public decency'. Neither these by-laws nor the confidential handbook for park keepers referred specifically to indecency between men and there seems in fact to have been more concern about heterosexual transgressions. From a sample of papers presented to the Parks and Open Spaces Committee during the period 1888–1918 it appears that cases of indecent exposure and sexual assault on young girls were reported by park keepers far more frequently than gross indecency between men. A certain pragmatism is suggested. Susan Pennybacker notes that despite 'the rhetoric of tight regulation park keepers were instructed to put by-laws into force "only when nuisance or damage is arising from the infraction of them"'. The men involved in consensual homosexual activity were unlikely to complain to the authorities about it and were also usually discreet given the potential penalties. Such behaviour thus caused less public 'nuisance' than more visible liaisons between men and women, and assaults on women and girls. Ives' scrapbook includes very few prosecutions resulting from activity in the parks. *London County Council Parks and Open Spaces: Staff Regulations and By-Laws* (1907), London Metropolitan Archive, PK/Gen/1/13; LCC Parks and Open Space Committee Papers (1888–1918), London Metropolitan Archive; Pennybacker, *A Vision for London, 1889–1914: Labour, Everyday Life and the London County Council Experiment* (London, 1995), p. 198.
104. The relative leniency may have been due to the reference the Salvation Army provided for Humphries. See LCC Parks and Open Space Committee

Papers (23 July–15 October 1909, p. 209), London Metropolitan Archive, LCC/Min/8892; and Pennybacker, *A Vision for London*, p. 192, fn. 188.

105. Pennybacker, *A Vision for London*.
106. *Ibid.*, pp. 212–13 and p. 225. The London County Council had to tread a fine line, however. When the Empire Theatre was closed – because of its prostitutes rather than its performances – there were vociferous protests from the public. In many ways the music halls provided a contained environment for 'lewd' behaviour, and, Pennybacker suggests, audiences often resented LCC interference. *Ibid.*, pp. 229–31. See also Chris Waters, 'Progressives, Puritans, and the Cultural Politics of the Council, 1889–1914', in Andrew Saint (ed.), *Politics and the People of London: The London County Council, 1889–1965* (London, 1989), p. 63
107. 'The Extraordinary Charge of Blackmailing', *Daily Chronicle*, 11 May 1895: p. 8.
108. 'A Remarkable Case', *Sun*, 9 September 1902, in Ives, 'Casebook', vol. III, p. 61.
109. 'The Studio Crimes: A Curious Verdict', *Daily Graphic*, 1 June 1906: p. 3.
110. George Ives, *A History of Penal Methods: Criminals, Witches, Lunatics* (London, 1914), p. 355.
111. Ives, 'Diary', vol. XXXVII, 21 July 1900, p. 92 (verso note).
112. *Ibid.*, vol. XXXI, 5 July 1894, p. 45.
113. Cited in Petrow, *Policing Morals*, p. 166.
114. 'Blackmail', 16 September 1908, in Ives, 'Casebook', vol. VII, p. 26. Newspaper not cited.
115. Frank Harris, *Oscar Wilde* (London, 1938), pp. 171–2.
116. Ives, 'Diary', vol. XLII, 10 March 1902, p. 63.
117. Henry Labouchere, *Truth*, 6 March 1890: p. 473.
118. On euphemism and unspeakability, see Cohen, *Talk on the Wilde Side*, p. 184; W. Cohen, *Sex Scandal: The Private Parts of Victorian Fiction* (Durham, NC, 1996), p. 91; Cocks, 'Nameless Offences', pp. 126–7 and introduction; and Eve Sedgwick, *The Epistemology of the Closet* (Berkeley, 1990), esp. ch. 5.
119. 'Seven Years for a Blackmailer', *Chronicle*, 12 March 1898: p. 7.
120. *Parliamentary Debates*, vol. 43 (London, 1912), col. 1858.
121. Mellors: 'West End Flat Scandal', *Reynolds*, 5 April 1906: p. 5; Goodchild: 'Other Serious Charges', *Reynolds*, 14 April 1895: p. 1; Wakley: 'The Studio Crime', *Daily Graphic*, 1 June 1906: p. 3.
122. 'Recorder's Regret: One of a Dangerous Gang', *Reynolds*, 6 May 1906: p. 4.
123. 'Masquerading as a Woman', 13 November 1908, in Ives, 'Casebook', vol. VII, p. 26. Newspaper not cited.
124. 'Masquerading as a Woman', 31 May 1908, in 'Casebook', vol. VII, p. 7. Newspaper not cited.
125. See, for example, 'Wilde/Some of the Mysteries of the Case/A List of Blanks Which Were Left Unfilled by the First Two Trials', *Star*, 28 May 1895: p. 2; and 'Some Mysteries of the Wilde Case', *Reynolds*, 2 June 1895: p. 5.

126. Ives, 'Diary', vol. XLII, 5 November 1902, p. 23.
127. *Parliamentary Debates*, vol. 341 (London, 1890), col. 1548; 'Our Old Nobility', *North London Press*, 28 September 1889: p. 5.
128. 'Our Old Nobility', *North London Press*.
129. 'The Scandals: Hackney Workmen Meet and Demand Equal Justice for Rich and Poor', *North London Press*, 14 December 1889: p. 5. Original emphasis.
130. On this point see Sinfield, *The Wilde Century*, p. 123.
131. Ives, 'Diary', vol. XLI, 13 September 1902, p. 108.
132. 'Male Prostitution', *Reynolds*, 26 May 1895: p. 1.
133. *Parliamentary Debates*, vol. 341 (London, 1890), col. 1605.
134. Hyde, *Cleveland Street*, p. 122.
135. Hyde, *Oscar Wilde*, p. 122.
136. Henry Labouchere, *Truth*, 6 March 1890: p. 473.
137. 'Wilde: Last Terrible Scene at the Great Trial', *Star*, 27 May 1895: p. 2.
138. 'The Case Ends with a Verdict Against Oscar', *Evening News*, 5 April 1895: p. 3; Hyde, *Oscar Wilde*, p. 273.
139. G. H. Mead, 'The Psychology of Punitive Justice', *American Journal of Sociology*, 23 (1918): 577–602, p. 590.
140. Walkowitz, *City of Dreadful Delight*, p. 84.
141. 'A Righteous Verdict', *Truth*, 30 May 1895: p. 332; 'Comment', *Daily Chronicle*, 26 May 1895: p. 4.
142. 'Wilde: Last Terrible Scene at the Great Trial', *Star*.
143. Cohen, *Talk on the Wilde Side*, pp. 193–5.
144. Michel Foucault, *Discipline and Punish: The Birth of the Prison*, trans. Alan Sheridan (London, 1977), parts 1 and 2.
145. 'The Last Scene', *Evening News*, 27 May 1895: p. 2.
146. 'About Oscar Wilde', *Reynolds*, 16 June 1895: p. 5.
147. *The Adult*, 2, 4 (May 1898): 121.
148. Ives, 'Diary', vol. XXIV, 31 May 1895, p. 42; and vol. XXV, 5 October 1895, p. 90.
149. *Ibid.*, vol. LIV, 19 November 1909, p. 13.
150. 'Diary', vol. LX, 9 July 1914, p. 112.
151. On this point, and the consequent cultural centrality of supposedly marginal figures like the homosexual, see Sinfield, *The Wilde Century*, p. 9; and Craig Owens, 'Outlaws: Gay Men in Feminism', in Alice Jardine and Paul Smith (eds.) *Men in Feminism* (New York, 1987), p. 231.

3 THE INVERTED CITY

1. George Bernard Shaw, 'The Prosecution of Mr Bedborough', *The Adult*, 2, 8 (September 1898): 230–1.
2. Jeffrey Weeks, *Coming Out: Homosexual Politics from the Nineteenth Century to the Present* (1979; London, 1990), p. 60. For Ellis' own account of the trial see H. Havelock Ellis, *A Note on the Bedborough Trial* (1898; New York, 1925).

3. Cited in Ellis, *A Note on the Bedborough Trial*, p. 8.

4. Letter, J. A. Symonds to Arthur Symons, 13 June 1892, cited by Roger Lhombreaud, *Arthur Symons: A Critical Biography* (London, 1963), p. 92.

5. On social purity see especially Edward Bristow, *Vice and Vigilance: Purity Movements in Britain Since 1700* (Dublin, 1977); Frank Mort, *Dangerous Sexualities: Medico-Moral Politics in England Since 1830* (London, 1987), pts. 3 & 4; Lucy Bland, *Banishing the Beast: English Feminism and Sexual Morality, 1885–1914* (London, 1995), pt. 2.

6. Gert Hekma, 'A History of Sexology: Social and Historical Aspects of Sexuality', in Jan Bremmer (ed.), *From Sappho to de Sade: Moments in the History of Sexuality* (London, 1989).

7. Richard von Krafft-Ebing, *Psychopathia Sexualis*, trans. F. J. Rebman (London, 1901), p. 330.

8. Charles Féré, *The Evolution and Dissolution of the Sexual Instinct* (1899; Paris, 1904), pp. 185 and 261–2.

9. James Burnet, 'Some Aspects of Neurasthenia', *The Medical Times and Hospital Gazette* (3 February 1906): 58–59.

10. *British Society for the Study of Sex Psychology: Policy and Principles: General Aims* (London, 1914). The conference, scheduled to take place in Berlin in November 1914, was cancelled at the outbreak of war.

11. E. M. Forster, *Maurice* (1914; London, 1972), p. 140.

12. See Sheila Rowbotham and Jeffrey Weeks, *Socialism and the New Life: The Personal and Sexual Politics of Edward Carpenter and Havelock Ellis* (London, 1977).

13. See Phyllis Grosskurth, *Havelock Ellis: A Biography* (London, 1980), ch. 13.

14. See William Cohen, *Sex Scandal: The Private Parts of Victorian Fiction* (Durham, NC: 1996); Ivan Dalley Crozier, 'The Medical Construction of Homosexuality and its Relation to the Law in Nineteenth-Century England', *Medical History*, 45 (2001): 61–82.

15. George Savage, 'Clinical Notes and Cases: Case of Sexual Perversion in a Man', *Journal of Mental Science*, 30 (1884): p. 390.

16. Richard von Krafft-Ebing, Psychopathia Sexualis; *with Especial Reference to Contrary Sexual Instinct*, trans. Charles Chaddock (London, 1892), p. v.

17. 'Reviews: *Psychopathia Sexualis*', *British Medical Journal*, 1 (24 June 1893): 1325.

18. 'The Origin of Moral Ideas', *Review of Reviews*, 38 (December 1908): 591.

19. Chris Waters, 'Havelock Ellis, Sigmund Freud and the State: Discourses of Homosexual Identity in Interwar Britain', in Lucy Bland and Laura Doan (eds.), *Sexology in Culture: Labelling Bodies and Desires* (Cambridge, 1998).

20. Magnus Hirschfeld's translated work includes *Sexual Pathology* (1917), *The Sexual History of the World War* (1930) and *Sexual Anomalies and Perversion* (1936). These texts were published without Hirschfeld's prior knowledge and, James Steakley suggests, were 'mutilations' rather than translations. James Steakley, '*Per Scientiam ad Justifiam*: Magnus Hirschfeld and the Sexual Politics of

Innate Homosexuality', in Vernon Rosario (ed.), *Science and Homosexualities* (London, 1997).

21. Edward Carpenter to George Ives, 3 May 1916, Ives Papers, box 1, folder 1, Harry Ransom Humanities Research Center, University of Texas at Austin. See also Weeks, *Coming Out*, p. 117.

22. See, for example, John Addington Symonds, *A Problem in Modern Ethics: An Inquiry into the Phenomenon of Sexual Inversion* (1891; London: 1896), chs. 4 and 5; Edward Carpenter, *Homogenic Love and its Place in a Free Society* (Manchester, 1894); and Carpenter, 'The Intermediate Sex', in *Selected Writings: Sex* (1908; London, 1984).

23. For more information on the British Society for the Study of Sex Psychology see Lesley A. Hall, '"Disinterested Enthusiasm for Sexual Misconduct": The British Society for the Study of Sex Psychology, 1913–47', *Journal of Contemporary History*, 30 (1995): 665–86.

24. Krafft-Ebing, *Psychopathia Sexualis*, p. 7.

25. *Ibid.*, p. 405.

26. Sidney Low, 'The Rise of Suburbia', *Contemporary Review*, 60 (October 1891): 545–57, p. 533. See also Daniel Pick, *Faces of Degeneration: A European Disorder, c.1848–1918* (Cambridge, 1989), esp. chs. 6 and 7; Sander Gilman and J. E. Chamberlain (eds.), *Degeneration: The Dark Side of Progress* (New York, 1985); and William Greenslade, *Degeneration, Culture and the Novel, 1880–1940* (Cambridge, 1994).

27. Arnold White, *The Problems of a Great City* (London, 1886), p. 49.

28. James Greenwood, *In Strange Company: Being the Experiences of a Roving Correspondent* (London, 1883), p. 217.

29. *Ibid.*, p. 186.

30. George Bernard Shaw, *The Sanity of Art: An Exposure of the Current Nonsense About Artists Being Degenerate* (London, 1908).

31. Max Nordau, *Degeneration* (1895; Lincoln, NE, 1993), p. 7.

32. *Ibid.*, p. 36.

33. *Ibid.*, pp. 538–9.

34. See Sally Ledger, *The New Woman: Fiction and Feminism at the* Fin de Siècle (Manchester, 1997), ch. 6; Ledger, 'The New Woman and the Crisis of Victorianism', in Ledger and Scott McCracken (eds.) *Cultural Politics at the* Fin de Siècle (Cambridge, 1995); and Linda Dowling, 'The Decadent and the New Woman', *Nineteenth Century Fiction*, 33, 4 (1979): 434–53.

35. Cesare Lombroso, 'Atavism and Evolution', *Contemporary Review*, 68 (July 1895): 42–9.

36. Ives, 'Diary', vol. LVII, 19 July 1912, p. 104.

37. *Policy and Principle*, p. 10.

38. Richard von Krafft-Ebing, *Nervosität und neurasthenische Zustände* (Vienna, 1895).

39. Féré, *Evolution and Dissolution*, p. 244.

40. John Clarke, *The Practitioner's Handbook: Hysteria and Neurasthenia* (London, 1905), pp. 171, 176. See also Hugh Campbell, *A Treatise on Nervous Exhaustion*

and Diseases Induced by It (London, 1874), p. 1; and George Beard, *A Practical Treatise on Nervous Exhaustion (or Neurasthenia)* (New York, 1880), p. 9.

41. J. A. Hobson, *The Psychology of Jingoism* (London, 1901), p. 8.
42. Georg Simmel, 'The Metropolis and Mental Life' (1903), in Richard Sennett (ed.), *Classic Essays on the Culture of Cities* (Englewood Cliffs, NJ, 1969), pp. 48 and 57.
43. August Forel, *The Sexual Question: A Scientific, Psychological, Hygienic and Sociological Study for the Cultured Classes*, trans. C. F. Marshall (London, 1908), pp. 326–30.
44. Clarke, *The Practitioner's Handbook*, p. 176.
45. Forel, *The Sexual Question*, p. 484.
46. Féré, *Evolution and Dissolution*, p. 297.
47. Cesare Lombroso, *Crime: Its Cause and Cure*, trans. Henry P. Horton (1899; London, 1911), p. 233. For a detailed analysis of the relationship between homosexuality and degeneration in the Wilde case see Michael Foldy, *The Trials of Oscar Wilde: Deviance, Morality and Late-Victorian Society* (New York, 1997), p. 145.
48. See Forel, *The Sexual Question*, pp. 254–7; Lombroso, *Crime*, p. 233; and 'Contra-Sexual Perversions', *British Medical Journal*, 1 (1 June 1895): 1225–6.
49. Harry Oosterhuis, 'Richard von Krafft-Ebing's "Step-Children of Nature": Psychiatry and the Making of Homosexual Identity', in Rosario, *Science and Homosexualities*, p. 80. Lawrence Birken develops a similar argument. See Lawrence Birken, *Consuming Desire: Sexual Science and the Emergence of a Culture of Abundance, 1871–1914* (London, 1988), p. 52.
50. Oosterhuis, 'Richard von Krafft-Ebing's "Stepchildren of Nature"', p. 85.
51. Krafft-Ebing, *Psychopathia Sexualis*, p. 321; Forel, *The Sexual Question*, p. 446; Féré, *Evolution and Dissolution*, p. 309.
52. Probably case study 36 in Ellis and J. A. Symonds, *Studies in the Psychology of Sex*, vol. 1, *Sexual Inversion* (London, April 1897). This edition is the only one to carry Symonds' name as co-author. At the insistence of Symonds' literary executor it was withdrawn from all subsequent editions, including the second of 1897.
53. See Grosskurth, *Havelock Ellis*, p. 144; Siobhan Somerville, 'Scientific Racism and the Homosexual Body', in Bland and Doan, *Sexology in Culture*.
54. Iwan Bloch, *The Sexual Life of Our Time in its Relation to Modern Civilisation*, trans. M. Eden Paul (London, 1908), p. 534.
55. This oppositional understanding of space and time is and was powerful and engrained, though deeply problematic. For a discussion of the relationship and the supposed subservience of space to time see Doreen Massey, 'Politics and Space/Time', in Michael Keith and Steve Pile (eds.), *Place and the Politics of Identity* (London, 1993).
56. Julia Kristeva, 'Women's Time' (1979), in Toril Moi (ed.), *The Kristeva Reader* (Oxford, 1986), pp. 191–2.
57. Bloch, *Sexual Life of Our Time*, p. 497.

58. Féré, *Evolution and Dissolution*, p. 190.
59. Forel, *The Sexual Question*, p. 243.
60. See Ellen Moers, *The Dandy: Brummel to Beerbohm* (Lincoln, NE, 1978).
61. Ellis, *Sexual Inversion* (April 1897), p. 140.
62. Jeffrey Weeks, *Sex, Politics and Society: The Regulation of Sexuality Since 1800* (London, 1981), p. 94. See also Randolph Trumbach, 'Gender and the Homosexual Role in Modern Western Culture: The 18th and 19th Century Compared', in D. Altman (ed.), *Homosexuality, Which Homosexuality?*, (London, 1989), p. 159.
63. Harry Oosterhuis, *Stepchildren of Nature: Krafft-Ebing, Psychiatry and the Making of Sexual Identity* (Chicago, 2000), p. 252. See also Birken, *Consuming Desire*, p. 128.
64. Oosterhuis, *Stepchildren of Nature*, part III.
65. Krafft-Ebing, *Psychopathia Sexualis*, pp. 198–9.
66. *Ibid.*, p. 270.
67. *Ibid.*, p. 414.
68. *Ibid.*, p. 417.
69. *Ibid.*, p. 273.
70. *Ibid.*, p. 259.
71. *Ibid.*, p. 245.
72. Féré, *Evolution and Dissolution*, p. 219.
73. *Ibid.*, p. 226.
74. Krafft-Ebing, *Psychopathia Sexualis*, p. 261.
75. *Ibid.*, p. 337.
76. Bloch, *Sexual Life of Our Time*, p. 514.
77. *Ibid.*
78. *Ibid.*, p. 518.
79. *Ibid.*, p. 545.
80. Carpenter, *Homogenic Love*, p. 30.
81. Ellis, *Sexual Inversion* (April 1897), p. 25.
82. *Ibid.*, p. 9. There was little consideration of working-class sexuality in any of these sexological texts, even though desire for working-class men was mentioned frequently. Bloch's analysis was as cursory as Ellis'. He merely suggested that working-class homosexuals were generally more intelligent than their peers. See Bloch, *Sexual Life of Our Time*, p. 502.
83. Ellis, *Sexual Inversion* (April 1897), p. 64. Gustavus Brooke (1818–66) was an Irish Shakespearean actor who impressed audiences in the West End theatres and on Broadway with his 'fine presence and noble voice'. *Dictionary of National Biography*, vol. II (Oxford, 1921), p. 422.
84. Havelock Ellis, *Studies in the Psychology of Sex*, vol. II, *Sexual Inversion* (Philadelphia, 1915), p. iii.
85. *Ibid.*, p. 177.
86. *Ibid.*, p. 178.
87. *Ibid.*, p. 179.

88. Ellis, *Sexual Inversion* (April 1897), p. 61; *The Memoirs of John Addington Symonds*, ed. Phyllis Grosskurth (London, 1984), p. 62; Wayne Koestenbaum, *Double Talk: The Erotics of Male Literary Collaboration* (London, 1989), p. 59.

89. Cited in Jane Caplan, '"Educating the Eye": The Tattooed Prostitute', in Bland and Doan, *Sexology in Culture*, p. 101. *Sex in Relation to Society* was volume VI of Ellis' *Studies in the Psychology of Sex*.

90. Laura Doan and Chris Waters note that Ellis was keen to challenge the supposed connection between effeminacy and male homosexuality, whilst paradoxically affirming ideas of lesbian 'mannishness'. See Laura Doan and Chris Waters, 'Homosexualities: Introduction', in Lucy Bland and Laura Doan (eds.), *Sexology Uncensored: The Documents of Sexual Science* (Cambridge 1998), p. 43.

91. Ellis, *Sexual Inversion* (April 1897), p. 15.

92. Xavier Mayne (pseud. Edward Stevenson), *The Intersexes: A History of Simisexualism as a Problem in Social Life* (Naples, 1908).

93. Rudi Bleys, *The Geography of Perversion: Male to Male Sexual Behaviour Outside the West and the Ethnographic Imagination, 1750–1918* (London, 1996) p. 81. See also Jonathan Dollimore for his discussion of the role of Africa as an homoerotic Utopia in André Gide's work. Jonathan Dollimore, *Sexual Dissidence: Augustine to Wilde, Freud to Foucault* (Oxford, 1991), p. 343.

94. Lisa Z. Sigel, *Governing Pleasures: Pornography and Social Change in England, 1815–1914* (New Brunswick, NJ, 2002), pp. 60 and 63.

95. 'The Arabian Nights', *The Edinburgh Review*, 164 (July 1886): 166–99, p. 185.

96. Richard Burton, 'Terminal Essay', in *The Arabian Nights*, vol. X (London, 1885), pp. 232 and 222.

97. *Ibid.*, p. 224.

98. *Ibid.*, p. 236.

99. Peter Mendes, *Clandestine Erotic Fiction in English 1800–1930* (Aldershot, 1993), pp. 32–9.

100. Dr Jacobus X [pseud. Louis Jarolliot], *Untrodden Fields of Anthropology: Observations on the Esoteric Manners and Customs of Semi-Civilised Peoples*, vol. I (Paris, 1898), p. xiii.

101. *Ibid.*, p. xx.

102. *Ibid.*, p. 107.

103. *Ibid.*, pp. 294 and 320.

104. *Ibid.*, pp. 99 and 118.

105. *Ibid.*, p. 126.

106. Burton, *The Arabian Nights*, p. 246.

107. *Ibid.*, p. 248.

108. Pisanus Fraxi, *Centuria Librorum Absconditorum* (London, 1879), p. 414; Burton, *The Arabian Nights*, pp. 248–1; Dr Jacobus X, *Untrodden Fields of Anthropology*, pp. 68–279; and Bloch, *Sexual Life of Our Times*, p. 515.

109. Jacobus X, *Crossways of Sex: A Study in Eroto-Pathology*, vol. II (Paris, 1904), pp. 108–43.

4 THE DECADENT CITY

1. Max Nordau, *Degeneration* (1895; Lincoln, NE, 1993), p. 9.
2. *Ibid.*, p. 15.
3. *Ibid.*, p. 10.
4. Regenia Gagnier, *Idylls of the Market Place: Oscar Wilde and the Victorian Public* (Aldershot, 1987), p. 138. See also Linda Gertner Zatlin, *Beardsley*, Japonisme, *and the Perversion of the Victorian Ideal* (Cambridge, 1997), p. 154.
5. Walter Pater, 'Conclusion', in *The Renaissance: Studies in Art and Poetry* (1873; Oxford, 1986), p. 153.
6. *Ibid.*, p. 152.
7. *Ibid.*
8. Oscar Wilde, 'The Decay of Lying'(1889), in *De Profundis and Other Writings*, ed. Hesketh Pearson (London, 1986), p. 82.
9. Richard Ellmann, *Oscar Wilde* (London, 1985), p. 225.
10. Jean Pierrot, *The Decadent Imagination, 1880–1900*, trans. Derek Coltman (Chicago, 1981), p. 8.
11. Charles Hirsch, '*Notice Bibliographique*', in *Teleny: Etude Physiologique* (Paris, 1934), p. 11. This translation is taken from Peter Mendes, *Clandestine Erotic Fiction in English 1800–1930* (Aldershot, 1993), appendix, p. 449.
12. Ellman, *Oscar Wilde*, p. 242; Jeremy Cooper, *Victorian and Edwardian Furniture and Interiors* (London, 1987), p. 120. For more on the fashion for *japanosme* see Ian Fletcher, 'Bedford Park: Aesthete's Elysium', in Ian Fletcher (ed.) *Romantic Mythologies* (London, 1967), p. 181; Zatlin, *Beardsley*; Cooper, *Victorian and Edwardian Furniture*, ch. 5.
13. Wilde, 'The Decay of Lying', p. 70.
14. Max Beerbohm, '1880', *The Yellow Book*, vol. IV (January 1895), p. 278.
15. Arthur Symons, 'The Decadent Movement in Literature', in *Selected Writings*, ed. Roger Holdsworth (Manchester, 1974), p. 72.
16. Pater, 'Conclusion', p. 152.
17. *Ibid.*, p. 186.
18. Edward Carpenter, *Iölaus: an Anthology of Friendship* (London, 1902).
19. Symons, 'The Decadent Movement in Literature', p. 78.
20. David Mickelsen, '*A Rebours*: Spatial Form', *French Forum*, 3, 1 (January 1978): 48–55, p. 53.
21. Edward Soja, *Post-modern Geographies: The Reassertion of Space in Critical Social Theory* (London, 1989), p. 34.
22. Joris-Karl Huysmans, *Against the Grain* (A Rebours), trans. John Howard (New York, 1922), p. vi.
23. Joris-Karl Huysmans, *Against Nature: A New Translation of* A Rebours, trans. Robert Baldick (London, 1959), p. 35. The 1959 translation agrees fairly well with the first complete English edition of 1926 and is used here because it is more widely available. The earlier translation of 1922, introduced by Ellis, is abridged and most homoerotic sequences omitted. Karl-Joris [*sic*] Huysmans, *Against the Grain* (A Rebours) (Paris, 1926).

24. Huysmans, *Against Nature* (1959), p. 111.
25. For a discussion of carnivalesque inversion see Peter Stallybrass and Allon White, *The Politics and Poetics of Transgression* (London, 1986), pp. 6–12.
26. Huysmans, *Against Nature* (1959), p. 111.
27. *Ibid.*, p. 112.
28. *Ibid.*, p. 113.
29. *Ibid.*, p. 115.
30. *Ibid.*, p. 116.
31. *Ibid.*, p. 22.
32. Huysmans, *Against the Grain* (1922), ch. 9.
33. On this point see Camille Paglia, *Sexual Personae: Art and Decadence from Nefertiti to Emily Dickinson* (New Haven, 1990), p. 431.
34. See R. K. Thornton, (ed.) *Poetry of the 'Nineties* (London, 1970), p. 57.
35. Holbrook Jackson, *The 1890s: A Review of Art and Ideas at the Close of the Nineteenth Century* (1913; London, 1927), p. 105.
36. Oscar Wilde, *The Picture of Dorian Gray* (1891; London, 1985), p. 5.
37. Brian Stableford (ed.) *The Dedalus Book of Decadence: Moral Ruins* (Sawtry, 1990), p. 51.
38. Jackson, *The 1890s*, p. 58.
39. See Ellen Moers, *The Dandy: Brummel to Beerbohm* (Lincoln, NE, 1978), p. 286.
40. Lord Alfred Douglas, '*Impression du Nuit*: London', in *The City of the Soul* (London, 1899), p. 65.
41. Arthur Symons, 'City Nights', in *The Collected Works of Arthur Symons*, vol. 1, *Poems* (London, 1924), p. 152.
42. See also Richard Le Galliene, 'A Ballad to London', in *Robert Louis Stevenson: An Elegy, and Other Poems Mainly Personal* (London, 1895), p. 26.
43. Oscar Wilde, 'Symphony in Yellow', in *The Complete Works of Oscar Wilde*, ed. J. B. Foreman (London, 1983), p. 808; '*Impression du Matin*', in Wilde, *Poems* (Boston, 1881), p. 85.
44. Cited in Richard Dellamora, *Masculine Desire: The Sexual Politics of Victorian Aestheticism* (Chapel Hill, NC, 1990), p. 208.
45. Wilde, *Dorian Gray*, p. 142.
46. Hirsch, '*Notice Bibliographique*', pp. 9–10; translation from Mendes, *Erotic Fiction*, p. 449.
47. On this point see Mendes, *Erotic Fiction*, p. 311.
48. *Teleny: Etude physiologique* (Paris, 1934), p. 16.
49. *Teleny, or The Reverse of the Medal* (1893; Ware, 1995), p. 33.
50. *Ibid.*, p. 36.
51. Wilde, *Dorian Gray*, p. 41.
52. *Ibid.*, p. 159.
53. *Ibid.*, p. 109.
54. Neil Bartlett, *Who was that Man? A Present for Mr Oscar Wilde* (London, 1988), p. 50.
55. Wilde, *Dorian Gray*, p. 55.

56. Christopher Breward, 'Fashion and the Man, From Suburb to City Street: The Cultural Geography of Masculine Consumption, 1870–1914', *New Formations*, 37 (Spring 1999): 47–70. For a wider discussion of consumerism and homosexuality see Gagnier, *Idylls of the Market Place*; and Rachel Bowlby, *Shopping With Freud* (London, 1993), ch. 2.

57. Wilde, *Dorian Gray*, p. 57.

58. *Ibid.*

59. The East End was described as 'a dark continent', a 'great dark region of poverty, misery, squalor and immorality' and 'a human wilderness of which nobody seemed to know anything'. It was also organic and devouring: 'a huge dragon, preying on mankind'. George Sims, *How the Poor Live* (London, 1883), p. 4; Andrew Mearns, *The Bitter Cry of Outcast London: An Inquiry into the Condition of the Abject Poor* (London, 1883), p. 2; Jack London, *The People of the Abyss* (London, 1903), p. 4; J. Milner Fothergill, 'The Town Dweller: His Needs and Wants' (1883), reprinted in Lynn and Andrew Lees (eds.), *The Rise of Urban Britain* (London, 1985), p. 109.

60. Wilde, *Dorian Gray*, p. 60.

61. *Ibid.*, p. 64.

62. Bowlby, *Shopping With Freud*, p. 11.

63. On this point see Paglia, *Sexual Personae*, p. 431.

64. Wilde, *Dorian Gray*, p. 139.

65. Laurence Senelick, 'Boys and Girls Together: Subcultural Origins of Glamour Drag and Male Impersonation on the Nineteenth-century Stage', in Lesley Ferris (ed.), *Crossing the Stage: Controversies in Cross-dressing* (London, 1993), p. 84.

66. Wilde, *Dorian Gray*, p. 121.

67. *Ibid.*, p. 167.

68. *Ibid.*, p. 87.

69. *Ibid.*, p. 88.

70. James Greenwood, *In Strange Company* (London, 1883), p. 186.

71. Wilde, *Dorian Gray*, p. 149.

72. George Gissing, *The Nether World* (1889; Oxford, 1999).

73. Greenwood, *In Strange Company*, p. 222.

74. *London by Night, or Gay Life in London* (London, c.1888), p. 7.

75. Bartlett, *Who Was That Man?*, p. 144.

76. Wilde, *Dorian Gray*, p. 145.

77. *Ibid.*, p. 207.

78. *Ibid.*, p. 80. Robert Machray, *The Night Side of London* (London, 1902), p. 36.

79. Steve Pile, *The Body and the City: Psychoanalysis, Space and Subjectivity* (London, 1996), p. 226.

80. Cited in Ed Cohen, *Talk on the Wilde Side: Towards a Genealogy of a Discourse on Male Sexualities* (London, 1993), p. 128.

81. Hugh E. M. Stutfield, 'Tommyrotics', *Blackwoods Edinburgh Magazine* (June 1895), 833–45, p. 841. See also L. Dowling, 'The Decadent and the New Woman', *Nineteenth Century Fiction*, 33, 4 (1979): 434–53.

82. Elaine Showalter, *Sexual Anarchy: Gender and Culture at the* Fin de Siècle (New York, 1990).
83. Steven Marcus, *The Other Victorians: A Study of Sexuality and Pornography in Mid Nineteenth-Century England* (London, 1966), p. 169.
84. *Teleny* (1893), p. 10.
85. *Ibid.*, p. 11.
86. *Ibid.*
87. *Teleny* (1934), p. 90.
88. *Teleny* (1893), p. 79.
89. *Ibid.*, p. 81.
90. *Ibid.*
91. *Ibid.*, p. 88.
92. *Ibid.*, p. 89.
93. *Ibid.*, pp. 89–90.
94. Bartlett, *Who Was That Man?*, p. 177.
95. *Teleny* (1893), p. 114.
96. Alan Sinfield, *The Wilde Century: Effeminacy, Oscar Wilde and the Queer Moment* (London, 1994), p. 138.
97. *Teleny* (1893), p. 130.
98. *Ibid.*
99. *Ibid.*, p. 113.
100. *Ibid.*, p. 158.
101. *Ibid.*, p. 153.
102. Lisa Z. Sigel, *Governing Pleasures: Pornography and Social Change in England, 1815–1914* (New Brunswick, NJ, 2002), p. 117.
103. Walter Benjamin, 'Paris, Capital of the Nineteenth Century', in *Reflections: Essays, Aphorisms and Autobiographical Writings*, ed. Peter Demetz, trans. Edmund Jephcott (New York, 1986), p. 158.
104. On this point see Stallybrass and White's consideration of the relationship between upstairs and downstairs in the upper-middle-and upper-class Victorian home. Stallybrass and White, *The Politics and Poetics of Transgression*, ch. 4.
105. G. S. Street, *The Autobiography of a Boy* (London, 1894), vii.
106. Robert Hichens, *The Green Carnation* (1894; London, 1992), p. 46.
107. *Ibid.*, p. 10.
108. *Ibid.*, p. 17.
109. *Ibid.*, p. 15. See also Charles Hichens, *Yesterday* (London, 1947), p. 70.
110. *The Green Carnation*, p. 60.
111. Street, *Autobiography of a Boy*, pp. 39 and 29.
112. Cited in Karl Beckson, *London in the 1890s: A Cultural History* (London, 1992), p. 64.
113. Grant Allen, 'The New Hedonism'. *Fortnightly Review*, 55, 327 (1 March 1894), 377–92, p. 381.
114. Cited in H. Montgomery Hyde, *The Trials of Oscar Wilde* (New York, 1973), p. 18.

115. 'What We Think: A Check to Cant', *Star*, 6 April 1894: p. 1.
116. 'Dangerous Infiltration', *Telegraph*, 6 April 1895: p. 4.
117. Talia Schaffer, '"A Wilde Desire Took Me": The Homoerotic History of *Dracula*', *English Literary History*, 61, 2 (Summer 1994): 381–425. Christopher Craft has also examined the strong homoerotic vein running through the novel. Christopher Craft, 'Kiss Me on Those Red Lips', in Elaine Showalter (ed.) *Speaking of Gender* (London, 1989).
118. Sinfield, *The Wilde Century*, p. 125.
119. Havelock Ellis, *Studies in the Psychology of Sex*, vol. II, *Sexual Inversion* (Philadelphia, 1915), p. 177; E. M. Forster, *Maurice* (1914; London, 1972), p. 140.
120. Jackson, *The 1890s*, p. 116
121. Oscar Wilde, '*De Profundis*', in De Profundis *and Other Writings*, ed. Hesketh Pearson (London, 1986), p. 208.
122. Frank Harris, *Oscar Wilde* (London, 1938), pp. 171–2.
123. Philip Hoare, *Wilde's Last Stand: Decadence, Conspiracy and the First World War* (London, 1997), p. 10.
124. Iwan Bloch, *Sexual Life in England: Past and Present*, trans. William Forstern (London, 1938), p. 420. For further discussion of the behaviour and theatricality of the Marquis see Martha Vicinus, 'Male Impersonation and Lesbian Desire', in Billie Melman (ed.), *Borderlines: Genders and Identities in War and Peace, 1870–1930* (London, 1998).
125. Hoare, *Wilde's Last Stand*, p. 15.
126. Wilde's *An Ideal Husband* was produced at the Coronet Theatre in 1899 for example, and *A Woman of No Importance* was staged in the West End at His Majesty's Theatre in the West End in 1907. Ives' friends took part in an unlicensed production of *Salome* in 1905. George Ives, 'Diary', vol. XLVIII, 19 October 1905, p. 4, Ives Papers, Harry Ransom Humanities Research Center, University of Texas at Austin.

5 THE HELLENIC CITY

1. John Addington Symonds, *A Problem in Modern Ethics: An Inquiry into the Phenomenon of Sexual Inversion* (1891; London, 1896), pp. 15, 77 and 13.
2. Edward Carpenter, *Homogenic Love* (Manchester, 1894), p. 15.
3. George Ives, 'Diary', vol. LV, 8 January 1911, p. 48; vol. LVII, 14 July 1912, p. 100. George Ives Papers, Harry Ransom Humanities Research Center, University of Texas at Austin.
4. See Morris B. Kaplan, *Sexual Justice: Democratic Citizenship and the Politics of Desire* (London, 1997), ch. 2.
5. See Michael Port, *Imperial London: Civil Government Building in London, 1850–1915* (New Haven, 1995); Donald Olsen, *The Growth of Victorian London* (London, 1976).
6. See Raymond Williams, *The Country and the City* (1973; London, 1985), p. 248; Martin Weiner, *English Culture and the Decline of the Industrial Spirit*,

1850–1980 (Cambridge, 1981), p. 49; Simon Schama, *Landscape and Memory* (London, 1995), pp. 181–4; and Glen Cavaliero, *The Rural Tradition in the English Novel, 1900–1939* (London, 1977), pp. 3–8.

7. Georg Simmel, 'The Metropolis and Mental Life' (1903), in Richard Sennett (ed.) *Classic Essays on the Culture of Cities* (Englewood Cliffs, NJ, 1969), p. 50.

8. Williams, *The Country and the City*, p. 256; Weiner, *English Culture*, p. 21.

9. On this point see Phillippe Joudel, 'Ruskin's Vision of Two Cities', in Jean-Paul Hulin and Pierre Coustillas (eds.), *Victorian Writers and the City* (Lille, 1979), p. 78.

10. For more on these movements see Logie Barrow, 'The Environment of Fellowship Around 1900', in Roy Porter and Sylvana Tomaselli (eds.), *The Dialectics of Friendship* (London, 1989); Alan Crawford, *C. R. Ashbee: Architect, Designer and Romantic Socialist* (London, 1985); Tony Brown (ed.), *Edward Carpenter and Late-Victorian Radicalism* (London, 1990); Sheila Rowbotham and Jeffrey Weeks, *Socialism and the New Life: The Personal and Sexual Politics of Edward Carpenter and Havelock Ellis* (London, 1977); Jeffrey Weeks, 'The Fabians and Utopia', in *Against Nature: Essays on History, Sexuality and Identity* (London, 1991).

11. On this point see John Paterson, *Edwardians: London Life and Letter, 1901–1914* (Chicago, 1996), p. 42; Lynne Hapgood, 'Urban Utopias: Socialism, Religion and the City', in Sally Ledger and Scott McCracken (eds.), *Cultural Politics at the* Fin de Siècle (Cambridge, 1995), p. 187.

12. Linda Dowling, *Hellenism and Homosexuality in Victorian Oxford* (New York, 1994), p. 31. For further accounts of the development of classical thought during the period see Richard Jenkyns, *The Victorians and Ancient Greece* (Oxford, 1980); Jenkyns, *Dignity and Decadence: Victorian Art and the Classical Inheritance* (London, 1991); and Louis Crompton, *Byron and Greek Love: Homophobia in Nineteenth-Century England* (London, 1985).

13. Charles Kingsley, 'Nausicaa in London; or the Lower Education of Women'(1873), in *Sanitary and Social Essays* (London, 1880), p. 107.

14. *Ibid.*, p. 115. See Bruce Haley, *The Healthy Body and Victorian Society* (Cambridge, MA, 1978), p. 259.

15. Matthew Arnold, *Culture and Anarchy*, ed. J. Dover Wilson (1869; Cambridge, 1948), p. 162. See also J. S. Mill, 'On Liberty' (1859), in *Utilitarianism, On Liberty and Considerations on Representative Government*, ed. H. B. Acton (London, 1972), pp. 112 and 130.

16. Dowling, *Hellenism and Homosexuality*, p. 77.

17. Recent commentators have argued that this holism was in fact fractured. See Paul Cartledge, Paul Millett and Sitta von Reden (eds.), *Kosmos: Essays in Order, Conflict and Community in Classical Athens* (Cambridge, 1998); David Cohen, *Law, Sexuality and the Enforcement of Morals in Classical Athens* (Cambridge, 1991).

18. See Richard Sennett, *Flesh and Stone: The Body and the City in Western Civilisation* (London, 1994), chs. 1 and 2.

19. Plutarch, *The Lives of the Noble Grecians and Romans*, trans. John Dryden (Chicago, 1990), p. 239.

20. John Addington Symonds, 'A Problem in Greek Ethics' (1883), in H. Havelock Ellis and John Addington Symonds, *Studies in the Psychology of Sex*, vol. I, *Sexual Inversion* (London, April 1897), p. 231. Ten copies of 'A Problem in Greek Ethics' had been previously published 'for the authors' use' in 1883.

21. John Addington Symonds, *Studies in the Greek Poets* (London, 1879), p. 437.

22. Walter Pater, 'Winckelmann', in *The Renaissance: Studies in Art and Poetry* (1873; Oxford, 1986), p. 143.

23. The art historian Alex Potts describes the conflict inherent in Pater's response to Greek statuary. He sought, Potts argues, 'an unperplexed realm of self-realisation and freedom' but in his accounts exposed 'complexities and erotic tensions'. Alex Potts, *Flesh and the Ideal: Winckelmann and the Origins of Art History* (New Haven, 1994), p. 239.

24. See Kaplan, *Sexual Justice*, ch. 2; Cohen, *Law, Sexuality and the Enforcement of Morals*, ch. 7.

25. Edward Carpenter, *My Days and Dreams* (London, 1918), pp. 67–8; John Addington Symonds, *The Memoirs of John Addington Symonds*, ed. Phyllis Grosskurth (London, 1984), p. 286; Ives, 'Diary', vol. LXX, 8 March 1917, p. 43.

26. Dowling, *Hellenism and Homosexuality*, pp. 2 and 134. See also Gert Hekma, 'Sodomites, Platonic Lovers, Contrary Lovers: The Background of the Modern Homosexual', *Journal of Homosexuality*, 16, 1/2 (1988), 433–57, p. 43.

27. Linda Dowling shows how in the 1870s Oxford Hellenism had been 'thrust into a scandalous visibility on the national stage' following a series of scandals and the publication of W. H. Mallock's *New Republic* in 1877. In the same year, in the *Contemporary Review*, Richard St John Tyrwhitt attacked Symonds for his failure to censure Greek homosexuality in his *Studies of the Greek Poets*. In 1899 Ives was asked to remove a line from a poem he submitted to an un-named magazine because it had 'a Greek tendency', and the warm review of Carpenter's *Iölaus* in the *Daily Chronicle* in 1902 was qualified by a criticism of the text's over-emphasis on 'the Greek institution of friendship between man and man'. Dowling, *Hellenism and Homosexuality*, p. 100; Richard St John Tyrwhitt, 'The Greek Spirit in Modern Literature', *Contemporary Review*, 29 (March 1877): 522–66, p. 557; Ives, 'Diary', vol. XXXV, 7 November 1899, p. 124; 'Comrades', *Daily Chronicle*, c.March 1902, in Ives, 'Casebook', vol. III, p. 47, Beinecke Rare Book and Manuscript Library, Yale University, MSS 14.

28. Timothy d'Arch Smith, *Love in Earnest: Some Notes on the Lives and Writings of English 'Uranian' Poets from 1889 to 1930* (London, 1970).

29. Laurel Brake, *Print in Transition, 1850–1910: Studies in Media and Book History* (Basingstoke, 2001), p. 142.

30. Lord Alfred Douglas, 'Prince Charming'; John Gambril Nicholson, 'On the River's Bank'; Theodore Wratislaw, 'The Salome of Aubrey Beardsley', *The Artist*, 14/15 (April 1894: 102, 105 and 100.

31. 'The New Chivalry', *The Artist*, 14/15 (April 1893): 102–3.

32. Lord Alfred Douglas to Charles Kains Jackson, 9 April 1894, Douglas Letters, Harry Ransom Humanities Research Center, University of Texas at Austin.
33. Brake, *Print in Transition*, p. 127.
34. Douglas to Jackson, 29 November 1893, Douglas Letters.
35. 'The Artist', *The Artist*, 14/15 (September 1894): 323.
36. Brake, *Print in Transition*, p. 127.
37. 'The Nude in Photography, with Some Studies Taken in the Open Air', *The Studio: An Illustrated Magazine of Fine and Applied Arts*, 1, 2 (June 1893): 104–7.
38. Lisa Z. Sigel, *Governing Pleasures: Pornography and Social Change in England, 1815–1914* (New Brunswick, NJ, 2002), pp. 117–18. See also Robert Aldrich, *The Seduction of the Mediterranean: Writing, Art and Homosexual Fantasy* (London, 1993); and John Pemble, *The Mediterranean Passion: Victorians and Edwardians in the South* (Oxford, 1987).
39. 'The Spirit of Ancient Greece Recreated for the Camera', *c.*July 1905, in Ives, 'Casebook', vol. v, p. 92. Magazine not cited.
40. In *Sexual Heretics* Brian Reade traces homoerotic poems using Hellenic and pastoral imagery to the *Art Review* and *The Athenaeum*; Laurel Brake notes Laurence Housman's drawing 'Death and the Bather' alongside other homoerotic material in the first issue of *The Pageant* (1896). Brian Reade (ed.), *Sexual Heretics: Male Homosexuality in English Literature from 1850–1900* (London, 1970), pp. 42 and 44; Brake, *Print in Transition*, pp. 127 and 296 (n29). Among the novels and collections of poetry are George Ives' *The Lifting of the Veil* (London, 1892), *Book of Chains* (London, 1896) and *Eros Throne* (London, 1900), A. W. Clarke's novel of platonic schoolboy friendship, *Jasper Tristram* (London, 1899), Horatio Brown's *Drift* (London, 1900), Carpenter's *Iölaus* (London, 1902), Forrest Reid's *The Garden God* (London, 1905), Montague Summers' *Antinous and Other Poems* (London, 1907), and John Gambril Nicholson's *Love in Earnest* (London, 1892), *A Chaplet of Southernwood* (Ashover, 1896) and *A Garland of Ladslove* (London, 1911).
41. 'From Month to Month', *The Artist*, 12/13 (1 April 1892): 113–15.
42. On this point see Brake, *Print in Transition*, p. 119.
43. Douglas to Kains Jackson, 29 November 1893, Douglas Letters.
44. Douglas to Jackson, 16 May 1894, Douglas Letters.
45. Symonds, *Memoirs*, pp. 62 and 186; George Augustus Sala, *London Up to Date* (London, 1894), p. 160.
46. Symonds, *Memoirs*, p. 186.
47. *Ibid.*, p. 187.
48. Morris B. Kaplan, 'Who's Afraid of Jack Saul?: Urban Culture and the Politics of Desire in Late-Victorian London', *GLQ*, 5, 3 (1999): 267–314, pp. 271–4.
49. Symonds, *Memoirs*, p. 191.
50. *Ibid.*, p. 268.
51. *Ibid.*, p. 254.
52. Kaplan, 'Who's Afraid of Jack Saul?', p. 277.
53. Symonds, *Memoirs*, p. 254.

54. Symonds to Carpenter, 21 January 1893, in *The Letters of John Addington Symonds: 1885–1893*, eds. Herbert Schueller and Robert Peters (Detroit, 1969), p. 808.
55. On this point see Matt Houlbrook, 'Soldier Heroes and Rent Boys: Homosex, Masculinities and Britishness in the Brigade of Guards, c.1900–60', paper submitted to the *Journal of British Studies*, July 2003, forthcoming, p. 23; Kaplan, 'Who's Afraid of Jack Saul?', p. 272; and Peter Stallybrass and Allon White, *The Politics and Poetics of Transgression* (London, 1986), ch. 4.
56. John Addington Symonds, *In the Key of Blue and Other Essays* (London 1893). On the mythology of Venice – a city Dorian Gray also relishes – see Tony Tanner, *Venice Desired* (London, 1992).
57. Henning Bech, *When Men Meet: Homosexuality and Modernity*, trans. Teresa Mesquit and Tim Davies (Cambridge, 1997), p. 108.
58. The poem is pasted into the manuscript of the 'Memoirs' held by the London Library and is not included in the published version edited by Grosskurth. It is accompanied by the words: 'this was clearly introduced under the influence of Walt Whitman'. Symonds, 'Memoirs', typescript from original ms, London Library, vol. 1, pp. 284–5. I am extremely grateful to Morris B. Kaplan for this reference.
59. Symonds, *Memoirs*, p. 167.
60. John Addington Symonds, *Walt Whitman: A Study* (London, 1893), p. 80.
61. Walt Whitman, 'City of Orgies', in *Walt Whitman: The Complete Poems*, ed. Francis Murphy (London, 1996), p. 158.
62. Carpenter wrote: 'I have said . . . nothing about the influence of Whitman – for the same reason that I have said nothing about the influence of the sun or the winds. These influences lie too far back and ramify too complexly to be traced.' Edward Carpenter, *Towards Democracy*, (1883–1902; London, 1985), p. 414. On Whitman's impact on Carpenter see Scott McCracken, 'Writing the Body: Edward Carpenter, George Gissing and Late Nineteenth-Century Realism', in Tony Brown (ed.), *Edward Carpenter and Late-Victorian Radicalism* (London, 1990).
63. Carpenter, *Towards Democracy*, p. 141.
64. *Ibid.*, p. 25.
65. Ibid., pp. 62–3.
66. McCracken, 'Writing the Body', p. 187.
67. Some utopias included visions of a reformed sexual life. Morris and Ellis imagined 'natural' – though exclusively heterosexual – expressions of desire, whilst Fourier described a commune where 'lesbians, pederasts, flagellants, and others with more recondite tastes such as heel scratching and eating live spiders will all have their desires recognised and satisfied'. John Carey (ed.), *The Faber Book of Utopias* (London, 1999), p. 212. See also Saskia Poldervaart, 'Theories About Sex and Sexuality in Utopian Socialism', *Journal of Homosexuality*, 29, 2/3 (1995): 41–67; and Barbara Taylor, *Eve and the New Jerusalem: Socialism and Feminism in the Nineteenth Century* (London, 1983).
68. Carpenter, *Towards Democracy*, p. 44.

69. See Chris Waters, 'Progressives, Puritans and the Cultural Politics of the Council, 1889–1914', in Andrew Saint (ed.), *Politics and the People of London: The London County Council, 1889–1965* (London, 1989), p. 58; and Stephen Kern, *The Culture of Time and Space, 1880–1918* (London, 1983), p. 175.

70. Carpenter, *Towards Democracy*, p. 36.

71. *Ibid.*, p. 34.

72. Gustave le Bon, *The Crowd: A Study of the Popular Mind* (London, 1896), p. 2.

73. See *ibid.*, J. A. Hobson, *The Psychology of Jingoism* (London, 1901), pp. 171–8.

74. Carpenter, *Some Friends of Walt Whitman*, (c.1898), published as a pamphlet (London, 1924); see also 'The Intermediate Sex' (1908), in *Selected Writings: Sex* (London, 1984).

75. Carpenter, *Towards Democracy*, p. 198; 'Wilde and Taylor Committed for Trial', *Reynolds*, 21 April 1895: p. 4.

76. Carpenter, *Towards Democracy*, p. 325.

77. *Ibid.*, pp. 323–4.

78. *Ibid.*, pp. 323–6.

79. Circulating ideas about the male homosexual were distinct from images of the lesbian, though there were also significant overlaps, relating in particular to Hellenism, performativity and sexological theory. See Martha Vicinus, 'The Adolescent Boy: *Fin de Siècle Femme Fatale? Journal of the History of Sexuality*, 5, 1 (1994): 90–114; Vicinus, 'Male Impersonation and Lesbian Desire', in Billie Melman (ed.) *Borderlines: Genders and Identities in War and Peace, 1870–1930* (London, 1998); Sarah Waters, '"The Most Famous Fairy in History": Antinous and Homosexual Fantasy', *Journal of the History of Sexuality*, 6 (1995–6): 194–230; Linda Dowling, 'The Decadent and the New Woman', *Nineteenth Century Fiction*, 33, 4 (1979): 434–53; E. Newton, 'The Mythic Mannish Lesbian: Radclyffe Hall and the New Woman', in Martin Duberman, Martha Vicinus and George Chauncey Jr, *Hidden from History: Reclaiming the Gay and Lesbian Past* (London, 1991); Deborah Epstein Nord, '"Neither Pair nor Odd": Female Community in Late Nineteenth-Century London', *Signs*, 15.4 (Summer 1990: 733–55); Rosemary Auchmuty, 'By Their Friends We Shall Know Them: The Lives and Networks of Some Women in North Lambeth, 1880–1940', in Lesbian History Group, *Not a Passing Phase: Reclaiming Lesbians in History, 1840–1985* (London, 1989); Laura Doan, *Fashioning Sapphism: The Origins of Modern Lesbian Culture* (New York, 2001).

80. Carpenter, *Towards Democracy*, pp. 323–4.

81. *Ibid.*, p. 233.

82. Ives, 'Diary', vol. XIX, 31 March, 1894, p. 67.

83. Carpenter spearheaded the protest about the British Library's cataloguing policy in 1911 and launched a defence fund for C. W. Daniel, the publisher of A. T. Fitzroy's *Despised and Rejected*, which was banned under the Defence of the Realm Act in 1918. He was also a member of the Free Press Defence Committee

founded in response to the arrest of George Bedborough in 1898. See Edward Carpenter to George Ives, 3 May 1916, George Ives Papers, box 1, folder 1, Harry Ransom Humanities Research Center, University of Texas at Austin; Edward Carpenter, appeal letter in support of C. W. Daniel, *c.*October 1918, BSSSP Papers, box 19, folder 2, Harry Ransom Humanities Research Center; 'An Appeal to the People', *The Adult*, 2, 7 (August 1898): 190–1. See also Jeffrey Weeks, *Coming Out: Homosexual Politics from the Nineteenth Century to the Present* (1979; London, 1990), p. 117.

84. Laurence Housman declined to join the Order on account of his lack of 'faith'; Ives described Symonds as a 'pioneer and leader of the faith'; and Carpenter noted that Symonds wrote sometimes 'with an ardour as almost a propagandist of the faith'. Explaining why he was 'taken for a Jesuit' in 1893, Ives observed: 'the charge arises of course from my connection with Us (O of C)'. Earlier, Wilde had facetiously suggested that Ives form a pagan monastery. In his work on the Bolton Whitmanite fellowship, H. G. Cocks outlines the importance of 'the Victorian search for the spirit' in conceptualisations of comradeship, homosociality and homosexuality. Ives' diary adds further weight to this claim. Stephen Yeo describes the importance of a similar idea of faith and spirit in contemporary socialist discourse. See Ives, 'Diary', vol. xviii, 10 December 1893, p. 64; vol. xiv, September 1892, verso note, p. 64; vol. xxii, 30 December 1894, p. 83; on Housman see Fiona MacCarthy, *The Simple Life: C. R. Ashbee in the Cotswolds* (Berkeley, 1981), p. 144; Carpenter, *Some Friends of Walt Whitman*, p. 12; H. G. Cocks, '*Calamus* in Bolton: Spirituality and Homosexual Desire in Late-Victorian England', *Gender and History*, 13, 2 (August 2001): 191–223; Stephen Yeo, 'A New Life: The Religion of Socialism in Britain, 1883–1896', *History Workshop Journal*, 4 (Autumn 1977): 44–56, p. 33. See also Weeks, *Coming Out*, part 4.

85. Ives, 'Service of Initiation' (1899), Ives Papers, box 5, folder 11, Harry Ransom Humanities Research Center.

86. Ives, 'Diary', vol. xli, 6 June 1902, p. 56; vol. xliv, 4 July 1904, p. 110.

87. *Ibid.*, vol. lix, 8 August 1913, p. 40.

88. *Ibid.*, vol. xxxix, 3 April 1901, p. 56.

89. The piece came as a direct response to the controversy which followed the appearance of Grant Allen's 'New Hedonism' in the *Fortnightly Review*. Allen's piece attacked the sexual double standard and the debilitated sexual culture of late Victorian society, but he later backtracked when it was suggested that his argument might legitimise same-sex relationships. Ives was dismayed at Allen's retraction and entered the fray with his piece, 'The New Hedonism Controversy'. Ives' piece was attacked in *Review of Reviews*. Grant Allen, 'The New Hedonism', *Fortnightly Review*, 55, 327 (1 March 1894): 377–92; T. G. Bonney, 'The New Hedonism', *The Humanitarian*, 5, 2 (August 1894): 106–13; Allen, 'About the New Hedonism', *The Humanitarian*, 5, 3 (September 1894): 181–5; George Ives, 'The New Hedonism Controversy', *The Humanitarian*, 5, 4 (October 1894): 292–7. Ives' piece was attacked in *The Review of Reviews*. 'In

Praise of Two Crimes', *Review of Reviews*, 10, 4 (October 1894): 356. See also Ives, 'Diary', vol. xxii, 6 October 1894–15 October 1894, pp. 2–14.

90. Ives, 'Diary', vol. xxix, 25 August 1896, p. 24.
91. *Ibid.*, vol. i, p. 1.
92. *Ibid.*, vol. xxii, 20 January 1895, p. 100.
93. *Ibid.*, vol. xxxviii, 12 November 1900, p. 62.
94. *Ibid.*, vol. xviii, 29 October 1893, p. 1.
95. *Ibid.*, vol. xxi, 27 August 1894, p. 57.
96. *Ibid.*, vol. xxix, 28 August 1896, p. 26.
97. *Ibid.*, vol. lx, 5 May 1914, p. 87.
98. John Stokes, 'Wilde at Bay: The Diaries of George Ives', *English Literature in Transition, 1880–1920*, 26, 3 (1983): 175–84, p. 177.
99. Ives, 'Diary', vol. l, 15 August 1906, p. 52.
100. Ives, 'Some Needs of a Great City', *The Saturday Review*, 11 November 1912: 609; 'Diary', vol. lvii, 26 January 1912, p. 15.
101. Ives, 'Diary', vol. l, 15 August 1907, p. 52.
102. On these groups see: Lucy Bland, *Banishing the Beast: English Feminism and Sexual Morality, 1885–1914* (London, 1995); Judith Walkowitz, *City of Dreadful Delight: Narratives of Sexual Danger in Late Victorian London* (London, 1992), ch. 5; and Lesley A. Hall, '"Disinterested Enthusiasm for Sexual Misconduct": The British Society for the Study of Sex Psychology, 1913–1947', *Journal of Contemporary History*, 30 (1995): 665–86.
103. Ives, 'Diary', vol. xix, 9 March 1894, p. 37.

EPILOGUE: PUBLIC SPACES/PRIVATE LIVES

1. Ives published three volumes of poetry in the 1890s and subsequently works on Graeco-Roman history, animal behaviour and the criminal law. C. Branco [*pseud.*], *The Lifting of the Veil* (London, 1892); anon., *Book of Chains* (published anonymously, London, 1896); and *Eros' Throne* (London, 1900); *A History of Penal Methods: Criminals, Witches, Lunatics* (London, 1914); *The Sexes, Structure and Extra-Organic Habits of Certain Animals* (London, 1918); *The Continued Extension of the Criminal Law* (London, 1922); *The Graeco-Roman View of Youth* (London, 1926); *Obstacles to Human Progress* (London, 1939).
2. *Man Bites Dog: The Scrapbook of an Edwardian Eccentric*, ed. Paul Sieveking (London, 1980).
3. Short accounts of Ives' life and reform work, his involvement in the British Society for the Study of Sex Psychology, his friendship with Wilde and his poetry appear in, respectively: Jeffrey Weeks, *Coming Out: Homosexual Politics from the Nineteenth Century to the Present* (1979; London, 1990), pp. 118–24 and pp. 130–6; Lesley A. Hall, '"Disinterested Enthusiasm for Sexual Misconduct": The British Society for the Study of Sex Psychology, 1913–47', *Journal of Contemporary History*, 30 (1995): 665–86; John Stokes, 'Wilde at

Bay: The Diaries of George Ives', *English Literature in Transition, 1880–1920*, 26, 3 (1983): 175–84; Timothy d'Arch Smith, *Love in Earnest: Some Notes on the Lives and Writing of English 'Uranian' Poets from 1889–1930* (London, 1970), pp. 110–14.

4. On this point see Regenia Gagnier, *Subjectivities: A History of Self-Representation, 1832–1920* (Oxford, 1991), p. 4.
5. Neil Bartlett brilliantly evokes the significance of an individual's ephemera in constructing – and indicting the gaps and inconsistencies in – his/her story. Neil Bartlett, *Who Was That Man? A Present for Mr Oscar Wilde* (London, 1988), pp. 25–6.
6. George Ives, 'Diary', vol. III, 21 May 1889, p. 27, Ives papers, Harry Ransom Humanities Research Center, University of Texas at Austin.
7. *Ibid.*, vol. XXIX, 21 August 17 1896, p. 16.
8. *Ibid.*, vol. VIII, 11 September 1890, p. 88
9. *Ibid.*, vol. IX, 6 December 1890, p. 66.
10. *Ibid.*, vol. VI, 13 January 1890, p. 91; vol. IX, 29 December, 1890, p. 79.
11. *Ibid.*, vol. XI, 6 October 1891, p. 72.
12. *Ibid.*, vol. XVIII, 23 December 1893, p. 78.
13. *Ibid.*, vol. XVII, 26 October 1893, p. 129.
14. 'London's Bachelors and Their Mode of Living', *Leisure Hour*, 35 (1886): 413–16, p. 415.
15. Ives, 'Diary', vol. XVII, 14 October 1893, p. 119.
16. *Ibid.*, vol. XVII, 28 October 1893, p. 131.
17. *Ibid.*, vol. XVII, 19 October 1893.
18. *Ibid.*, vol. XIII, 31 May 1892, p. 36.
19. *Ibid.*, vol. XIII, 30 June 1892, p. 49.
20. *Ibid.*, vol. XVII, July 29 1893, p. 18.
21. George Ives, 'The New Hedonism Controversy', *The Humanitarian*, 5, 4 (October 1894): 292–7; Ives, 'Diary', vol. XXII, 6 October 1894, p. 2.
22. Ives, 'Diary', vol. XXII, 6 and 12 October 1894, p. 11.
23. 'In Praise of Two Crimes', *Review of Reviews*, 10, 4 (October 1894): 356. See also Ives, 'Diary', vol. XXII, 6 October 1894–15 October 1894, pp. 2–14.
24. Ives, 'Diary', vol. XXII, 1 January 1895, p. 86.
25. *Ibid.*, vol. XLVIII, 14 February 1906, p. 63.
26. *Ibid.*, vol. XLIX, 14 February 1906, p. 63.
27. Donald Olsen, *The Growth of Victorian London* (London, 1976), p. 244.
28. Ives, 'Diary', vol. XLVII, 4 June 1905, p. 20.
29. *Ibid.*, vol. LIV, 15 May 1910, p. 77; vol. L, 1 October 1907, p. 102; vol. II, 21 July 1888, p. 87, verso note.
30. *Ibid.*, vol. XI, 4 July 1891, p. 20.
31. *Ibid.*, vol. XXXIX, 22 March 1901, p. 43.
32. Ives, 'Casebook', vol. VI, p. 49, Ives Papers, Beinecke Rare Book and Manuscript Library, Yale University, MSS 14.
33. Ives 'Diary', vol. LVIII, 10 February 1913, p. 78.

34. Wilde to Ives, 12 February 1900, cited in Stokes, 'Wilde at Bay', p. 183.
35. See H. G. Cocks, 'Nameless Offences: Homosexual Desire in the Nineteenth Century', ts, forthcoming (London 2003), fo. 326.
36. See Michel de Certeau, *The Practice of Everyday Life*, trans. Steven Rendell (Berkeley, 1988), part 3; see also Steve Pile, *The Body and the City: Psychoanalysis, Space and Subjectivity* (London, 1996).
37. Ives, 'Diary', vol. XLVI, 17 February 1905, p. 63; vol. X, 22 April 1891, p. 98.

Bibliography

ARCHIVAL SOURCES

Bodleian Library: John Johnson Ephemera Collection.
Harry Ransom Humanities Research Center, University of Texas at Austin: George
  Ives Papers; British Society for the Study of Sex Psychology Papers; Lord Alfred
  Douglas Letters.
Beinecke Rare Book and Manuscript Library, Yale University: George Ives
  Casebooks.
London Metropolitan Archives: London County Council Archive, Minutes and
  Committee Papers.

NEWSPAPERS AND PERIODICALS

*The Daily Chronicle, Evening News, Pall Mall Gazette, Reynolds, Star, Telegraph,
Illustrated London News, Illustrated Police News, Daily Chronicle, Truth* and
The Times were consulted extensively for the period 1885–1914. *The Artist
and Journal of Home Culture and Modern Man* was consulted for the periods
1888–95 and 1908–11 respectively. Individual articles are not listed here.

PRIMARY SOURCES

Abbot, Evelyn. *Pericles and the Golden Age of Athens.* London: Putnams, 1891.
'About the New Hedonism'. *The Humanitarian,* 5, 3 (September 1894): 181–5.
'Afternoons in Studios: Henry Scott Tuke at Falmouth'. *The Studio,* 5 (June 1895):
  90–5.
Allen, Grant. 'The New Hedonism'. *Fortnightly Review,* 55, 327 (1 March 1894):
  377–92.
'The Arabian Nights'. *The Edinburgh Review,* 164 (July 1886): 166–99.
Arnold, Matthew. *Culture and Anarchy.* Ed. J. Dover Wilson. 1869; Cambridge:
  Polity, 1948.
Baedeker, Carl. *London and its Environs: a Handbook for Travellers.* London:
  Dunlau, 1881; 1885; 1898; 1905; 1911.
Ballet, Gilbert. *Neurasthenia.* London: Henry Kimpton, 1908.
Barton-Baker, H. *Stories of the Streets of London.* London: Chapman and Hall, 1899.

Beard, George. *A Practical Treatise on Nervous Exhaustion (or Neurasthenia): Its Symptoms, Nature, Sequences, Treatment.* New York: William Wood, 1880.

Beerbohm, Max. '1880'. *The Yellow Book*, 4 (January 1895): 278.

Bennet, Cyril. *The Modern Malady or Sufferers from Nerves.* London: Edward Arnold, 1890.

Bland, Lucy and Laura Doan. *Sexology Uncensored: The Documents of Sexual Science.* Cambridge: Polity Press, 1998.

Bloch, Iwan. *Sexual Life in England: Past and Present.* Trans. William Forstern. London: Francis Aldor, 1938.

  The Sexual Life of Our Time in its Relation to Modern Civilisation. Trans. M. Eden Paul. London: Rebman, 1908.

Bon, Gustave Le. *The Crowd: A Study of the Popular Mind.* London: Fisher Unwin, 1896.

Bonney, T. G. 'The New Hedonism'. *The Humanitarian*, 5, 2 (August 1894): 106–13.

Booth, Charles, *Life and Labour of the People of London*, 1st series, vol. IV, *Poverty.* 1889; London: Macmillan, 1902.

Braddon, Mary. *Lady Audley's Secret.* 1862; Oxford: Oxford University Press, 1987.

British Society for the Study of Sex Psychology: Policy and Principles: General Aims. London: The British Society for the Study of Sex Psychology, 1914.

Brown, Horatio. *Drift.* London: Grant Richards, 1900.

Burnet, James. 'Some Aspects of Neurasthenia'. *The Medical Times and Hospital Gazette.* (3 February 1906): 58–9.

Burton, Richard. *The Arabian Nights.* 10 vols. London: Smithers, 1885.

'Lord Byron'. *Don Leon.* London: 1866.

Cabanés, Dr. *Curious Bypaths of History; Being Medico-Historical Studies and Observations.* Paris: Charles Carrington, 1898.

Campbell, Harry. *Differences in the Nervous Organisation of Men and Women.* London: H. K. Lewis, 1891.

Campbell, Hugh. *A Treatise on Nervous Exhaustion and the Diseases Induced by It.* London: Longmans, 1874.

Carpenter, Edward. *Homogenic Love and its Place in a Free Society.* Manchester: Labour Press Society, 1894.

  'The Intermediate Sex'. In *Selected Writings: Sex.* 1908; London Gay Men's Press, 1984.

  Iölaus: an Anthology of Friendship. London: Swann Sonnenschien, 1902.

  Love's Coming-of-Age: A Series of Papers on the Relations Between the Sexes. 1896; London: George Allen, 1913.

  My Days and Dreams. London: Allen and Unwin, 1918.

  Some Friends of Walt Whitman. c.1898; London: British Society for the Study of Sex Psychology, 1924.

  Towards Democracy. 1883–1902; London: Gay Men's Press, 1985.

Casement, Roger. *The Black Diaries.* Eds. Peter Singleton-Gates and Maurice Girodias. London: Olympia, 1959.

The Chameleon: A Bazaar of Dangerous and Smiling Chances, 1, 1 (1894).

Chancellor, E. Beresford. *Wanderings in Piccadilly, Mayfair and Pall Mall*. London: Alston Rivers, 1907.

Clarke, John. *The Practitioner's Handbook: Hysteria and Neurasthenia*. London: Bodley Head, 1905.

Clouston, T. S. 'The Neurosis and Psychosis of Decadence'. *British Medical Journal* 2 (30 July 1898): 302–6.

'Contra-Sexual Perversions'. *British Medical Journal*, 1 (1 June 1895): 1225–6.

Crackenthorpe, Montague. 'Population and Progress'. *Fortnightly Review*, 80 (December 1906): 1001–16.

Darwin, Charles. *The Descent of Man and Selection in Relation to Sex*. London: John Murray, 1874.

Douglas, Lord Alfred. *The City of the Soul*. London: Grant Richards, 1899.

  The Rossiad. 1914; London: Dawson and Son, 1916.

Du Maurier, George. *Trilby*. 1894; Oxford: Oxford University Press, 1995.

Ellis, H. Havelock. *The Criminal*. London: Walter Scott, 1890.

  A Note on the Bedborough Trial. 1898; New York: privately printed, 1925.

  The Nineteenth Century: A Dialogue in Utopia. London: Grant Richards, 1900.

  Studies in the Psychology of Sex, vol. I, *Sexual Inversion*. Watford: University Press, October 1897.

  Studies in the Psychology of Sex, vol. II, *Sexual Inversion*. Philadelphia: F. A. Davis, 1901.

  Studies in the Psychology of Sex, vol. II, *Sexual Inversion*. Philadelphia: F. A. Davis, 1915.

  Studies in the Psychology of Sex, vol. III, *Erotic Symbolism*. 1912; New York: Random House, 1936.

  Studies in the Psychology of Sex, vol. VI, *Sex in Relation to Society*. 1910; London: Heinemann, 1937.

  The Task of Social Hygiene. London: Constable and Co., 1912.

Ellis, H. Havelock and J. A. Symonds. *Studies in the Psychology of Sex*, vol. I, *Sexual Inversion*. London: Wilson and Macmillan, April 1897.

Féré, Charles. *The Evolution and Dissolution of the Sexual Instinct*. Paris: Charles Carrington, 1904.

Fitzgerald, Percy. *Music Hall Land*. London, 1890.

Fitzjames Stephens, Sir James. *Digest of the Criminal Law: Crimes and Punishments*. London: Macmillan, 1904.

Ford, Ford Madox. *The Soul of London: A Survey of a Modern City*. 1905; London: Everyman, 1995.

'Foreign Undesirables'. *Blackwood's Magazine*, 169 (February 1901): 279–89.

Forel, August. *The Sexual Question: A Scientific, Psychological, Hygienic and Sociological Study for the Cultured Classes*. Trans. C. F. Marshall. London: Rebman, 1908.

Forster, E. M. *The Longest Journey*. 1907; London: Penguin, 1972.

  Maurice. 1914; London: Penguin, 1972.

The New Collected Short Stories. Ed. P. N. Furbank. London: Sidgwick and Jackson, 1984.

Fraxi, Pisanus. Catena Librorum Tacendorum: *Being Notes Bio-, Biblio-, Econo-Graphical and Critical on Curious and Uncommon Books*. London: privately printed, 1885.

Centuria Librorum Absconditorum: *Being Notes Bio-, Biblio-, Econo-Graphical and Critical on Curious and Uncommon Books*. London: privately printed, 1879.

Index Librorum Prohibitorum: *Being Notes Bio-, Biblio-, Econo-Graphical and Critical on Curious and Uncommon Books*. London: privately printed, 1877.

Freud, Sigmund. 'Three Essays on the Theory of Sexuality' (1905). *In On Sexuality*. Trans. James Strachey. London: Penguin, 1991.

Gallienne, Richard Le. *Robert Louis Stevenson: An Elegy, and Other Poems Mainly Personal*. London: John Lane, 1895.

Gissing, George. *In The Year of Jubilee*. 1894; London: Everyman, 1994.

The Nether World. 1889; Oxford: Oxford University Press, 1999.

Greenwood, James. *In Strange Company: Being the Experiences of a Roving Correspondent*. London: Vizetelly, 1883.

Hell Upon Earth, or the Town in Uproar. London: 1729.

Henley, W. E. and William Nicholson. *London Types*. London: Heinemann, 1898.

Hichens, Robert. *The Green Carnation*. 1894; London: Heineman, 1992.

Hobson, J. A. *The Psychology of Jingoism*. London: Grant Richards, 1901.

Holloway, Robert. *The Phoenix of Sodom or the Vere Street Coterie*. London: 1813.

Housman, A. E. *Collected Poems and Selected Writing*. Ed. Christopher Ricks. London: Allen Roe, 1988.

Hume, Fergus. *The Piccadilly Puzzle: A Mysterious Story*. London: D. V. White and Co., 1889.

Huysmans, Joris-Karl. *Against the Grain* (A Rebours). Trans. John Howard. New York: Lieber and Lewis, 1922.

Against the Grain (A Rebours). Trans. unspecified. Paris, Groves & Michaux, 1926.

Against Nature: A New Translation of A Rebours. Trans. Robert Baldick. London: Penguin, 1959.

Imre: A Memorandum. Naples: The English Book Press, 1908.

Ives, George. *Book of Chains*. Published anonymously, London: Swan Sonnenschien, 1896.

Casebook (1894–1949). MSS 14, The George Ives Papers in the Beinecke Rare Book and Manuscript Library, Yale University.

The Continued Extension of the Criminal Law. London: J. E. Francis, 1922.

Diary (1886–1949). Harry Ransom Humanities Research Center, University of Texas at Austin.

Eros Throne. London: Swan Sonnenschien, 1900.

The Graeco-Roman View of Youth. London: Cayme Press, 1926.

A History of Penal Methods: Criminals, Witches, Lunatics. London: Stanley Paul, 1914.

The Lifting of the Veil by C. Branco [pseud.]. London: Swan Sonnenschein, 1892.

Man Bites Dog: The Scrapbook of an Edwardian Eccentric. Ed. Paul Sieveking. London: Jay Landesman, 1980.

'The New Hedonism Controversy'. *The Humanitarian*, 5, 4 (October 1894): 292–7.

Obstacles to Human Progress. London: Allen and Unwin, 1939.

The Sexes, Structure and Extra-Organic Habits of Certain Animals. London, Unwin, 1918.

'Some Needs of a Great City'. *The Saturday Review* (11 November 1912): 609.

Jackson, Holbrook. *The 1890s: A Review of Art and Ideas at the Close of the Nineteenth Century.* 1913; London: Jonathan Cape, 1927.

Jacobus X [pseud. Louis Jarolliot]. *Crossways of Sex: A Study in Eroto-Pathology,* vol. II. Paris: British Bibliophiles Society, 1904.

The Ethnology of the Senses: Studies and Researches into its Abuses, Perversions, Follies, Anomalies and Crimes. Paris: Charles Carrington, 1899.

Untrodden Fields of Anthropology: Observations on the Esoteric Manners and Customs of Semi-Civilised Peoples. Paris: Charles Carrington, 1898.

Johnson, Lionel. *The Collected Poems.* Ed. Ian Fletcher. London: Garland, 1982.

Keating, P., ed. *Into Unknown England, 1866–1913: Selections from the Social Explorers.* Manchester: Manchester University Press, 1976.

Kingsford, Charles. *The Early History of Piccadilly, Leicester Square, Soho, and their Neighbourhood.* Cambridge: Cambridge University Press, 1925.

Kingsley, Charles. *Sanitary and Social Essays.* London: Macmillan, 1880.

Krafft-Ebing, Richard von. *Nervosität und neurasthenische Zustände.* Vienna: Alfred Holder, 1895.

Psychopathia Sexualis, *with Especial Reference to Contrary Sexual Instinct: a medico-legal study.* Trans. Charles Chaddock. London: Davis, 1892.

Psychopathia Sexualis. Trans. F. J. Rebman. London: Rebman, 1901.

The Law Reports: Digest of Cases, 1865–1890. London: Council of Law Reporting, 1892.

The Law Reports: Digest of Cases, 1891–1900. London: Council of Law Reporting, 1901.

The Law Reports: King's Bench Division, 1913. London: Council of Law Reporting, 1913.

The Law Reports: Queen's Bench Division, 1896. London: Council of Law Reporting, 1896.

The Lives of Boulton and Park: Extraordinary Revelations. London: George Clark, c.1870.

Lombroso, Cesare. 'Atavism and Evolution'. *Contemporary Review*, 68 (July 1895), 42–9.

Crime: Its Cause and Cure. Trans. Henry P. Horton. 1899; London: Heinemann, 1911.

London, Jack. *The People of the Abyss.* London: Macmillan, 1903.

London by Night, or Gay Life in London. London: c.1888. John Johnson Collection, Bodleian Library, Oxford.

'London's Bachelors in London and their Mode of Living'. *Leisure Hour*, 35 (1886): 413–16.

Low, Sidney. 'The Rise of Suburbia'. *Contemporary Review*, 60 (October 1891): 545–57.

Machray, Robert. *The Night Side of London*. London: John MacQueen, 1902.

Massingham, H. 'The Great London Dailies'. *Leisure Hour*, 41 (1891–2): 231.

Masterman, Charles. *The Heart of Empire*. London: Fisher Unwin, 1901.

Mayhew, Henry. *London Labour and London Poor: The Condition and Earnings of Those That Will Work, Cannot Work, and Will Not Work*. London: Griffin, 1861.

Mayne, Xavier (pseud. Edward Stevenson). *The Intersexes: A History of Simisexualism as a Problem in Social Life*. Naples: 1908.

McCormick, Ian, ed. *Secret Sexualities: a Sourcebook of Seventeenth and Eighteenth Century Writing*. London: Routledge, 1997.

Mearns, Andrew. *The Bitter Cry of Outcast London: An Inquiry into the Condition of the Abject Poor*. London: Hunt, Barnard and Co., 1883.

Mill, John Stuart. *Utilitarianism, On Liberty and Considerations on Representative Government*. Ed. H. B. Acton. London: Dent, 1972.

Moore, William. 'The Necessity of Re-establishing the Contagious Diseases Act'. *The Humanitarian*, 5, 4 (October 1894): 285–91.

Morgan, G. Osborne. 'Are We Really So Bad? Word on Lady Jeunes's London Society'. *Contemporary Review*, 62 (July 1892): 85–92.

Morris, William. *The Earthly Paradise: A Poem*. London: F. S. Ellis, 1868.

    News from Nowhere and Other Writings. Ed. Clive Wilmer. 1890; London, Penguin 1993.

Nettle, Humphrey. *Sodom and Onan: A Satire*. London, 1772.

Nevill, Ralph and Charles Jerningham. *Piccadilly to Pall Mall: Manners, Morals and Man*. London: Duckworth, 1908.

Nicholson, John Gambril. *A Chaplet of Southernwood*. Ashover: Murray, 1896.

    A Garland of Ladslove. London, 1911.

    Love in Earnest: Sonnets, Ballades, and Lyrics. London: E. Stock, 1892.

Noble, James Ashcroft. 'The Fiction of Sexuality'. *Contemporary Review*, 67 (April 1895): 490–8.

Noel, Roden. *Essays in Poetry and Poets*. London: Kegan Paul, 1886.

Nordau, Max. *Degeneration*. 1895; Lincoln: University of Nebraska Press, 1993.

'The Nude in Photography, with Some Studies Taken in the Open Air'. *The Studio: An Illustrated Magazine of Fine and Applied Arts*, 1, 2 (June 1893): 104–7.

O'Connor, T. P. 'The New Journalism'. *The New Review*, 1, 5 (October 1889): 423–34.

Oldershaw, Lucian, ed. *England: A Nation, Being the Papers of the Patriots' Club*. London: R. Brimley Johnson, 1904.

'The Origin of Moral Ideas'. *Review of Reviews*, 38 (December 1908): 591.

Paris by Day and Night. London: Daisy Bank, *c*.1890.

Parker, George. *A View of Society and Manners in High and Low Life*. 2 vols. London: 1781.

Parliamentary Debates, vol. 300. London, 1885.
　vol. 341. London, 1890.
　vol. 64. London, 1898.
　vol. 43. London, 1912.
Parliamentary Papers: Reports from the Commissioners: Police, London. 1882–1916.
Pascoe, Charles. *London of Today: An Illustrated Annual Publication*. London: Simpkin, Marshall, Hamilton, 1894.
Pater, Walter. *Essays on Literature and Art*. Ed. Jennifer Uglow. London: Dent, 1990.
　Greek Studies: A Series of Essays, 1895; London: Macmillan, 1901.
　The Renaissance: Studies in Art and Poetry. Ed. Adam Phillips. 1873; Oxford: Oxford University Press, 1986.
　Selected Writing of Walter Pater. Ed. Harold Bloom. New York: Signet, 1974.
The Phoenix of Sodom, or the Vere Street Coterie. London, 1813.
'Piccadilly'. *Chambers Journal of Popular Literature, Science, and Art*, 9, 444 (2 July 1892): 417–420.
Plutarch. *The Lives of the Nobel Grecians and Romans*. Trans. John Dryden. Chicago: University of Chicago Press, 1990.
'In Praise of Two Crimes'. *The Review of Reviews*, 10, 4 (October 1894): 356.
Public General Acts, 4 Geo. London, 1824.
Public General Acts, 44 and 45 Vict. London, 1861.
Public General Acts, 48–9 Vict. London, 1885.
Public General Acts, 61–2 Vict. London, 1898.
Public General Acts, 2–3 Geo. V. London, 1912.
Ransome, Arthur. *Bohemia in London*. London: Chapman and Hall, 1907.
Reade, A. A. *The Tragedy of the Streets*. Manchester: Reade, 1912.
Reade, Brian, ed. *Sexual Heretics: Male Homosexuality in English Literature from 1850–1900: An Anthology*. London: Routledge and Kegan Paul, 1970.
Reaney, G. S. 'The Moral Aspect'. In *The Problems of a Great City*. Ed. Arnold White. London: Remington, 1886.
Reid, Forrest. *The Garden God: A Tale of Two Boys*. London: David Nutt, 1905.
'Reviews: *Psychopathia Sexualis*'. *British Medical Journal*, 1 (24 June 1893): 1325.
Rimbault, E. F. *Soho and its Associations: Historical, Literary and Artistic*. London: Dula, 1895.
Sala, George. *London Up To Date*. London: Adam and Charles Black, 1894.
Satan's Harvest Home, or the Present State of Whorecraft, Pimping, Adultery, Fornication, Sodomy, Procuring and the Game of Flats. London: 1749.
Savage, George. H. 'Clinical Notes and Cases: Case of Sexual Perversion in a Man'. *The Journal of Mental Science*, 30 (1884): 390–1.
Select Trials for Murder, Robbery, Burglary, Rapes, Sodomy, Coining, Forgery and Pyracy at the Sessions House in the Old Bailey From the Years 1720–1732. 2 vols. London, 1735.
Select Trials for Murder, Robbery, &.C at the Sessions House in the Old Bailey From 1720–1741. 4 vols. London, 1742.

Select Trials for Murder, Robbery, Burglary, &.C in the Old Bailey From 1741 to the Present Year. 4 vols. London, 1764.

Shaw, George Bernard. 'The Prosecution of Mr Bedborough'. *The Adult*, 2, 8 (September 1898): 230–1.

The Sanity of Art: An Exposure of the Current Nonsense About Artists Being Degenerate. London: New Age Press, 1908.

Showalter, Showalter, ed. *Daughters of Decadence: Women Writers of the* Fin de Siècle. New Brunswick, NJ: Rutgers, 1993.

Sims, George. *How the Poor Live*. London: Chatto and Windus, 1883.

Living London: Its Work and Its Play; Its Humour and Its Pathos; Its Sights and Its Scenes. London: Cassel, 1901–3 and 1906.

Sins of the Cities of the Plain, or Recollections of a Mary-Ann with Short Essays on Sodomy and Tribadism. London, 1881.

Stableford, Brian, ed. *The Dedalus Book of Decadence: Moral Ruins*. Sawtry: Dedalus, 1990.

Stevenson, Robert Louis. *The Strange Case of Dr Jekyll and Mr Hyde*. 1886; London: Penguin, 1994.

Stoker, Bram. *Dracula*. 1897; Oxford: Oxford University Press, 1983.

Strachey, Lytton. *Lytton Strachey By Himself: A Self-Portrait*. Ed. Michael Holroyd. London: Vintage, 1994.

Street, G. S. *The Autobiography of a Boy*. London: Matthews and Lane, 1894.

Stutfield, Hugh. E. M. 'Tommyrotics'. *Blackwoods Edinburgh Magazine* (June 1895): 833–45.

Summers, Montague. *Antinous and Other Poems*. London: Sisleys, 1907.

Symons, Arthur. *The Collected Works of Arthur Symons*. London: Martin Secker, 1924.

'The Decadent Movement in Literature' (1893). *Arthur Symons: Selected Writings*. Ed. Roger Holdsworth. Manchester, Carcanet Press: 1974.

Symonds, John Addington. *In the Key of Blue and Other Prose Essays*. London: Elkin Matthews, 1893.

The Letters of John Addington Symonds: 1885–1893. Eds. Herbert Schueller and Robert Peters. Detroit: Wayne State University Press, 1969.

The Memoirs of John Addington Symonds. Ed. Phyllis Grosskurth. London: Hutchinson, 1984.

'A Problem in Greek Ethics'. In H. Havelock Ellis and John Addington Symonds, *Studies in the Psychology of Sex*, vol. 1, *Sexual Inversion*. London: Wilson and Macmillan, April 1897.

A Problem in Modern Ethics: An Inquiry into the Phenomenon of Sexual Inversion. 1891; London, 1896.

Studies in the Greek Poets. London: Smith, Elder and Co., 1879.

Walt Whitman: A Study. London: John C. Nimmo, 1893.

Tames, Richard. *Soho Past*. London, 1894.

Taylor, Tom. *Leicester Square: Its Associations and Its Worthies. London*. Bickers and Son, 1874.

Teleny: Etude physiologique. Paris, 1934.

Teleny, or The Reverse of the Medal. 1893; Ware: Wordsworth, 1995.

Tempted London. London: Hodder and Stoughton, 1889.

Thornbury, Walter. *Old and New London: A Narrative of its History, its People and its Places.* London: Cassell, 1873–8, 1897.

Timbs, John. *Clubs and Club Life in London.* London: Chatto and Windus, 1908.

'The Trial and Conviction of Several Reputed Sodomites, Before the Right Honourable Lord Mayor and Recorder of London, at Guildhall, the 20th day of October, 1707'. In Ian McCormick, ed., *Secret Sexualities: a Sourcebook of Seventeenth and Eighteenth Century Writing.* London: Routledge, 1997.

Tyrwhitt, Richard St John. 'The Greek Spirit in Modern Literature'. *Contemporary Review,* 29 (March 1877): 522–66.

A View of the Town in an Epistle to a Friend in the Country: A Satire. London: 1735.

Walker, Quentin Thomas. 'On Clubs'. *Leisure Hour,* 35 (1986): 415.

Walling, W. M. *Sexology.* Philadelphia: Puritan Press, 1902.

Ward, Ned. *Satyrical Reflections on Clubs in 29 Chapters.* London: 1710.

Weininger, Otto. *Sex and Character.* London: Heinemann, 1906.

Westermarck, Edward. *The Origin and Development of Moral Ideas.* London: Macmillan, 1908.

Wheatley, Henry. *Round About Piccadilly and Pall Mall; or a Ramble from the Haymarket to Hyde Park.* London: 1870.

White, Arnold. *The Problems of a Great City.* London: Remington, 1886.

White, Arnold, ed. *The Destitute Alien in Britain: A Series of Papers Dealing with the Subject of Foreign Pauper Immigration.* London: Swann Sonnenschein, 1892.

Whitman, Walt. *Leaves of Grass.* 1855; New York: Airmont, 1965.

Walt Whitman: The Complete Poems. Ed. Francis Murphy. London, 1996.

Wilde, Oscar. *The Artist as Critic: Critical Writings of Oscar Wilde.* Ed. Richard Ellmann. London: W. H. Allen, 1970.

Complete Works of Oscar Wilde. Ed. J. B. Foreman. London: Collins, 1983.

De Profundis and Other Writings. Ed. Hesketh Pearson. London: Penguin, 1986.

Four Letters by Oscar Wilde (which were not included in the English edition of De Profundis*).* London: privately printed, 1906.

The Importance of Being Earnest. 1895; London: Nick Hern Books, 1997.

More Selected Letters of Oscar Wilde. Ed. Rupert Hart-Davis. Oxford: Oxford University Press, 1989.

The Picture of Dorian Gray. 1891; London: Penguin; 1985.

Poems. Boston: Robert Bros.1881.

Selected Letters of Oscar Wilde. Ed. Rupert Hart-Davis. Oxford: Oxford University Press, 1979.

Wilkins, W. H. *The Alien Invasion.* London: Methuen, 1892.

Willis, W. N. *White Slaves in a Piccadilly Flat.* London: Anglo-Easton, 1915.

Western Men with Eastern Morals. London: Stanley Paul, 1912.

Yokel's Preceptor, or More Sprees in London! London: H. Smith, *c.*1855.

SECONDARY SOURCES

Ackerly, J. R. *My Father and Myself.* London: Bodley Head, 1968.

Adburgham, Alison. *Shopping in Style: London from the Restoration to Edwardian Elegance.* London: Thames and Hudson, 1979.

Aldrich, Robert. *The Seduction of the Mediterranean: Writing, Art and Homosexual Fantasy.* London: Routledge, 1993.

Altman, D., ed. *Homosexuality, Which Homosexuality?* London: Gay Men's Press, 1989.

Aronson, Theo. *Prince Eddy and the Homosexual Underworld.* London: John Murray, 1994.

Attick, Richard. *Evil Encounters: Two Victorian Sensations.* London: John Murray, 1987.

Bailey, Peter. 'Conspiracies of Meaning: Music Hall and the Knowingness of Popular Culture', *Past and Present*, 144 (August 1994): 138–71.

'Parasexuality and Glamour: The Victorian Barmaid as Cultural Prototype'. *Gender and History*, 2, 2 (Summer 1990): 148–72.

Bailey, Victor, ed., *Policing and Punishment in Nineteenth-Century Britain.* London: Croom Helm, 1981.

Bakhtin, Mikhail. *The Bakhtin Reader.* Ed. Pam Morris. London: Edward Arnold, 1994.

Rabelais and his World. Trans. H. Iswolsky. Bloomington: Indiana University Press, 1984.

Barret-DuCrocq, Françoise. *Love in the Time of Victoria: Sexuality, Class and Gender in Nineteenth-Century London.* Trans. John Howe. London: Verso, 1991.

Barthes, Roland. *Mythologies.* Trans. Annette Lavers. London: Jonathan Cape, 1972.

Bartlett, Neil. *Who Was That Man? A Present for Mr Oscar Wilde.* London: Serpent's Tail, 1988.

Bech, Henning. *When Men Meet Men: Homosexuality and Modernity.* Trans. Teresa Mesquit and Tim Davies. Cambridge: Polity Press, 1997.

Beckson, Karl. *London in the 1890s: A Cultural History.* London: W. W. Norton, 1992.

Beer, Gillian. *Arguing with the Past: Essays in Narrative from Woolf to Sidney.* London: Routledge, 1989.

Darwin's Plots: Evolutionary Narrative in Darwin, George Elliot and Nineteenth-Century Fiction. London: Routledge, 1985.

Forging the Missing Link: Interdisciplinary Stories. Cambridge: Cambridge University Press, 1991.

Open Fields: Science in Cultural Encounter. Oxford: Oxford University Press, 1996.

Bell, David and Gill Valentine, eds. *Mapping Desire: Geographies of Sexualities.* London: Routledge, 1995.

Benjamin, Walter. *Reflections: Essays, Aphorisms and Autobiographical Writings.* Ed. Peter Demetz, trans. Edmund Jephcott. New York: Schochen Books, 1986.

Berman, Marshall. *All That Is Solid Melts into Air: The Experience of Modernity.* New York: Simon and Schuster, 1982.

Betsky, Aaron, *Queer Space: Architecture and Same-Sex Desire.* New York: William Marrow, 1997.

Birken, Lawrence. *Consuming Desire: Sexual Science and the Emergence of a Culture of Abundance, 1871–1914.* London: Cornell University Press, 1988.

Bland, Lucy. *Banishing the Beast: English Feminism and Sexual Morality, 1885–1914.* London: Penguin, 1995.

Bland, Lucy, and Laura Doan, eds. *Sexology in Culture: Labelling Bodies and Desires.* Cambridge: Polity Press, 1998.

Bleys, Rudi. *The Geography of Perversion: Male to Male Sexual Behaviour Outside the West and the Ethnographic Imagination, 1750–1918.* London: Cassell, 1996.
‘Homosexual Exile: The Textuality of the Imaginary Paradise, 1800–1980’. *Journal of Homosexuality*, 25, 1/2 (1993): 165–79.

Boone, Joseph and Michael Cohen, eds. *Engendering Men: The Question of Male Feminist Criticism.* London: Routledge, 1990.

Boswell, John. *Christianity and Social Tolerance: Gay People in Western Europe from the Beginning of the Christian Era to the Fourteenth Century.* Chicago: University of Chicago Press, 1980.
The Marriage of Likeness: Same-Sex Unions in Pre-Modern Europe. London: Harper Collins, 1995.

Bowlby, Rachel. *Shopping with Freud.* London: Routledge, 1993.

Brake, Laurel. *Print in Transition, 1850–1910: Studies in Media and Book History.* Basingstoke: Palgrave, 2001.

Brake, Laurel, Aled Jones and Lionel Madden, eds. *Investigating Victorian Journalism.* London: MacMillan, 1990.

Brantlinger, Patrick. *Rules of Darkness: British Literature and Imperialism, 1830–1914.* Ithaca: Cornell University Press, 1988.

Bray, Alan. *Homosexuality in Renaissance England.* London: Gay Men's Press, 1982.

Brecher, Edward. *The Sex Researchers.* London: André Deutsch, 1970.

Bremmer, Jan, ed. *From Sappho to de Sade: Moments in the History of Sexuality.* London: Routledge, 1989.

Breward, Christopher. ‘Fashion and the Man, From Suburb to City Street: The Cultural Geography of Masculine Consumption, 1870–1914’. *New Formations*, 37 (Spring 1999): 47–70.
The Hidden Consumer: Masculinities, Fashion and City Life, 1860–1914. Manchester: Manchester University Press, 1999.
‘ “On the Bank's Threshold”: Administrative Revolutions and the Fashioning of Masculine Identities at the Turn of the Century’. *Parallax*, 5 (September 1997): 109–23.

Briggs, Asa. *Victorian Cities.* Harmondsworth: Pelican, 1963.

Bristow, Edward. *Vice and Vigilance: Purity Movements in Britain Since 1700.* Dublin: Gill and Macmillan, 1977.

Bristow, Joseph, ed. *Sexual Sameness: Textual Differences in Lesbian and Gay Writing.* London: Routledge, 1992.

Brown, Tony, ed. *Edward Carpenter and Late-Victorian Radicalism*. London: Frank Cass, 1990.

Bruns, Gerald. 'Cain: or, The Metaphorical Construction of Cities'. *Salmagundi*, 74–5 (Spring/Summer 1987): 70–86.

Buck-Morss, Susan. 'The City of Dreamworld and Catastrophe'. *October*, 73 (Summer 1995): 3–26.

Bullough, Vern. *Science in the Bedroom: A History of Sex Research*. New York: Basic Books, 1994.

Burford, C. J. *The 'Orrible Synne: A Look at London Lechery from Roman to Cromwellian Times*. London: Calder and Boyars, 1973.

Burgin, Victor, James Donald and Cora Kaplan, eds. *Formations of Fantasy*. London: Methuen, 1986.

Burke, Peter and Roy Porter, eds. *The Social History of Language*. Cambridge: Cambridge University Press, 1987.

Language, Self and Society. Cambridge: Polity Press, 1991.

Burlington, Russell. *Forrest Reid: A Portrait and a Study*. London: Faber and Faber, 1953.

Calligaris, Contardo. 'Memory Lane: a Vindication of Urban Life'. *Critical Quarterly*, 36, 4 (Winter 1994): 56–73.

Carey, John. *The Intellectuals and the Masses*. London: Faber and Faber, 1992.

Carey, John, ed. *The Faber Book of Utopias*. London: Faber and Faber, 1999.

Cartledge, Paul, Paul Millett and Sitta von Reden, eds. *Kosmos: Essays in Order, Conflict and Community in Classical Athens*. Cambridge: Cambridge University Press, 1998.

Castells, Manuel. *The City and the Grass Roots: A Cross-Cultural Theory of Urban Social Movements*. London: Edward Allen, 1983.

Cavaliero, Glen. *The Rural Tradition in the English Novel, 1900–1939*. London: Macmillan, 1977.

Certeau, Michel de. *The Practice of Everyday Life*. Trans. Steven Rendell. Berkeley: University of California Press, 1988.

Chauncey, George. *Gay New York: The Making of the Gay Male World, 1890–1940*. London: Flamingo, 1995.

Chesney, Kellow. *The Victorian Underworld*. London: Temple Smith, 1970.

Clarke, I. F. *Voices Prophesying War*. Oxford: Oxford University Press, 1992.

Cocks, H. G. '*Calamus* in Bolton: Spirituality and Homosexual Desire in Late-Victorian England', *Gender and History*, 13, 2 (August 2001): 191–223.

'Nameless Offences: Homosexual Desire in the Nineteenth Century'. Ts, forthcoming with I. B. Taurus, 2003.

Cohen, David. *Law, Sexuality and the Enforcement of Morals in Classical Athens*. Cambridge: Cambridge University Press, 1991.

Cohen, Ed. *Talk on the Wilde Side: Towards a Genealogy of a Discourse on Male Sexualities*. London: Routledge, 1993.

Cohen, William A., *Sex Scandal: The Private Parts of Victorian Fiction*. Durham, NC: Duke University Press, 1996.

Collins, Marcus, ed. *The Permissive Society and its Enemies*. London, Rivers Oram, 2003.

Columina, Beatrix, ed. *Sexuality and Space*. New York: Princeton, 1992.

Colebrook, Claire. *New Literary Histories: New Historicism and Contemporary Criticism*. Manchester: Manchester University Press, 1997.

Compagnon, Antoine. 'The Street as Passser-by'. *Critical Quarterly*, 36, 4 (Winter 1994): 73–8.

Cooper, Davina. *Sexing the City: Lesbian and Gay Politics Within the Activist State*. London: Rivers Oram, 1994.

Cooper, Emmanuel. *The Sexual Perspective: Homosexuality and Art in the Last Hundred Years in the West*. London: Routledge, 1994.

Cooper, Jeremy. *Victorian and Edwardian Furniture and Interiors*. London: Thames and Hudson, 1987.

Coote, Stephen, ed. *The Penguin Book of Homosexual Verse*. London: Penguin, 1983.

Corbin, Alain. *Time, Desire and Horror: Towards a History of the Senses*. Trans. Jean Birrel. Cambridge: Polity Press, 1995.

Cowling, Mary. *The Artist as Anthropologist: The Representation of Type and Character in Victorian Art*. Cambridge: Cambridge University Press, 1989.

Crawford, Alan. *C. R. Ashbee: Architect, Designer and Romantic Socialist*. London: Yale University Press, 1985.

Croft-Cooke, Rupert. *Feasting With Panthers: A New Consideration of Some Late Victorian Writers*. London: W. H. Allen, 1967.

Crompton, Louis. *Byron and Greek Love: Homophobia in Nineteenth-Century England*. London: Faber and Faber, 1985.

Crozier, Ivan Dalley. 'The Medical Construction of Homosexuality and its Relation to the Law in Nineteenth-Century England'. *Medical History*, 45 (2001): 61–82.

Dannecker, Martin. *Theories of Homosexuality*. London: Gay Men's Press, 1981.

Davenport-Hines, Richard. *Sex, Death and Punishment: Attitudes to Sex and Sexuality in Britain Since the Renaissance*. London: Fontana, 1990.

Davidoff, Leonore and Catherine Hall. *Family Fortunes: Men and Women of the English Middle Class, 1780–1850*. London: Hutchinson, 1987.

Davies, Gill. 'Foreign Bodies: Images of the London Working Class at the End of the Nineteenth Century'. *Literature and History*, 14, 1 (Spring 1988): 64–80.

Dellamora, Richard. *Masculine Desire: The Sexual Politics of Victorian Aestheticism*. Chapel Hill: University of North Carolina Press, 1990.

Dixon, Joy. 'Sexology and the Occult: Sexuality and Subjectivity in the Theosophical New Age'. *Journal of the History of Sexuality*, 7, 3 (1997): 409–33.

Doan, Laura, *Fashioning Sapphism: The Origins of Modern Lesbian Culture*. New York: Columbia University Press, 2001.

Dollimore, Jonathan. *Sexual Dissidence: Augustine to Wilde, Freud to Foucault*. Oxford: Clarendon, 1991.

Dowling, Linda. 'The Decadent and the New Woman'. *Nineteenth Century Fiction*, 33, 4 (1979): 434–53.

Hellenism and Homosexuality in Victorian Oxford. New York: Cornell University Press, 1994.

Language and Decadence in the Victorian Fin de Siècle. Princeton: Princeton University Press, 1986.

Driver, Felix and David Gilbert, eds. *Imperial Cities: Landscapes, Display and Identities*. Manchester: Manchester University Press, 1999.

Duberman, Martin, Martha Vicinus and George Chauncey Jr. *Hidden from History: Reclaiming the Gay and Lesbian Past*. London: Penguin, 1991.

Duncan, James and David Ley, eds. *Place, Culture and Representation*. London: Routledge, 1993.

Dynes, Wayne. *Encyclopaedia of Homosexuality*. London: Garland, 1990.

Dyos, H. J. *Exploring the Urban Past: Essay in Urban History by H. J. Dyos*. Eds. David Cannadine and David Reeder. Cambridge: Cambridge University Press, 1982.

Dyos, H. J. and Michael Wolff. *The Victorian City: Images and Reality*. 2 vols. London: Routledge and Kegan Paul, 1973.

Eagleton, Terry. *Ideology*. London: Longman, 1994.

Eckardt, Wolf von, Sander Gilman and J. Edward Chamberlain. *Oscar Wilde's London*. London: Michael O'Mara, 1988.

Edwards, Catherine. *Writing Rome: Textual Approaches to the City*. Cambridge: Cambridge University Press, 1996.

Ellmann, Richard. *Oscar Wilde*. London: Penguin, 1985.

Erber, Nancy and George Robb, eds. *Disorder in the Court: Trials and Sexual Conflict at the Turn of the Century*. Basingstoke: Macmillan, 1999.

Ericson, Richard, Patricia Baranek and Janet Chan. *Visualising Deviance: A Study of News Organisation*. Milton Keynes: Open University Press, 1987.

Ferris, Lesley, ed. *Crossing the Stage: Controversies in Cross-Dressing*. London: Routledge, 1993.

Fisher, N. R. E, ed. *Social Values in Classical Athens*. London: Dent, 1976.

Fisher, Trevor. *Scandal: The Sexual Politics of Late Victorian Britain*. Stroud: Alan Sutton, 1995.

Fitzgerald, Mike, Gregor McLennan and Jennie Pawson. *Crime and Society: Readings in History and Theory*. London: Routledge, 1981.

Fitzroy, A. T. *Despised and Rejected*. 1918; London: Gay Men's Press, 1988.

Fletcher, Ian, ed. *Decadence and the 1890s*. London: Edward Arnold, 1979.

Romantic Mythologies. London: Routledge and Kegan Paul, 1967.

Foldy, Michael. *The Trials of Oscar Wilde: Deviance, Morality and Late-Victorian Society*. New York: Yale University Press, 1997.

Foucault, Michel. *Discipline and Punish: The Birth of the Prison*. Trans. Alan Sheridan. London: Penguin, 1977.

Foucault Live: Interviews, 1966–1984. New York: Columbia University Press, 1989.

The History of Sexuality, vol. 1, *An Introduction*. Trans. Robert Hurley, 1976; London: Penguin, 1990.

'Of Other Spaces'. *Diacritics*, 16 (1986): 22–7.

Fout, John, ed. *Forbidden History: The State, Society and the Regulation of Sexuality in Modern Europe.* Chicago: University of Chicago Press, 1992.

Fraçouer, Robert. *A Descriptive Dictionary and Atlas of Sexology.* London: Greenwood, 1991.

Fraser, David and Anthony Sutcliffe. *The Pursuit of Urban History.* London: Arnold, 1983.

Fraser, W. Hamish. *The Coming of the Mass Market.* London: Macmillan, 1981.

Furbank, P. N. *E. M. Forster: A Life.* London: Secker and Warburg, 1978.

Gagnier, Regenia. *Idylls of the Market Place: Oscar Wilde and the Victorian Public.* Aldershot: Scolar Press, 1987.

  Subjectivities: A History of Self-Representation, 1832–1920. Oxford: Oxford University Press, 1991.

Gainer, Bernard. *The Alien Invasion: The Origin of the Alien's Act of 1905.* London: Heinemann, 1972.

Gardiner, James. *Who's a Pretty Boy Then: One Hundred and Fifty Years of Gay Life in Pictures.* London: Serpent's Tale, 1996.

Gatrell, V. A. C, Bruce Lenman and Geoffrey Parker, eds. *Crime and the Law: the Social History of Crime in Western Europe since 1500.* London: Europa, 1980.

Gay, Peter. *Freud for Historians.* Oxford: Oxford University Press, 1985.

Gilbert, Pamela, ed., *Imagined Londons.* New York: State University of New York Press, 2002.

Gille, Didier. 'Macuration and Purification'. *Zone*, 1, 2 (1986): 226–84.

Gilman, Sander and J. E. Chamberlain, eds. *Degeneration: The Dark Side of Progress.* New York: Columbia University Press, 1985.

Goldberg, Isaac. *Havelock Ellis: A Biographical and Critical Survey.* London: Constable and Co., 1926.

Goldberg, Jonathan. *Reclaiming Sodom.* London: Routledge, 1994.

Greenberg, David. *The Construction of Homosexuality.* Chicago: University of Chicago Press, 1988.

Greenslade, William. *Degeneration, Culture and the Novel, 1880–1940.* Cambridge: Cambridge University Press, 1994.

Grosskurth, Phyllis. *Havelock Ellis: A Biography.* London: Allen Lane, 1980.

  John Addington Symonds: A Biography. London: Longmans, 1964.

Grosz, Elizabeth. *Space, Time and Perversion: Essays on the Politics of Bodies.* London: Routledge, 1995.

Gunn, Simon and R. J. Morris, eds. *Identities in Space: Contested Terrains in the Western City Since 1850.* Aldershot: Ashgate, 2001.

Haley, Bruce. *The Healthy Body and Victorian Society.* Cambridge, MA: Harvard University Press, 1978.

Hall, Catherine. *White, Male and Middle Class: Explorations in Feminism and History.* Cambridge: Polity Press, 1992.

Hall, Lesley A. '"Disinterested Enthusiasm for Sexual Misconduct": The British Society for the Study of Sex Psychology, 1913–47'. *Journal of Contemporary History*, 30 (1995): 665–86.

Hallam, Paul. *The Book of Sodom.* London: Verso, 1993.

Halperin, David. 'Forgetting Foucault: Acts, Identities, and the History of Sexuality.' *Representations*, 63 (Summer 1998): 93–120

Hammond, M. G. L. and H. H. Scullard. *The Oxford Classical Dictionary*. Oxford: Clarendon Press, 1970.

Harris, Frank. *Oscar Wilde*. London: Constable and Co., 1938.

Harris, José. *Private Lives, Public Spirit: A Social History of Britain, 1870–1914*. Oxford: Oxford University Press, 1993.

Harvey, A. D. 'Prosecutions for Sodomy in England at the Beginning of the Nineteenth Century'. *Historical Journal*, 21, 4 (1978): 939–48.

Harvey, David. *Consciousness and the Urban Experience*. Oxford: Blackwell, 1985.

Hebdige, Dick. *Subculture: The Meaning of Style*. London: Methuen, 1979.

Hekma, Gert. 'Sodomites, Platonic Lovers, Contrary Lovers: The Background of the Modern Homosexual'. *Journal of Homosexuality*, 16, 1/2 (1988): 433–57.

Hekma, Gert, Harry Oosterhuis and James Steakley. 'Leftist Sexual Politics and Homosexuality: A Historical Overview'. *Journal of Homosexuality*, 29, 2/3 (1995): 1–32.

Hibbert, Christopher. *London: Biography of a City*. London: Longman, 1969.

Hibbert, Christopher and Ben Weinreb, eds. *The London Encyclopaedia*. London: Macmillan, 1995.

Hichens, Robert. *Yesterday*. London: Cassell, 1947.

Higgs, David, ed. *Queer Sites: Gay Urban Histories Since 1600*. London: Routledge, 1999.

Hitchcock, Tim. 'Redefining Sex in the Eighteenth Century'. *History Workshop Journal*, 41 (Spring 1996): 73–90.

Hoare, Philip. *Wilde's Last Stand: Decadence, Conspiracy and the First World War*. London: Duckworth, 1997.

Hobsbawm, Eric. *Industry and Empire*. London: Penguin, 1969.

Hobsbawm, Eric and Terrence Ranger. *The Invention of Tradition*. Cambridge: Cambridge University Press, 1983.

Houlbrock, Matt. 'Lady Austin's Camp Boys: Constituting The Queer Subject in 1930s London'. *Gender and History*, 14, 1 (2002): 31–61.

'The Private World of Public Urinals: London 1918–57'. *London Journal*, 25, 1 (2000): 52–70.

'Soldier Heroes and Rent Boys: Homosex, Masculinities and Britishness in the Brigade of Guards: c.1900–60'. *Journal of British Studies*. Forthcoming, July 2003.

'"A Sun Among Cities": Space, Identities and Queer Male Practices, London 1918–57', PhD Thesis, University of Essex (2002).

'Towards a Historical Geography of Sexuality', *Journal of Urban History*, 2, 4 (2001): 497–504.

Hulin, Jean-Paul and Pierre Coustillas, eds. *Victorian Writers and the City*. Lille: Publications de l'Université de Lille, 1979.

Hull, Isobel. 'The Bourgeoisie and Its Discontents: Reflections of Nationalism and Respectability'. *Journal of Contemporary History*, 17, 2 (1982): 247–68.

Hyam, Ronald. *Britain's Imperial Century: 1815–1914*. London: Batsford, 1976.

Empire and Sexuality – The British Experience. Manchester: Manchester University Press, 1990.

Hyde, H. Montgomeny. *The Cleveland Street Scandal*. London: W. H. Allen, 1976.

The Other Love: An Historical and Contemporary Survey of Homosexuality in Britain. London: Heinemann, 1970.

The Trials of Oscar Wilde. London: New York, Dover, 1973.

Inglis, Brian, *Roger Casement*. Belfast: Blackstaff Press, 1993.

Innes, Christopher, *A Sourcebook on Naturalistic Theatre*. London: Routledge, 2000.

Jardine, Alice and Paul Smith, eds. *Men in Feminism* (New York: Methuen, 1987).

Jeffs, William Patrick. '"Man's World" and Manly Comradeship: Language, Politics, and Homosexuality in Walt Whitman's Works'. *Journal of Homosexuality*, 23, 4 (1992): 19–41.

Jeffries, Sheila, ed. *The Sexuality Debates*. London: Routledge, 1987.

Jenkyns, Richard. *Dignity and Decadence: Victorian Art and the Classical Inheritance*. London: Harpers and Collins, 1991.

The Victorians and Ancient Greece. Oxford: Blackwell, 1980.

Johnson, R. V. *Aestheticism*. London: Methuen, 1969.

Jones, Gareth Stedman. *Languages of Class*. Cambridge: Cambridge University Press, 1983.

Outcast London: A Study in the Relationship Between Classes in Victorian Society. Oxford: Clarendon, 1971.

Joyce, Patrick. *Democratic Subjects: The Self and the Social in Nineteenth-Century England*. Cambridge: Cambridge University Press, 1994.

Kaplan, Morris B. *Sexual Justice: Democratic Citizenship and the Politics of Desire*. London: Routledge, 1997.

'Who's Afraid of Jack Saul?: Urban Culture and the Politics of Desire in Late-Victorian London', *Gay and Lesbian Quarterly*, 5, 3 (1999): 267–314.

Kearney, Patrick. *History of Erotic Literature*. London: Macmillan, 1982.

Kidd, Alan and David Nicholls, eds. *Gender, Civic Culture and Consumerism*. Manchester: Manchester University Press, 1999.

Keating, J. *Working Class Stories of the 1890s*. London: Routledge and Kegan Paul, 1971.

Keith, Michael and Steve Pile, eds. *Place and the Politics of Identity*. London: Routledge, 1993.

Kellogg, Stuart, ed. *Literary Visions of Homosexuality*. New York: Haworth Press, 1983.

Kern, Stephen. *The Culture of Time and Space, 1880–1918*. London: Weidenfeld and Nicholson, 1983.

Khoury, Elias. 'The Memory of the City'. *Grand Street*, 54 (October 1995): 137–43.

Koestenbaum, Wayne. *Double Talk: The Erotics of Male Literary Collaboration*. London: Routledge, 1989.

Kristeva, Julia. *The Kristeva Reader*. Ed. Toril Moi. Oxford: Basil Blackwood, 1986.

Lafitte, François. 'Homosexuality and the Law'. *British Journal of Delinquency*, 9, 1 (July 1958): 8–19.

Langdon, Susan, ed. *From Pasture to Polis: Art in the Age of Homer*. Columbia: University of Missouri Press, 1993.

Laqueur, Thomas. *The Making of Sex: Body and Gender from the Greeks to Freud*. Cambridge, MA: Harvard University Press, 1990.

Lauretis, Teressa de. 'Queer Theory: Lesbian and Gay Sexualities. An Introduction'. *Differences: A Journal of Feminist Cultural Studies*, 3, 2 (1991): iii–xviii.

Lawrence, Jon and Miles Taylor. 'The Poverty of Protest: Gareth Stedman Jones and the Politics of Language – a Reply'. *Social History*, 18, 1 (1993): 1–15.

Ledger, Sally. *The New Woman: Fiction and Feminism at the* Fin de Siècle. Manchester: Manchester University Press, 1997.

Ledger, Sally and Scott McCracken, eds. *Cultural Politics at the* Fin de Siècle. Cambridge: Cambridge University Press, 1995.

Lees, Andrew. *Cities Perceived: Urban Society in European and American Thought, 1820–1940*. Manchester: Manchester University Press, 1985.

Lees, Lynn and Andrew, eds. *The Rise of Urban Britain*. London and New York: Garland, 1985.

Lefebvre, Henri. *Everyday Life in the Modern World*. Trans. Sacha Rabinovitch. New Brunswick: Transaction, 1990.

The Production of Space. Trans. Donald Nicholson-Smith. Oxford: Blackwell, 1991.

Lehner, Johanna and Ernst. *Folklore and Symbolism of Flowers, Plants and Trees*. New York: Tudor Publishing, 1960.

Lesbian History Group, *Not a Passing Phase: Reclaiming Lesbians in History, 1840–1985*. London: Women's Press, 1989.

Lester, John. A. *Journey Through Despair, 1880–1914: Transformations in British Literary Culture*. Princeton: Princeton University Press, 1968.

Lhombreaud, Roger. *Arthur Symons: A Critical Biography*. London: Unicorn Press, 1863.

Longaker, Mark. *Ernest Dowson*. 1945; Philadelphia, University of Pensylvania Press, 1968.

Loveland, Ian, ed. *Frontiers of Criminality*. London: Sweet and Marshall, 1995.

MacCarthy, Fiona. *The Simple Life: C. R. Ashbee in the Cotswolds*. Berkeley: University of California Press, 1981.

MacCubbin, Robert, ed. *'Tis Nature's Fault: Unauthorised Sexuality During the Enlightenment*. Cambridge: Cambridge University Press, 1987.

Mackenzie, John. *Propaganda and Empire: The Manipulation of Public Opinion, 1880–1960*. Manchester: Manchester University Press, 1984.

Malinowsky, Bronislow. *Sex, Culture and Myth*. London: Hart-Davis, 1963.

Malinowsky, Sharon, ed. *Gay and Lesbian Literature*. Detroit: St James Press, 1994.

Mangan, J. A. and James Walvin, eds. *Manliness and Morality: Middle-Class Masculinity in Britain and America, 1800–1940*. Manchester: Manchester University Press, 1987.

Marcus, Steven. *The Other Victorians: A Study of Sexuality and Pornography in Mid Nineteenth-Century England*. London: Weidenfeld and Nicolson, 1966.

Massey, Doreen. 'Places and their Pasts'. *History Workshop Journal*, 39 (Spring 1995): 182–92.

McCalman, Iain. *Radical Underworld: Prophets, Revolutionaries and Pornographers in London, 1795–1840*. Cambridge: Cambridge University Press, 1988.

McLaren, Angus, *The Trials of Masculinity: Policing Sexual Boundaries, 1870–1930*. Chicago: Chicago University Press, 1997.

Mead, G. H. 'The Psychology of Punitive Justice'. American Journal of Sociology, 23 (1918): 577–602.

Melman, Billie (ed.). *Borderlines: Genders and Identitites in War and Peace, 1870–1930*. London: Routledge, 1998.

Mendes, Peter. *Clandestine Erotic Fiction in English 1800–1930*. Aldershot: Scolar Press, 1993.

Merck, Mandy. *Perversion: Deviant Readings*. London: Virago, 1993.

Meyers, Jeffrey. *Homosexuality and Literature, 1890–1930*. Montreal: Queen's University of Press, 1977.

Michasiw, Kim. 'Camp, Masculinity, Masquerade'. *Differences*, 6, 2 and 3 (Summer/Fall 1994): 146–73.

Mickelsen, David. '*A Rebours*: Spatial Form'. *French Forum*, 3, 1 (January 1978): 48–55.

Miller, D. A. *The Novel and the Police*. Berkeley: University of California Press, 1988.

Miller, Michael. *The* Bon Marché: *Bourgeois Culture and the Department Store, 1869–1920*. London: Allen and Unwin, 1981.

Miller, Neil. *Out of the Past: Gay and Lesbian History From 1869 to the Present*. London: Vintage. 1995.

Moers, Ellen. *The Dandy: Brummel to Beerbohm*. Lincoln: University of Nebraska Press, 1978.

Moran, Leslie. *The Homosexual(ity) of Law*. London: Routledge, 1996.

Mort, Frank. *Cultures of Consumption: Masculinity and Social Space in Twentieth-Century Britain*. London: Routledge, 1996.

Dangerous Sexualities: Medico-Moral Politics in England Since 1830. London: Routledge, 1987.

Mosse, George. 'Naturalism and Respectability: Normal and Abnormal Sexuality in Nineteenth Century'. *Journal of Contemporary History*, 17, 2 (April 1992): 221–46.

Nead, Lynda. *Myths of Sexuality: Representation of Women in Victorian Britain* Oxford: Blackwell, 1988.

Victorian Babylon: People, Street and Images in Nineteenth-Century London. New Haven: Yale University Press, 2000.

Nord, Deborah Epstein. '"Neither Pair nor Odd": Female Community in Late Nineteenth-Century London', *Signs*, 115 (1990).

Walking the Victorian Streets: Women, Representation and the City. Ithaca, NY: Cornell University Press, 1995.

Norton, Rictor. *Mother Clap's Molly House: The Gay Subculture in England, 1700–1830.* London: Gay Men's Press, 1992.

The Myth of the Modern Homosexual: Queer History and the Search for Cultural Unity. London: Cassell, 1997.

Olsen, Donald. *The City as a Work of Art: London, Paris, Vienna.* New Haven: Yale University Press, 1986.

The Growth of Victorian London. London: Penguin, 1976.

Oosterhuis, Harry. 'Homosexual Emancipation in Germany Before 1933: Two Traditions'. *Journal of Homosexuality*, 22, 1/2 (1991): 1–27.

Stepchildren of Nature: Krafft-Ebing, Psychiatry and the Making of Sexual Identity. Chicago: University of Chicago Press, 2000.

Paglia, Camille. *Sexual Personae: Art and Decadence from Nefertiti to Emily Dickinson.* New Haven: Yale University Press, 1990.

Parker, Andrew, Mary Russo, Doris Sommer and Patricia Yaeger, eds. *Nationalisms and Sexualities.* London, Routledge, 1992.

Paterson, John. *Edwardians: London Life and Letters, 1901–1914.* Chicago: Ivan Dee, 1996.

Pearsal, Ronald. *The Worm in the Bud: The World of Victorian Sexuality.* London: Weidenfeld and Nicholson, 1969.

Pemble, John. *The Mediterranean Passion: Victorians and Edwardians in the South.* Oxford: Clarendon, 1987.

Penn, Donna. 'Queer: Theorising Politics and History'. *Radical History Review*, 62 (Spring 1995): 24–40.

Pennybacker, Susan. *A Vision for London, 1889–1914: Labour, Everyday Life and the London County Council Experiment.* London: Routledge, 1995.

Peterkin, Allan. *One Thousand Beards: A Cultural History of Facial Hair.* Vancouver: Arsenal Pulp Press, 2002.

Petrow, Stefan. *Policing Morals: The Metropolitan Police and the Home Office, 1870–1914.* Oxford: Clarendon Press, 1994.

Pick, Daniel. *Faces of Degeneration: A European Disorder, c.1848–1918.* Cambridge: Cambridge University Press, 1989.

Pick, John. *The West End: Mismanagement and Snobbery.* Eastbourne: Olford, 1983.

Pierrot, Jean. *The Decadent Imagination, 1880–1900.* Trans. Derek Coltman. Chicago: University of Chicago Press, 1981.

Pile, Steve. *The Body and the City: Psychoanalysis, Space and Subjectivity.* London: Routledge, 1996.

Poldervaart, Saskia. 'Theories About Sex and Sexuality in Utopian Socialism'. *Journal of Homosexuality*, 29, 2/3 (1995): 41–67.

Poovey, Mary. *Making a Social Body: British Cultural Formation, 1830–1864.* Chicago: University of Chicago Press, 1995.

Port, Michael. *Imperial London: Civil Government Building in London, 1850–1915.* New Haven: Yale University Press, 1995.

Porter, Kevin and Weeks, Jeffrey. *Between the Acts: Lives of Homosexual Men, 1885–1967.* London: Routledge, 1991.

Porter, Roy. *London: A Social History.* London: Hamish Hamilton, 1994.

Porter, Roy, ed. *Rewriting the Self: Histories from the Renaissance to the Present.* London: Routledge, 1997.

Porter, Roy and Lesley Hall. *The Facts of Life: The Creation of Sexual Knowledge in Britain, 1650–1950.* London, Routledge, 1995.

Porter, Roy and G. S. Rousseau, eds. *Sexual Underworlds of the Enlightenment.* Manchester: Manchester University Press, 1987.

Porter, Roy and Mikulás Teich, eds. Fin de Siècle *and its Legacy.* Cambridge: Cambridge University Press, 1990.

Sexual Knowledge, Sexual Science: The History of Attitudes to Sexuality. Cambridge: Cambridge University Press, 1994.

Porter, Roy and Sylvana Tomaselli, eds. *The Dialectics of Friendship.* London: Routledge, 1989.

Rape: An Historical and Cultural Enquiry. Oxford: Blackwell, 1986.

Potts, Alex. *Flesh and the Ideal: Winckelmann and the Origins of Art History.* New Haven: Yale University Press, 1994.

Powell, Kerry. *Oscar Wilde and the Theatre of the 1890s.* Cambridge: Cambridge University Press, 1990.

Prendergast, Christopher. *Paris and the Nineteenth Century.* Oxford: Blackwell, 1992.

Preston, Peter. *Writing the City: Eden, Babylon and the New Jerusalem.* London: Routledge, 1994.

Querrien, Ann. 'The Metropolis and the Capital'. *Zone*, 1, 2 (1986): 218–26.

Radzinowicz, Leon and Roger Hood. *The History of Criminal Law and its Administration from 1750*, vol. v, *The Emergence of Penal Policy.* London: Stevens and Son, 1986.

Rappaport, Erica. *Shopping for Pleasure: Women in the Making of London's West End.* Princeton: Princeton University Press, 2000.

Rawcliffe, Michael. *Victorian London.* London: Batsford, 1985.

Read, Donald. *England, 1868–1914.* London: Longmans, 1979.

Robertson, W. Graham. *Time Was – The Reminiscences of W. Graham Robertson.* London: Hamish Hamilton, 1931.

Roose-Evans, James. *London Theatre, from the Globe to the National.* Oxford: Phaidon Press, 1977.

Roper, Lyndal. *Oedipus and the Devil: Witchcraft, Sexuality and Religion in Early Modern Europe.* London: Routledge, 1994.

Roper, Michael and John Tosh, eds. *Manful Assertions: Masculinities in Britain Since 1800.* London: Routledge, 1991.

Rosario, Vernon. *The Erotic Imagination: French Histories of Perversity.* Oxford: Oxford University Press, 1997.

Rosario, Vernon, ed. *Science and Homosexualities.* London: Routledge, 1997.

Rose, Jonathan. *The Edwardian Temperament, 1895–1919.* Ohio: Ohio University Press, 1986.

Rosenwein, Barbara H. 'Worrying About Emotions in History. *American Historical Review*, 107, 3 (June 2002): 821–45.

Ross, Ellen, *Love and Toil: Motherhood in Outcast London, 1870–1918*. Oxford: Oxford University Press, 1993.

Roughhead, William. *Bad Companions*. Edinburgh: Green & Son, 1930.

Rowbotham, Sheila, and Jeffrey Weeks. *Socialism and the New Life: The Personal and Sexual Politics of Edward Carpenter and Havelock Ellis*. London: Pluto, 1977.

Rutherford, Johnathan, ed. *Identity, Community, Culture and Difference*. London: Lawrence and Wishart, 1990.

Said, Edward. *Orientalism: Western Conceptions of the Orient*. London: Penguin, 1991.

Saint, Andrew, ed. *Politics and the People of London: The London County Council, 1889–1965*. London: Hambeldon Press, 1989.

Saint, Andrew and Gillian Darley. *The Chronicles of London*. London: Weidenfeld and Nicolson, 1994.

Samuel, Raphael, ed. *Patriotism: The Making and Unmaking of British National Identity*, vol. I, *History and Politics*. London: Routledge, 1989.

Sawyer, Roger. *Casement: The Flawed Hero*. London: Routledge, 1984.

Schaffer, Talia. '"A Wilde Desire Took Me": The Homoerotic History of *Dracula*'. *English Literary History*, 61, 2 (Summer 1994): 381–425.

Schama, Simon. *Landscape and Memory*. London: Harper Collins, 1995.

Schivelbusch, Wolfgang. *Disenchanted Night: The Industrialisation of Light in the Nineteenth Century*. Trans. Angela Davies. Oxford: Berg, 1988.

Schorske, Carl. Fin de Siècle *Vienna: Politics and Culture*. London: Weidenfeld and Nicolson, 1979.

Searle, G. R. *Eugenics and Politics in Britain, 1900–1914*. Leyden: Noordhoff International, 1976.

Sedgwick, Eve. *Between Men: English Literature and Male Homosocial Desire*. New York: Columbia University Press, 1985.

The Epistemology of the Closet. Berkeley: University of California Press, 1990.

Sennett, Richard. *Flesh and Stone: The Body and the City in Western Civilisation*. London: Faber and Faber, 1994.

Sennett, Richard, ed. *Classic Essays on the Culture of Cities*. Englewood Cliffs, NJ: Prentice Hall, 1969.

Sergeant, Bernard. 'Paederasty and Political Life in Archaic Greek Cities'. *Journal of Homosexuality*, 25, 1/2 (1993): 147–64.

Service, Alastair. *Edwardian Architecture: A Handbook to Building Design*. London: Thames and Hudson, 1977.

Shephard, Francis. *London 1808–1870: The Infernal Wen*. London: Secker and Warburg, 1971.

Shires, Lynda, ed. *Rewriting the Victorians: Theory, History and the Politics of Gender*. London: Routledge, 1992.

Showalter, Elaine. *Sexual Anarchy: Gender and Culture at the* Fin de Siècle. New York: Viking, 1990.

Showalter, Elaine, ed. *Daughters of Decadence: Women Writers of the* Fin de Siècle. New Brunswick, NJ: Rutgers, 1993.

Speaking of Gender. London: Routledge, 1989.

Sigel, Lisa Z. *Governing Pleasures: Pornography and Social Change in England, 1815–1914*. New Brunswick, NJ: Rutgers, 2002.

Silverman, Kaja. *Male Subjectivity at the Margins*. London: Routledge, 1992.

Simpson, Colin, Chester Lewis and David Leitch. *The Cleveland Street Affair*. Boston: Brown Little, 1976.

Sinfield, Alan. *Faultlines: Cultural Materialism and the Politics of Dissident Reading*. Berkeley: University of California Press, 1992.

The Wilde Century: Effeminacy, Oscar Wilde and the Queer Moment. London: Cassell, 1994.

Small, Ian, ed. *The Aesthetes: A Sourcebook*. London: Routledge and Kegan Paul, 1979.

Smith, F. B. 'Labouchere's Amendment to the Criminal Law Amendment Bill'. *Historical Studies*, 17 (October 1976): 165–73.

Smith, Michael. *The City and Social Theory*. Oxford: Blackwell, 1980.

Smith, Timothy d'Arch. *Love in Earnest: Some Notes on the Lives and Writings of English 'Uranian' Poets from 1889–1930*. London: Routledge and Kegan Paul, 1970.

Soja, Edward. *Post-modern Geographies: The Reassertion of Space in Critical Social Theory*. London: Verso, 1989.

Soloway, Richard. 'Counting the Degenerates: The Statistics of Race Degeneration in Edwardian England'. *Journal of Contemporary History*, 17, 1 (January 1982): 137–65.

Somerville, Siobhan. 'Scientific Racism and the Emergence of the Homosexual Body'. *Journal of the History of Sexuality*, 5, 2 (1994): 243–66.

Stallybrass, Peter and Allon White. *The Politics and Poetics of Transgression*. London: Methuen, 1986.

Stokes, John. 'Wilde at Bay: The Diaries of George Ives'. *English Literature in Transition, 1880–1920*, 26, 3 (1983): 175–84.

Stokes, John, ed. Fin de Siècle/Fin du Globe: *Fears and Fantasies of the Late Nineteenth-Century*. London: Macmillan, 1992.

Strachey, Lytton. *The Shorter Strachey*. Eds. Michael Holroyd and Paul Levy, London: Hogarth Press, 1980.

Sulloway, Frank. *Freud, Biologist of the Mind: Beyond the Psychoanalytic Legend*. London: Harvard University Press, 1992.

Summers, Anne. 'Militarism in Britain Before the Great War'. *History Workshop Journal*, 1, 2 (Autumn 1976): 104–23.

Tanner, Tony. *Venice Desired*. London: Blackwell, 1992.

Taylor, Barbara. *Eve and the New Jerusalem: Socialism and Feminism in the Nineteenth Century*. London: Virago, 1983.

Thornton, R. K., ed. *Poetry of the 'Nineties*. London: Penguin, 1970.

Tosh, John. *The Pursuit of History: Aims, Methods, and New Directions in the Study of Modern History*. New York: Longman, 1991.

Trumbach, Randolph. 'London's Sodomites: Homosexual Behaviour and Western Culture in the Eighteenth Century'. *Journal of Social History*, 11, 1 (1977–8): 1–34.

Tully, James. *Meaning and Context: Quentin Skinner and his Critics*. Cambridge: Polity Press, 1988.

Vanita, Ruth. *Sappho and the Virgin Mary: Same-Sex Love and the English Literary Imagination*. New York: Columbia University Press, 1996.

Varias, Alexander. *Paris and the Anarchists: Aesthetes and Subversives During the Fin de Siècle*. London: Macmillan, 1997.

Vernon, James, 'Who's Afraid of the "Linguistic Turn"? The Politics of Social History and its Discontents'. *Social History*, 18, 1 (1993): 81–5.

Veeser, H. Aram, ed. *The New Historicism Reader*. London: Routledge, 1994.

Vicinus, Martha. 'The Adolescent Boy: *Fin de Siècle* Femme Fatale?' *Journal of the History of Sexuality*, 5, 1 (1994): 90–114.

Upchurch, Charles. 'Forgetting the Unthinkable: Cross-dressers and British Society in the case of the Queen vs Boulton and Others'. *Gender and History*, 12, 1 (2000), 127–57.

Waitey, Bernard. 'The Language and Imagery of "Class" in Early Twentieth-Century England (c.1900–1925)'. *Literature and History*, 4 (Autumn 1976): 30–55.

Walkowitz, Judith. *City of Dreadful Delight: Narratives of Sexual Danger in Late Victorian London*. London: Virago, 1992.

　Prostitution and Victorian Society: Women, Class and the State. Cambridge: Cambridge University Press, 1980.

Waters, Sarah. ' "The Most Famous Fairy in History": Antinous and Homosexual Fantasy'. *Journal of the History of Sexuality*, 6 (1995–6): 194–230.

Weale, Adrian. *Patriot Traitors: Roger Casement, John Amerty and the Real Meaning of Treason*. London: Viking, 2001.

Weber, Eugen. 'Pierre de Courbertin and the Introduction of Organised Sport in France'. *Journal of Contemporary History*, 5, 3 (1970): 3–26.

Weeks, Jeffrey. *Against Nature: Essays on History, Sexuality and Identity*. London: River Oram Press, 1991.

　Coming Out: Homosexual Politics from the Nineteenth Century to the Present. 1979; London: Quartet, 1990.

　Sex, Politics and Society: The Regulation of Sexuality Since 1800. London: Longman, 1981.

　Sexuality and Its Discontents: Meanings, Myths and Modern Sexualities. London: Routledge, 1985.

Weightman, Gavin. *Bright Lights, Big City: London Entertained, 1830–1950*. London: Collins, 1992.

Weiner, Martin. *English Culture and the Decline of the Industrial Spirit, 1850–1980*. Cambridge: Cambridge University Press, 1981.

White, Chris, ed. *Nineteenth-Century Writing on Homosexuality*. London: Routledge, 1999.

White, Stephen, ed. *The Margins of the City: Gay Men's Urban Lives*. Aldershot: Arena, 1999.

Wiener, Joel, ed. *Papers for the Millions: The New Journalism in Britain 1850 –1914*. New York: Greenwood Press, 1988.

Williams, Raymond. *Communications*. London: Penguin, 1976.

   The Country and the City. London: Hogarth Press, 1985.

   Culture and Society: Coleridge to Orwell. London: Hogarth Press, 1987.

   Keywords: A Vocabulary of Culture and Society. London: Croam Helm, 1976.

   Politics and Letters: Interviews with New Left Review. London: New Left Books, 1979.

   Problems of Materialism and Culture. London: Verso, 1980.

Wilson, Elizabeth. *The Sphinx and the City: Urban Life, the Control of Disorder, and Women*. London: Virago, 1991.

Wood, Anthony. *Nineteenth Century Britain, 1815–1914*. London: Longman, 1982.

Wotherspoon, Garry. *City of the Plain: History of a Gay Subculture*. Sydney: Hale and Iremonger, 1991.

Yeo, Stephen. 'A New Life: The Religion of Socialism in Britain, 1883–1896, *History Workshop Journal*. 4 (Autumn 1977): 44–56.

Young, Ian. *The Male Homosexual in Literature: A Bibliography*. Metuchen: Scarecrow Press, 1973.

Zatlin, Linda Gertner. *Beardsley, Japonisme, and the Perversion of the Victorian Ideal*. Cambridge: Cambridge University Press, 1997.

Index

CAMBRIDGE STUDIES IN NINETEENTH-CENTURY
LITERATURE AND CULTURE

General editor
Gillian Beer, *University of Cambridge*

Titles published

Printed in Great Britain
by Amazon

47781109R00147